The Human Tradition in Imperial Russia

The Human Tradition around the World
Series Editors: William H. Beezley and Colin M. MacLachlan

The Human Tradition in Imperial Russia

Edited by
Christine D. Worobec

ROWMAN & LITTLEFIELD PUBLISHERS, INC.
Lanham • Boulder • New York • Toronto • Plymouth, UK

ROWMAN & LITTLEFIELD PUBLISHERS, INC.

Published in the United States of America
by Rowman & Littlefield Publishers, Inc.
A wholly owned subsidiary of The Rowman & Littlefield Publishing Group, Inc.
4501 Forbes Boulevard, Suite 200, Lanham, Maryland 20706
www.rowmanlittlefield.com

Estover Road, Plymouth PL6 7PY, United Kingdom

British Library Cataloguing in Publication Information Available

Library of Congress Cataloging-in-Publication Data

The human tradition in imperial Russia / edited by Christine D. Worobec.
    p. cm. — (The human tradition around the world)
  Includes bibliographical references and index.
  ISBN-13: 978-0-7425-3736-1 (cloth : alk. paper)
  ISBN-10: 0-7425-3736-6 (cloth : alk. paper)
  ISBN-13: 978-0-7425-3737-8 (pbk. : alk. paper)
  ISBN-10: 0-7425-3737-4 (pbk. : alk. paper)
  ISBN-13: 978-0-7425-5790-1 (electronic)
  ISBN-10: 0-7425-5790-1 (electronic)
  1. Russia—Social conditions. 2. Russia—History—1613–1917. I. Worobec, Christine.
  HN523.H84 2009
  947—dc22

                                                                          2008036419

Printed in the United States of America

∞™ The paper used in this publication meets the minimum requirements of American
National Standard for Information Sciences—Permanence of Paper for Printed Library
Materials, ANSI/NISO Z39.48-1992.

To the victims of the shootings at
Northern Illinois University
14 February 2008

Contents

Introduction

Christine D. Worobec

"Imperial Russia"—the two-and-a-half centuries from the reign of Peter the Great (1682–1725) until the February Revolution of 1917—conjures up the image of a sprawling state apparatus that at times sought to infuse change into Russian and non-Russian societies. It nevertheless always stopped short of reforming the centralized and undemocratic political system called autocracy until its hand was finally forced in 1905 by a revolutionary flood of strikes and political demands for civil liberties and political representation. But even then, reforms came too little and too late. Individuals of all classes and ethnicities in early March 1917 welcomed Nicholas II's abdication and a world without the Romanov dynasty and autocracy.

Until the 1970s and the embrace of interdisciplinary social historical methodologies, historians of Russia in the West focused their attention on the reforming and nonreforming tendencies of individual tsars. They attempted to explain what had gone wrong with Russia and why it did not follow a liberal political path, in spite of a glimmer of hope in 1905 with the creation of a representative political body called the Duma and rising expectations after the February Revolution of 1917, when the Provisional Government promised liberal reforms. That weak government could not withstand the vagaries of World War I, an exhausted economy, and a more popular Bolshevik Party led by Vladimir Lenin that promised to introduce socialism and egalitarianism in Russia. The Provisional Government simply vanished in the October Revolution of 1917.

Since the 1970s, historians have focused more and more attention on how various classes and communities lived within Imperial Russia and were influenced not only by political but also by economic and social developments. As more and more voices were uncovered among workers, peasants, and women, not every discovery related to politics. Yet the knowledge that revolution occurred in 1905 and twice in 1917 continued to shape the ways in which this history was written because those cataclysmic events had to be explained. The revolutions themselves carried with them a certain aura of inevitability that came to an end in 1991 with the collapse of communism and the splintering of the colossal empire that had been called the Soviet Union.

With the 1991 revolution, even the Russians themselves began to question the inevitability of the Bolshevik victory in October 1917. However, in doing so they became nostalgic for the grandeur of the imperial period, especially the reign of the last tsar, Nicholas II, when officials tried to create representative government in response to revolution and encourage agricultural modernization in order to stem further revolutions. They tended to ignore, on the one hand, the halfhearted nature of the experiment with constitutional government, the disparities in wealth among classes, and Nicholas's disastrous foreign policy measures, including the unnecessary Russo-Japanese War of 1904–1905. On the other hand, nostalgic Russians also underestimated the degree to which an educated civil society that clamored for serious political reform had developed in the immediate prerevolutionary period and were hostile to the national movements among non-Russians that were demanding autonomy within the empire or in some cases outright independence.

The collapse of the Soviet Union in 1991 brought with it another change that has begun to alter the way in which Western historians view the imperial period. Archives opened within the Russian Federation and the successor states, including collections that had been off-limits to historians of Imperial Russia in both the East and West. Scholars, including those in this volume, seized an unprecedented opportunity to uncover the lives of ordinary subjects of the realm. With the enrichment of social history by cultural history, historians began asking new questions and examining both unpublished and previously published cultural artifacts to illuminate the human tradition within Imperial Russia.

Many of the stories contained in this collection are microstudies of individual or group experiences, or events that occurred at different points in the history of Imperial Russia. In this regard the volume follows the lead of William Husband's companion edited volume on modern Russia in the Human Tradition series "by focusing on the role of individuals and groups previously underrepresented in scholarship."[1] The chapters are similarly organized chronologically, beginning with Peter I's dress reforms in the early eighteenth century and concluding with poets arising out of a stratified and largely urban working class between the revolutions of 1905 and 1917. Through the chronological sweep of more than two centuries, the pieces introduce readers to some of the major changes in Imperial Russian history and their consequences.

Imperial Russian history is usually broken down into two periods, punctuated by the Crimean War (1853–1856) and the abolition of serfdom in 1861. The first period, beginning in the late seventeenth century, witnessed the adoption of Western ideas, education, and culture to what was a predominantly Orthodox Christian society, on the one hand, and the entrenchment of serfdom, an unfree labor system that exploited the bulk of the population, on the other. Due to the expansion of this economic system, Westernization was initially not as widespread as it might have been. Serfdom had long disappeared from Western Europe. Further east, however, for economic and military reasons arising out of Ivan IV's devastating domestic and foreign policies, serfdom gradually evolved in the late sixteenth and early seventeenth centuries. It became solidified by law in 1649, and enveloped more and more populations as Russia expanded its boundaries in the seventeenth and eighteenth centuries to become one of the world's major empires. The imported Western ideas, however, eventually resulted in a reassessment of the unfree labor system, the beginnings of a backlash against an autocratic and unrepresentative form of government, the raising of the issue of women's emancipation, and finally the abolition of serfdom in 1861.

Emancipation of the serfs ushered in the second period of Imperial Russian history, bringing with it urbanization, industrialization, and a series of other reforms to modernize Russia. While the empire remained predominantly rural, it was profoundly changed by the tremendous growth of the capital cities of Moscow and St. Petersburg, the railroad, the development of a national market, and the swelling of educated society that was no longer confined to a tiny elite. An unwise foreign policy decision in 1904 to challenge Japan's imperialistic ventures coupled with economic and social changes precipitated a revolution in 1905 that introduced a limited constitutional monarchy. This experiment with representative government was severely challenged, however, not only by Nicholas II's reluctance to accept limitations on his authority but more importantly by the costly and devastating First World War. The war displaced millions of people, caused millions of deaths, and disrupted a fragile industrial economy. Had it not been for that war, the radicalization of the general populace might not have been as extreme.

The reconstruction of personal and group histories provides important correctives to these traditional grand narratives of Russian history by nuancing and complicating them. The laconic entries in the late eighteenth-century diary of the merchant Ivan Tolchenov, discussed in chapter 3, shed light on not only an individual's experiences but also the shaping of a personal identity. From court records we learn in chapter 2 about the travails of the unmarried vagrant serf woman Mar'ia Semenova, who was caught up in the web of an eighteenth-century society that had totally marginalized her. Owned by a monastic institution, Mar'ia had no rights whatsoever but only the obligations of labor and obedience to her master. When she chose to renege on those responsibilities, she became the victim of a punitive and ultimately weak state that could not tolerate any challenge to public and social order. We also witness the ways in which Evdokiia Kulikova, the upwardly mobile peasant migrant to St. Petersburg at the end of the nineteenth century and the subject of chapter 9, was more successful than Semenova in being able to create a new persona for herself. The abolition of the unfree labor and economic system of serfdom in 1861 created new, if still limited, opportunities for peasants. Those who were able to migrate to the cities could find employment opportunities as domestics, prostitutes, factory workers, and tradespeople. Salaries and wages gave people some independence and respectability that they had not enjoyed previously. While not all of these experiences were necessarily without hardship, some individuals, like Kulikova, could become upwardly mobile. Nonetheless, Kulikova's transformation from a peasant migrant into a modern urban woman was at the same time held back by the Russian Orthodox Church's strictures against divorce as well as by legal limitations on divorce and separation from a spouse. Similarly, Masia Zalkind, a Jewish woman in Lithuania at the turn of the twentieth century, described in chapter 10, found herself trapped by community notions and a court system that judged her guilty of murdering her husband due to the discord in her marriage. In chapter 11 we read about domestic servants at the beginning of the twentieth century organizing themselves, while chapter 12 reconstructs the ways in which worker-poets wrote about a better future as they expressed their human dignity. In some of these cases, the revolutions of 1905 and 1917 were not that far away; in others those cataclysmic events were irrelevant. All of these individual and group histories, however, reveal the daily negotiations that individuals had to enter into with authority figures, be they government officials, religious leaders, individuals of another class, or even members of their own class.

These micro-histories and events also contain themes that cross historical periods. As David Ransel has written elsewhere, "The rich texture of a close-up view of an event or life gives new vitality and complexity to concepts like state and society."[2] Whether through the lens of the individual biography of Mar'ia Semenova or the collective story of a rebellion of serfs on a landowner's estate located in a village called Bernovo in 1827, as described in chapter 5, we learn about the ways in which individuals on their own or in a group failed at resisting authority they perceived to be arbitrary. Their attempts were nonetheless no less sincere than those of members of educated society. In the postemancipation period after 1861, informed individuals from the middling and upper classes sought to bring reforms to both Siberia and the empire as a whole through the contested celebration of the tricentennial anniversary of the annexation of that immense territory, a story reconstructed in chapter 7. It was the nature of resistance that had changed in this event: here educated members of society used the public forum of newspapers to voice their concerns and ambitions rather than the tactics of disobedience and refusal to carry out their obligations as had the Bernovo serfs. The growth of a civil society that was trying to reform the autocratic system without the benefits of popular representation through incremental and peaceful means was demonstrated as well by worker-poets in their writings between the 1905 and 1917 revolutions (see chapter 12). In the early twentieth century domestic servants in St. Petersburg also tried to better their positions through the peaceful attempt at creating labor associations. All of these acts of resistance contrasted with the attempts at social reconciliation that had been part of late eighteenth-century educated understandings of how their society and polity were so well integrated, the subject of chapter 4. Nonetheless, the playwrights of this earlier enlightenment period, when society as well as the government embraced the same faith in God-given order, were laying the foundations for the later public discussions.

Some of the stories in this collection deal with transformations on either a national or individual level. Standing close to seven feet tall and towering over his subjects and empire, Peter I and his elongated shadow permeate the volume. Much has been written on the issue of whether Peter was as revolutionary as the nineteenth century immortalized him in the Westernizer-Slavophile debate. That intellectual debate among a small but significant cohort of noblemen and professionals surfaced in the 1830s and 1840s. It either praised or vilified this tsar's attempt to bring Russia out of its Eastern Orthodox isolation and make Russia a Westernized state and full player on the Western diplomatic stage.

The Westernizers, as their name suggests, criticized pre-Petrine Russia as being bankrupt of cultural ideas and significance. Blaming Eastern Orthodoxy for retarding Russia's cultural, social, economic, and even political development, they heralded Western European triumphs of humanism and individualism, which they credited to the Renaissance (which did not occur in Russia) and the development of capitalism. They advanced the notion that Peter had a blank slate upon which to effect tremendous change.

The Slavophiles, on the other hand, countered this myth by pointing to the ways in which pre-Petrine Russia and its non-Western ways were to be applauded and extended. While both the Westernizers and Slavophiles were opposed to the system of serfdom and governmental censorship, the Slavophiles argued that the autocracy was a perfect type of governmental system when it kept itself confined to defending its subjects and giving communities autonomy.

Championing Russia's exceptionalism, they pointed to the superiority of both collectivism, which they saw perfectly epitomized by the Russian peasant commune, and Orthodoxy, which they believed would save all mankind. As in any such debate, mythmaking about the past was harnessed to contemporary issues of the early nineteenth to mid-nineteenth century—whether Russia had progressed since the time of Peter the Great or regressed, whether Russia should reform itself and become more like the West or attempt to undo those Western influences that actually predated Peter's reign by a few centuries.

In architecture and technology, Western inventions and practices came to Muscovite Russia as early as the fifteenth century in the reign of Ivan III (1462–1505) and increased with the gunpowder revolution of the sixteenth and seventeenth centuries. The Dormition Cathedral (1475–1479) in the center of the Kremlin, while Byzantine in its interior and external onion domes, was nonetheless the masterpiece of the Renaissance Italian architect Aristotele Fioravanti, who applied "Western construction techniques to create height, mass, and interior space."[3] Other Kremlin buildings of this period reflected similar Italianate influences. Portraiture, once prohibited by the Russian Orthodox Church, was introduced in the late sixteenth century. It became fairly commonplace among the aristocracy in the latter part of the seventeenth century. Peter I's own father, Tsar Aleksei Mikhailovich (1645–1676), after prohibiting Western clothing and other customs in 1675, did not follow his own prescriptions in his private life. Ultimately and ironically, the most significant Western-style reform came during Aleksei's reign with the corrections that were introduced to Orthodox ritual and practice by Ukrainian ecclesiastics who had fled Catholic Poland-Lithuania in the mid-seventeenth century. Those corrections unleashed a church schism that ultimately weakened the state church and fostered religious dissent that continued to grow in the eighteenth and nineteenth centuries.

While Western influences ensured that the Muscovite state was not as isolated as the Slavophiles later claimed, some of Peter's reforms were on such a vast scale that they began a dramatic transformation of Muscovy. Peter's changing the state's name to Imperial Russia in 1721 presaged the imagining of a different sort of polity, one that harkened back to the ancient Roman Empire. At the same time the new Russia did not lose its Orthodox pedigree as the heir to Byzantium and a more recent biblical evocation of a new Jerusalem. The opening chapter's introduction to and reintepretation of all of Imperial Russian history through the prism of a single Petrine reform—the prohibition of Russian dress in favor of utilitarian Western attire—gives us a sense of the colossal change that occurred, one that Peter himself could not have predicted. It began with the upper and urban classes, to be sure, but eventually affected all classes and groups within the society. The wrenching of Russians out of their loose-fitting robes launched a fascination with Parisian fashion, the growth of a fashion industry and garment trade, and in the last half of the nineteenth century ready-to-wear clothing. Peter's demands that men shave their beards or be fined, that women of the upper classes come out of the isolation of their households, that the elites adopt the manners of "civilized" society, among others, were not simply cosmetic changes. They inaugurated an interest in all things Western, not the least among which figured the importance of literacy and education. A number of Peter's new bureaucratic and educational institutions survived until 1917 and even later. They were paradoxically set in motion and made possible by the retention and expansion of the unfree labor system of serfdom, which exploited a huge population that made conspicuous consumption possible, manned a growing army, and built the western city of St. Petersburg out of malaria-infested swamps.

Returning to clothing for a moment—many of the chapters reflect on the ways in which clothing became tied up in individual identities. The stylishness of feminist aristocratic women's attire in the mid-nineteenth century, as described in chapter 6, contrasted sharply with the dress that nihilist (those who rejected the status quo) and revolutionary women preferred. The radicals set themselves off from their mothers and sisters by eschewing the latest Parisian fashions in favor of simple unadorned dark clothing, shorn hair, and granny glasses so that they could be spotted on the streets as making profound statements about their antiestablishment ways. The elegance of the gowns of upper-class feminists, nevertheless, aided them in making inroads into court and other social circles to plead the case of women's emancipation and have those pleas taken seriously, at least by some men. These women's transformation occurred as a result of some of the same stirrings that produced nihilists and revolutionaries, including the growth of literacy and education for women, the development of a significant print literature, the abolitionist movements in both the English-speaking world and Russia, and finally emancipation of the serfs in Russia in 1861. Working within the system undoubtedly had some advantages for aristocratic feminists, while at the same time these very women protected nihilist women and reached out to urban women who lived in poverty, demonstrating to them the virtues of self-help and education.

Near the end of the nineteenth century the migrant Evdokiia Kulikova was aided in her transformation by being able to shed the coarser clothing and full-head covering of a peasant woman for tasteful ready-to-wear clothing and a fashionable hairdo in St. Petersburg. She would have fit in with a broader urban population where appearing to be a member of the lower middle class became easier with the amenities and opportunities available in the city. However, as chapter 8 reminds us, not all transformations were complete. Dress did not necessary make the person. Well-healed strangers and tricksters in St. Petersburg could easily take advantage of unsuspecting recent rural migrants unaccustomed to city life by robbing them of their possessions or selling them adulterated goods.

As the reader may have already surmised, several chapters focus on women's experiences in Imperial Russia. Despite the growth of a substantial literature on Russian women in particular, that knowledge has not entered the mainstream textbooks on Russian history. This volume thus serves as an important supplement to those texts. Women were very much actors within Russian society. They came into contact with authority figures, challenged restrictions on their lives, reflected the immense changes that Westernization and secularization brought to their societies, and in some cases organized themselves to champion better conditions for themselves and others. Some, such as the eighteenth-century vagrant Mar'ia Semenova and early twentieth-century wife Masia Zalkind, were victims of their larger societies. Semenova ran afoul of draconian laws that interfered in all aspects of daily life, while Zalkind suffered from the various marital expectations of men and women within her Jewish community, Jewish attitudes toward marital discord, and the politics of divorce in a small Lithuanian town. At the turn of the twentieth century the migrant Kulikova emerged more victorious from her encounter with authorities in gaining separation from her spouse, but nonetheless had to contend repeatedly with a paternalistic and inefficient officialdom.

Finally, the chapters on a Jewish community in modern Lithuania and civil society in Siberia near the end of the nineteenth century remind us of imperial Russia's status as a multinational and multiconfessional empire. Siberia had been conquered by the beginning of the seventeenth century as a result of fur trappers and salt merchants searching for new supplies. These entrepreneurs claimed the vast lands of what became known as Siberia as belonging to the tsar, with disregard for the native peoples living there. Other acquisitions were products of wars, beginning with Ivan IV's annexation of Kazan and Astrakhan in the mid-sixteenth century and culminating in the battles over control of the Caucasus region in the mid-nineteenth century. The significant Jewish presence in the empire came about through successive partitions of independent Poland in the late eighteenth century by not only Russia, but also Prussia and Austria. In the imperial period the autocracy co-opted new areas by providing Russian noble status to their non-Russian elites and welcoming them into government service. At the same time, Russian officials were wary of non-Russian and non-Orthodox groups that could be disruptive to the law and order or were perceived, as in the case of Siberian and Turkish tribes, as being less civilized than their Slavic counterparts. As chapter 7 points out, various liberal reforms of the 1860s and 1870s were not extended to Siberia, a "colony" that had become a strange mixture of penal areas and thriving towns and villages. In the case of the Jewish population, measures were in place to prohibit freedom of movement of Jews throughout the empire. At the same time, the government respected the religious autonomy of Jews and Muslims, providing their religious leaders with authority over important rites of passage in daily life, from birth to marriage to death. Nevertheless, as chapter 10 demonstrates, growing secularization of marriage in the late nineteenth century and the modern concept of love began to erode local customs and create tensions among Jews. This situation created the rising and sometimes unmet expectation among some members of the community, especially women, that justice could be found in the state courts.

No collection such as this can be exhaustive in its subject matter. The twelve chapters presented here must be understood as merely scratching the surface of life in the Russian Empire. Nevertheless, they do enrich our understanding of the human experience in Imperial Russia. Individuals, groups, and events raised out of obscurity remind us of the messiness of everyday life, people's dreams and frustrations, as well as their sense of self and the community around them.

Russian terms in this volume have been transliterated following the Library of Congress system, with the exception of the names of certain monarchs such as Peter I (rather than Petr I) and Catherine II (rather than Ekaterina II), whose names are commonly Anglicized. All dates are recorded in the old style according to the Julian calendar, which was eleven days behind the Gregorian calendar in the eighteenth century, twelve days behind in the nineteenth century, and thirteen days behind in the following century. Abbreviated archival citations follow the practices of individual Russian archives.

NOTES

1. William B. Husband, ed., *The Human Tradition in Modern Russia* (Wilmington, DE: Scholarly Resources, 2000), xvi.

2. David L. Ransel, "An Eighteenth-Century Russian Merchant Family in Prosperity and Decline," p. 256 in *Imperial Russia: New Histories for the Empire*, ed. Jane Burbank and David L. Ransel (Bloomington: Indiana University Press, 1998).

3. Catherine Evtuhov, David Goldfrank, Lindsey Hughes, and Richard Stites, *A History of Russia: Peoples, Legends, Events, Forces* (Boston: Houghton Mifflin, 2004), 110.

Chapter One

Fashion and the Rise of Consumer Capitalism in Russia

Christine Ruane

Economists and historians have traditionally credited major technological changes such as the invention of the spinning jenny and the development of the railroad as serving as catalysts for such monumental changes as industrialization and urbanization that transformed largely rural economies and societies into modern ones. They do not usually see individual actions of rulers as producing fundamental social and economic changes. In contrast, Christine Ruane vividly demonstrates how a single decree on the part of Peter I (1682–1725), which mandated that Russian urban dwellers wear European clothing, spurred a variety of changes in Russia that forever changed that country's landscape and Russian identity. Indeed Peter's sartorial campaign was but one of many reforms that reflected Peter's determination to make Russia a major European power and his new city of St. Petersburg a European cultural center.

Although Western cultural and technological influences had begun to enter the Orthodox Muscovite state in the late fifteenth century, they became much more pronounced in the seventeenth century as a result of the Polish invasion of Russia, Muscovy's expansion into Ukraine, and the influence of bishops from Ukraine on the Russian Orthodox Church's religious practices. Peter's father, Tsar Aleksei Mikhailovich (1645–1676), introduced Western theater and ballet at court. However, these Western influences, while helping to fuel a church schism, did not revolutionize Russian cultural practices, which remained tied to a xenophobic religious system. In fact, Tsar Aleksei and Peter's half brother, Tsar Fedor, even prohibited Russians from wearing foreign dress. Ultimately, however, European influences would prevail as Russia continued to pursue expansionist policies in the west and south and desperately needed up-to-date European technologies.

Peter I's exposure as an adolescent to Moscow's foreign community and fascination with Western military technology and the art of shipbuilding led him to take two tours of Western Europe (in 1697–1698 and in 1717). He was the first Russian ruler to travel to the West. Upon his return from his first trip, he launched his social engineering project of making the Russians modern and "civilized" by turning them into Europeans. Peter was particularly attracted by the Europeans' culture, efficiency, and ease of movement. And true to his autocratic nature, he was determined to change fundamental aspects of Russia overnight with the might of his pen. As Ruane points out, that change was much slower than Peter envisioned, but it was revolutionary all the same. Peter's decree on dress eventually spawned a Russian fashion industry, a commercial revolution, and a new Russian identity. More importantly, it dramatically transformed everyday life. After the 1861 emancipation peasants began to exchange their hand-sewn attire fashioned out of homespun cloth for factory-made cloth and eventually ready-to-wear clothing. With those exchanges came expectations for a better life. Spanning the period between 1701 and 1917, Ruane's chapter provides a wonderful overview of all of Imperial Russian history through the lens of clothing and fashion.

Why do clothes matter? What do they tell us about political imperatives and class differences in Imperial Russia? Why did it take two centuries for all the ramifications of Peter's 1701 decree to play themselves out? What implications can you draw from the fact that Peter's Westernization project did not involve the abolition of serfdom but rather an intensification of that unfree labor system? Did Russia become a Westernized nation?

In 1701 Tsar Peter I of Russia issued the following decree:

> All residents of the city of Moscow including those serfs who come to the city to trade, but excluding the clergy and agricultural laborers, must wear German dress.[1] Outerwear must consist of French or Saxon coats, and underneath men must wear camisoles [sleeved vests], breeches, boots, shoes, and German hats. And they must ride in German saddles. Women of all ranks—women of the clergy, wives of officers, musketeers, and soldiers—and their children must wear German dress, hats, skirts, and shoes. From this day forward no one will be allowed to wear Russian dress, Caucasian caftans, sheepskin coats, pants, or boots, nor will anyone be permitted to ride in Russian saddles. Finally, artisans will not be allowed to make or trade [in these goods].

Those who entered the city gates in Russian dress were to be fined while those who produced or sold Russian clothing faced unspecified forms of "dreadful punishment."[2] This decree marked the beginning of the Russian revolution in dress. Although the decree referred only to residents of Moscow, it soon became clear that the tsar wanted all members of urban society to abandon their traditional clothing in favor of Western European dress.

For most of us, who are used to thinking of our choice of clothing as a personal act, Peter's command seems particularly arbitrary and authoritarian. But the tsar had a plan for his kingdom: he wanted Russia to become a major player in European political life. This meant that Russia had to modernize its army, economy, and way of life along Western European lines. Peter understood that one important step toward acceptance by Western Europeans was to dress like they did. The goal of the dress reform then was twofold. First, if they wore European dress, Russians would no longer be readily identifiable as Russians. They could mix and mingle with ease in the European capitals, and Western Europeans could no longer think of them as uncivilized barbarians. Second, wearing European clothes would help Russians think of themselves as Europeans. Dress plays a key role in self-representation in any society. If Russians were going to become Europeans, they had to dress the part. Peter clearly believed that his dress reform along with his other cultural reforms would help to create a modern Europeanized elite in Russia. European technology and culture were the tools that the tsar used to transform Russia into a major world power.

In order to understand the radical nature of Peter's dress decree, a few words need to be said about what had constituted "Russian" clothing. In general, all Russians wore loose-fitting clothing that completely covered the body. Married women even covered their hair with various kinds of headdresses and scarves. Both sexes wore linen in summer and wool and fur in the winter. The elite often used silks imported from Persia and Italy and expensive furs such as mink and lynx to make their garments. Men wore tunic shirts with loose pants over which they would wear knee-length or floor-length caftans. Women's wardrobes included underdresses that covered the entire body. They then placed different skirts and jumpers over these garments. In winter they wore full-length coats made from sheepskins or fur.

There was no such thing as "Russian" dress until the eighteenth century. Russians belonged to a number of different Slavic and Finnish tribes, and these people maintained their regional identity by wearing clothing that identified them as Muscovites, Cheremis, or Mordovians. Embroidery, headdresses, length of sleeves, and styles of caftans gave those people we call Russians an opportunity to distinguish themselves along tribal lines. In 1701 Peter's decree labeled all these different forms of costume as Russian dress. Tribal and regional differences came to be seen as variants of Russian ethnic dress. The colorful mélange of costumes became a single category.

While Peter's edict created the category of Russian dress, its real purpose was to introduce European fashions. Eighteenth-century European clothing differed dramatically from the garments worn in Russia. Women bared their arms and bosoms, wearing corsets to alter the natural shape of their bodies. They covered their hair with elaborate powdered wigs. Men wore tight-fitting breeches and waistcoats revealing every curve of the male physique. Moreover, European dress was governed by the concept of fashion. Fashion is the continual and rapid change in clothing styles. As it evolved in Europe, fashion dictated that clothing styles vary with each season and from one year to the next. Fashionable Europeans abandoned their garments when they went out of style, not when they were worn out. This meant that those who wished to dress in the latest fashions had to spend more money and time preparing their wardrobes. Because of the expense involved, only royal courts and wealthy aristocrats could afford to dress in the latest styles. Individuals who were less well-off financially either wore the elite's cast-off clothing or wore copies made from less-expensive materials. Thus, Peter's dress decree introduced not only new clothes but also new attitudes toward clothing into Russian society.

But how was Peter going to enforce his dress decree? The tsar began his attempt to change his subjects' sartorial habits by insisting that all government officials from the highest to the lowest wear European dress. Peter himself set the tone. His personal wardrobe consisted of beautifully crafted court dress worn for state occasions and simple breeches and waistcoats for daily wear. After 1701 the tsar appeared in paintings, sculptures, and other forms of representation wearing only Western European clothing. Peter also ordered uniforms based upon European designs for his new army and navy. These uniforms introduced European clothing to the thousands of men serving in the military. The new uniforms helped to provide a sense of cohesiveness and discipline that paved the way for a Russian victory over the Swedes in the Great Northern War. Civil servants were likewise forced to wear European dress.

Having introduced a European look for his military and civil servitors, Peter set out to transform high society. He did this by moving the capital from Moscow to his new city of St. Petersburg, which was designed to resemble the European capitals that he had visited in 1698. New palaces, government buildings, elegant stores, and townhouses were built along the swampy banks of the Neva River. Peter introduced new forms of sociability—balls, assemblies, theaters—where Russians had to conduct themselves according to European rules of etiquette. These activities required the proper form of clothing, which meant only European dress was allowed. Here again, the royal family played a key role. Peter's second wife, Catherine; her daughters; and their attendants all dressed in elegant gowns and wigs, setting the tone for other female courtiers to follow, while the males dressed like European gentlemen.

It is difficult to ascertain at this point in time just how readily Russians adopted Western European modes of dress. According to eighteenth-century sources, young men and women eagerly donned the new clothes. Like young people the world over, they were attracted to the new and innovative. Their parents proved less willing. Some wore European dress in public and Russian clothing at home. Others simply refused to comply and were fined accordingly. But open defiance of the tsar's dress reform became increasingly more difficult. Peter made his dress reform along with his other cultural innovations congruent with his political power. Those who wished to succeed in Russia quickly conformed to the new form of dress and lifestyle.

By the second half of the eighteenth century, it was apparent that Peter's dress reform had prevailed. After Peter's death in 1725, the Russian court continued to set the tone for elegance in dress. The emperors and empresses who succeeded Peter spent lavish amounts of money on their wardrobes. When Empress Elizabeth died in 1762, her attendants counted fifteen thousand dresses in her closets. At the same time, the Russian nobility, in an effort to imitate the royal standard, also spent large sums on fashionable clothing. Those beneath the aristocracy—writers, bureaucrats, doctors, and artists—tried to imitate the elite by wearing Western dress. In 1784 the Russian government established uniforms for civil servants using European fashions as the basis for their design. Each government agency developed a particular kind of uniform for its employees. The rich colors of the military and civilian uniforms enlivened the streets of St. Petersburg. Even royal and aristocratic servants wore special livery at work. By 1800 Russia had become a collage of dress styles. High society wore the latest French fashions; the middle urban ranks wore slightly out-of-date European styles. Servants, clerks, and others who worked in urban establishments usually wore some kind of European clothing. Urban manual laborers, most of whom were serfs, combined elements from Russian and European dress together. In the countryside, the provincial nobility wore fashionable clothing while their serfs continued to wear traditional ethnic dress.

Peter's dress decree did more than introduce European fashions into Russia—it created a whole new industry. By forbidding artisans to make or trade in Russian dress, the tsar was attempting to force them to learn how to make the new clothes or face starvation. Thankfully for the artisans, this part of Peter's decree proved impossible to enforce, his threats of dreadful punishment not withstanding. But the creation of a market for Western European clothing did give rise to a serious problem for Russians. How were they to acquire French fashions living so far from Paris? The royal family and the wealthiest aristocrats could import their clothing from Europe, but what about the other members of the court, urban society, and the military? How could they find artisans knowledgeable in European design to sew their uniforms and elegant fashions? The only solution to this difficulty was to invite foreign artisans to set up shop in Russia. In 1700 Peter introduced the labor recruitment contract, which permitted skilled artisans to come to Russia for a particular length of time during which they would practice their trade and teach Russian craftsmen and women their skills. A small number of European entrepreneurs came to Moscow and Petersburg to capitalize on the new Russian market for fashionable clothing throughout the eighteenth and nineteenth centuries.

The foreign tailors and dressmakers who arrived in Russia brought with them a well-established system of making and selling clothes that had evolved in Western Europe during the early modern period. Parents apprenticed their sons and daughters to tailors and dressmakers. According to the terms of the contract, the artisans agreed to teach the youngsters the craft and provide food and lodging for a set period of time, usually two or three years. Upon completion of the apprenticeship, the apprentices would find employment as journeymen to learn more about the craft. When the journeymen felt ready, they took a test before a board of master craftsmen. A successful outcome allowed the newly certified artisans to set up their own shops. Having opened up their own business, tailors and dressmakers either traveled to their clients' homes, or they measured and fitted clients in their shops. The best ateliers had beautifully appointed dressing rooms to make the customers feel pampered and comfortable. Eighteenth- and nineteenth-century dress also required a large number of accessories—hats, shoes, shawls, gloves, and stockings—to complete the look. Tailors and dressmakers frequently accompanied their clients to retail stores with lovely glass cases that sold these accessories. Polite, well-dressed salesclerks waited upon the customers, informing them of the cost of each item, collecting money, and making sure that the packages were delivered to the customer.

This system was now transplanted into the world of Russian commerce. The foreign tailors and dressmakers who journeyed to Russia recruited a new labor pool that consisted of serfs and children drawn from the urban classes. The key to success in the garment trades lay in the ability to fit clothing properly. Neighbors took delight in ridiculing those unfortunate creatures that appeared in public in ill-fitting garments. But sewing a garment to fit each individual was a tricky business. Before uniform sizing of garments developed in the second half of the nineteenth century, each tailor and dressmaker developed his or her own system of measurement. Artisans were usually loath to share their measurement system with their employees because this information would allow employees to compete with their former employers for clients. Under the terms of their contracts, foreign artisans were supposed to teach their Russian workers the fine art of European tailoring, but most refused to share the secrets of successful tailoring. As a result, Russian artisans found it difficult to break the hold that foreign tailors and dressmakers had in the fashion trades, and Russian garments acquired the reputation of being shoddy and inferior when contrasted with fashions made by foreign artisans.

A similar problem existed in retailing apparel. By the end of the eighteenth century, foreign entrepreneurs set up shops in close proximity to one another, creating fashionable shopping districts like those in Paris or London. These European entrepreneurs brought with them new business practices that by the mid-nineteenth century included fixed prices and advertising. These innovations differed sharply with Russian commercial practices. Russian retailing consisted of open-air markets and trading rows. There were no fixed prices as in the European stores, but instead loud haggling over prices. All social groups mixed and mingled in the marketplaces where wily merchants hawked their wares. Goods were displayed on the ground or on wooden countertops instead of glass cases and elegant window displays. No individual could leave a Russian shop without making a purchase—it was the salesclerk's job to ensure that customers bought something. The cool civility of European browsing had no place here. The entire atmosphere in the Russian markets was boisterous and noisy. Because European retailers tended to segregate themselves into exclusive shopping districts, Russian consumers faced a constant choice of whether to shop in elegant European boutiques or in the Russian markets and trading rows. And because Russian goods had a poor reputation when compared with European manufactures, those who could afford to do so shopped at European-style stores for garments manufactured by foreign artisans. One mid-nineteenth-century author offered this advice to his fellow countrymen: "If you have just come to Moscow and you feel you need to have a suit made, then I implore you do not order it on the Pokrovka, or across the Moskva River, in Lefortovo or Gruzinakh; you will perish . . . they will make you a suit in accordance with a fashion which has never existed, you will be dressed worse than a newcomer from the provinces. Hurry to the Tverskaia or Kuznetskii Bridge, address yourself to Zanftleben, to Samias, Reno, Otto, Muller, Tepfer, Lyuk."[3]

The Russian preference for clothing made and sold by foreigners could not be allowed to continue. Foreign craftsmen charged high prices for their goods and services, and that meant that only the wealthiest Russians could afford them. But, as the demand for these goods began to grow, particularly during the nineteenth century, Russian entrepreneurs needed to learn how to compete with foreigners by beating them at their own game. In 1829 businessmen and women organized the first exhibit of Russian manufactured goods, which included a number of fashion goods. They outlined the task they faced in rather dramatic terms:

> In order to understand the truth, it is necessary only to look at, first, the poor, half-wild existence of this country's inhabitants where no industrial development has penetrated, and, then, at the contented and luxurious life of the state where manufacturing and trade flourish. On the one side, poverty and none of life's necessities. On the other, a contentment with everything and even superfluous luxury. There, rank coarseness and ignorance. Here, civility, education, refined taste, and politeness. . . . In short, there stands a coarse son of wild Mother Nature and here stands an educated citizen of civilized society.[4]

A backward, crude, and ignorant land stood side by side with a civilized and refined order with the power of the new industrial revolution behind it. The only way to unite them was to follow the path of education, industrialization, and refinement.

To achieve independence from foreign competition, the Russian fashion industry first had to establish itself as a fashion center. The way to do that was to establish a reliable source of fashion news in Russia. In Europe the proper dress had become so important for any kind of social or economic success that most newspapers and periodicals devoted some space to reporting the latest fashions. In response to these changes, European publishers created the fashion magazine. To ease anxiety about what the current fashions were, these beautifully illustrated magazines reported in great detail on the latest styles. Beginning in the 1820s a group of enterprising men and women set out to create a Russian fashion magazine. The idea behind the magazines was to feature Russian commentary and expert advice on the latest European fashions. Publishers devoted equal coverage to the latest fashions in both Paris and Petersburg using both foreign and Russian commentators. The columnists advised readers to follow the lead of the Petersburg elite because they knew what the latest fashions were and what fashions were best suited to the rigors of the Russian climate. The magazines featured stories and advertisements about native designers, stores, and goods. The special blend of foreign and Russian features proved an enormous success. It now became much easier for Russians to obtain fashion information and to feel confident in developing their own style in dress.

As news about the latest fashions became more available through the periodical press, tailors and dressmakers found it easier to serve the needs of their customers. Clients often brought copies of their favorite magazine to their tailors and dressmakers and asked them to create an outfit for them based upon a particular fashion plate. An experienced artisan could use the picture as a guide and create an almost exact copy of the original, altered to fit the personal style of the client. For those garment workers who could read, this process was much easier because each fashion plate was accompanied by detailed instructions. This growing familiarity with European design eliminated much of the awkwardness of earlier Russian copies. By the last third of the nineteenth century, Russian fashion houses emerged. Nadezhda Lamanova established the most prominent house of women's fashions and her clients included members of the royal family and high society. Other Russians, recognizing that foreign names still had much cachet, tried to disguise their origins by using foreign names for their firms. One such designer, Olga Bul'benkova, created the firm of Madame Olga that was also very popular with Russian high society. Finally, Lev Bakst, the costume designer for the Ballets Russes, helped to revolutionize French high fashion through his brilliant designs. Bakst designed colorful, flowing costumes modeled after antiquity that emphasized the graceful movements of his dancers. French fashion designers took this radical new look and transformed the heavily corseted, hourglass silhouettes of the 1900s into a more natural look for women. In two hundred years, Russians had gone from mere imitators of European dress to fashion innovators.

Another important change was the introduction of ready-to-wear clothing. Ready-to-wear garments were made from precut fabric and sewn in sweatshops. Most ready-to-wear manufacturers operated combined wholesale and retail operations. Middlemen organized the sweatshops, which were usually hot, airless garrets crowded with garment workers of both sexes who toiled for twelve or more hours a day, six days a week. Sweatshops were enormously popular with manufacturers because they required little overhead. The vast supply of garment workers meant that wages were low. Manufacturers could then charge less than tailors and dressmakers for their work but still make handsome profits. Once the garments were stitched together, they were placed in retail outlets where consumers could buy them off the rack. There was no need for several fittings to ensure a proper fit. Most retail outlets that sold ready-to-wear offered whatever alterations might be needed for a small fee. Ready-to-wear saved consumers time and money. It helped fill the growing demand for fashionable clothing in Russia during the second half of the nineteenth century. Now, individuals who could not afford custom-made attire could afford ready-to-wear, allowing many more workers and peasants to wear Western fashions. Male migrant workers quickly abandoned their peasant clothing when they found work in urban settings, and many peasant girls tried to purchase "city clothes" for their dowries.

The rise of ready-to-wear was part of a larger retail transformation in nineteenth-century Russia. Because Russians used the Western European fashion industry as their model, they quickly adopted most of the new European retailing practices. One of the most important of these new retailing strategies was the development of advertising. The earliest success story in advertising was the Singer sewing machine. The Singer Sewing Machine Company proved remarkably innovative in creating a market for the new machine and then in persuading consumers to prefer Singer machines over those of its competitors. Singer became synonymous with the sewing machine in Europe and America. In Russia, salesmen for the company set up retail operations in the big cities and tiny hamlets all across the empire. They sold the machines on installment plans, thereby allowing consumers to use the machines before they had finished paying for them. For those who made their living as garment workers this was a distinct advantage. Another important retail innovation was the creation of the department store. These stores gathered together all sorts of goods under one roof. In Russia, the most famous department stores included Miur and Merilees in Moscow and Military Officers' Store in St. Petersburg. Using elaborate window displays, the retailers enticed customers with one-stop shopping. Department store owners bought large quantities of goods and sold them as quickly as possible. They also used installment plans, credit, and periodic sales to reduce their inventories. Clothing manufacturers also adopted these commercial innovations to increase their sales. Ready-to-wear clothing stores such as M. and I. Mandl', the Alekseev Brothers, and N. I. and G. E. Petukhov and Son used sales and credit to lure customers. Because large department and specialty stores were practical only in big cities, retailers used mail-order catalogues to increase their clientele. The development of the railroad and improvements in the postal service in nineteenth-century Russia allowed consumers the possibility of ordering goods through the mail. By 1914, Russian department and specialty stores were sending goods as far away as Vladivlostok and Manchuria.

Peter's dress revolution had a profound impact on Russian life. As the years went by, Russians grew more comfortable in European fashions. Once the elite adopted European dress as their own, other social groups followed their example. In order to gain acceptance in society, professionals, businessmen, and the artistic community had to learn how to dress à la mode. This was made easier and less costly when Russia developed a ready-to-wear clothing industry beginning in the 1870s. The working poor in both the city and the countryside adopted European dress when they could. Urban workers frequently had to dress in Western clothing as part of their employment, but peasants also bought European gowns and suits to wear for special occasions. Those who could not afford whole outfits began buying factory-made cloth from which they made their work clothes as well as boots, hats, coats, and shawls.

The creation of a fashion industry to supply Russians with European dress also had an important impact on the Russian economy and in particular on the development of Russian capitalism. Much has been written about Russian industrial development, but little has been said about small-scale, consumer-oriented industries like fashion. Yet, from the early eighteenth century onward, entrepreneurs worked hard to meet constantly growing consumer demand for European fashions. Government dress codes may have helped to initiate the fashion market, but it was consumer demand that sustained it. Entrepreneurs helped to expand this new market by developing a fashion press and by adopting retail innovations that had worked well in Western Europe. Although Russian markets and fairs persisted into the twentieth century, Westernized retail stores eclipsed them in commercial importance by the eve of World War I.

It is important to keep in mind that these cultural and economic developments were uneven in nature. Certainly not all peasants could afford or obtain fashions in the new retail establishments. And when they did manage to purchase city clothes, educated society roundly criticized them for purchasing "luxury" goods instead of life's necessities. This criticism suggests that the most important accomplishment of the fashion industry was creating the desire in all Russians to wear fashionable dress. This ability to imagine a different world, a world filled with material goods of all kinds, is a powerful but often overlooked contribution of consumer capitalism. Russians learned to dream about a better and more comfortable life for themselves and their families.

But if Russian capitalists were effective in promoting such dreams, they were unable to fulfill them to everyone's satisfaction. Workers and peasants could not afford to buy ready-to-wear fashions in great quantities; for them, such clothes remained luxury items. This meant that their dream of a better life remained just out of reach and added to their sense of alienation and discontent. Eventually that discontent erupted into revolution in 1905 and 1917. Their economic and political frustrations exploded into violence, bringing down the Romanov dynasty and the capitalist system that supported it. But even though the Bolshevik government abolished capitalism, it did not demand that Russians return to traditional dress. While the economic system that created the fashion industry was gone, Russians continued to dress in European clothing. Peter the Great's revolution in dress was a success.

NOTES

1. During Peter's day the adjective *German* had two meanings in Russian. The first was used to describe ethnic Germans living in Central Europe. *German* was also used to describe all foreigners, especially those from Europe. The word *nemetskii* is derived from the Russia word for "deaf" (*nimoi*). Foreigners were thus "deaf" to the

Russian language. Peter's use of "German dress" in his edict means European dress and not German ethnic costume.

2. *Polnoe sobranie zakonov Rossiiskoi Imperii s 1649 goda*, ser. 1, vol. 4, no. 1741, 1, and no. 1887, 182.

3. As the names suggest, these shops are German or Austrian ateliers. "Vneshnii vid Moskvy srediny XIX veka," *Moskva v ee proshlom i nastoiashchem* 10–11 (1911): 49.

4. *Opisanie pervoi publichnoi vystavki rossiiskoi manufakturnykh izdelii v Sankt-Peterburge 1829 goda* (St. Petersburg: Tipografiia Ekspeditsii zagotovleniia Gosudarstvennykh bumag, 1829), 28, 32–33.

SUGGESTED READINGS

Bonnell, Victoria E., ed. *The Russian Worker: Life and Labor under the Tsarist Regime*. Berkeley: University of California Press, 1983.

Glinka, V. M. *Russkii voennyi kostium XVIII–nachala XX veka*. Leningrad: Khudozhnik RSFSR, 1988.

Hughes, Lindsey. *Russia in the Age of Peter the Great*. New Haven, CT: Yale University Press, 1998.

Korshunova, T. T. *Kostium v Rossii XVIII–nachala XX veka: Iz sobraniia Gosudarstvennogo Ermitazha*. Leningrad: Khudozhnik RSFSR, 1979.

Molotova, L. N., and N. N. Sosina. *Russkii narodnyi kostium: Iz sobraniia Gosudarstvennogo muzeia etnografii narodov SSSR*. Leningrad: Khudozhnik RSFSR, 1984.

Onassis, Jacqueline, ed. *In the Russian Style*. New York: Viking Press, 1976.

Roosevelt, Priscilla. *Life on the Russian Country Estate: A Social and Cultural History*. New Haven, CT: Yale University Press, 1995.

Ruane, Christine. *The Empire's New Clothes: A History of the Russian Fashion Industry, 1700–1917*. London: Yale University Press, 2009.

Shepelev, L. E. *Tituly, mundiry, ordena v Rossiiskoi imperii*. Leningrad: Nauka, 1991.

Wortman, Richard S. *Scenarios of Power: Myth and Ceremony in Russian Monarchy*. 2 vols. Princeton, NJ: Princeton University Press, 1995, 2000.

Chapter Two

How One Runaway Peasant Challenged the Authority of the Russian State

The Case against Mar'ia Semenova

Christine D. Worobec

Feofan Prokopovich (1681–1736), a brilliant orator and theologian, is best known for being an apologist for Peter I's absolutist authority and the author of substantial portions of the Spiritual Regulation of 1721, which turned the Russian Orthodox Church into a bureaucratic arm of the state. Nevertheless, Prokopovich was also a bishop with ecclesiastical authority over the faithful in his diocese. First bishop of Pskov (1718–1725) and then, upon Peter's death, archbishop of Novgorod (1725–1736), Prokopovich had the responsibility to ensure the spiritual health of his flock. It is in his capacity as a bishop of the Russian Orthodox Church that we meet Prokopovich in this chapter. Having already given the eulogy for Peter I and spoken at the coronation ceremonies for Peter's wife, Catherine I (1725–1727), and niece, Anna Ivanovna (1730–1740), Prokopovich had to deal with the much less lofty subjects of the crown, the majority of whom were serfs owned by noblemen and the church.

Over a few centuries monasteries had accumulated significant landed property through grants from individual tsars and private donations. Beginning in the fifteenth century, the St. Cyril monastery in the White Sea area rewarded these donations and other gifts such as money, icons, chalices, crosses, and books with eternal prayers for patrons or their relatives (depending on the nature of the bequests). That practice soon spread to other monastic institutions, although there were opponents within the monastic clergy who in the early sixteenth century were unsuccessful in championing the ancient practice of monastic poverty as well as several sixteenth-century decrees that tried to outlaw donations of land. Clearly, believers' concerns about their salvation triumphed over such objections. With the land grants came peasant laborers. Although a 1497 decree limited the movement of debt-free peasants on all estates, whether church or privately owned, to two weeks a year, they were legally free. Labor shortages as a result of Ivan IV's domestic politics and disastrous wars against Livonia in the second half of the sixteenth century, however, began the process of tying the population to the land. With the abolition of peasants' freedom of movement in the late sixteenth century and the entrenchment of the unfree labor system of serfdom in the law code of 1649, monastic institutions became major serf owners and were very much a part of the serf economy until Catherine II's 1764 secularization of monastic lands. Thereafter, monastic serfs were transferred to the ownership of the state.

The protagonist of this story was a serf by the name of Mar'ia Semenova (b. 1687), who challenged the social order by running away from her owner, the St. George monastery in Novgorod province, and becoming a social nuisance. Not only was she a vagrant but also a mother out of wedlock and an alleged sorcerer, who went so far as to pretend that she was possessed by demons. As you read about Semenova's actions and her tragic past, you will need to consider how such a lower-class woman could pose a threat to the autocratic regime. Why did the state impose such high penalties as corporal punishment and hard labor for crimes that today would appear to be harmless? What do those penalties indicate about the real power of the eighteenth-century Russian government? Why was the newly rationalist church so concerned with combating certain religious practices and beliefs (such as demonic possession) that had been a part of Orthodox believers' understanding of their world for centuries, ultimately creating a fissure between popular practice and official prescriptions? Why was the Orthodox Church involved in policing morality in addition to spiritual matters? Finally, what does Semenova's story reveal about women's positions in a hierarchical patriarchal society?

In the fall of 1732 near the ancient St. George monastery, located just outside the city of Novgorod on the left bank of the River Volkhov, the forty-five-year-old peasant woman Mar'ia Semenova attracted public notice. Periodically, passersby and the monastery's residents found her experiencing horrifying seizures of demonic possession. Lying prostrate with a distended stomach, she spoke in a male voice and made beastly sounds. More astounding was the fact that in the midst of her delirium witnesses reported a reptilian-like creature emerging from her mouth. Onlookers understood Semenova to be tormented by demons; in fact, word quickly spread that twenty-seven evil spirits inhabited her body. Concerned about the effect that Semenova was having on the residents of Novgorod, who viewed her affliction as some preternatural sign that presumably could result in other persons becoming possessed, authorities brought the demoniac to the attention of the second highest ecclesiastical official in the realm, Feofan (Prokopovich), archbishop of Greater Novgorod and Greater Lutsk. The archbishop, in turn, launched an investigation that ultimately brought the wrath of church and state upon Semenova's head for carrying out "utterly God-hating and offensive, never-before-heard-of deeds." Semenova, as it turned out, had committed a number of crimes that defied various laws designed to wrest control over individuals whom the autocracy perceived to be a threat to the social order. As far as church and state were concerned, she epitomized the unruly woman par excellence.[1]

Demonic possession was not an unusual occurrence in eighteenth-century Russia. The phenomenon was part of the ancient church tradition from which Orthodoxy sprang. Christ himself had been a famed exorcist whose healing powers attracted believers from far and wide. With the Christianization of Rus' in 988 and the gradual spread of that monotheistic religion among the populace, demonic possession became part of the cultural landscape. Ascetic monks repeatedly waged battles against demons, and sometimes succumbed to their wiles temporarily. Only exorcisms, communion, holy oil, and the intercession of saints could combat the unclean spirits. Over the course of many centuries, a ritual of demon possession evolved in which the possessed experienced seizures during the divine liturgy or in the presence of holy objects. They convulsed uncontrollably, tore at their hair and clothing, made animal sounds, swore, and blasphemed. Witnesses believed these actions to be products of the demons who inhabited the demoniacs' bodies and who could not tolerate holy symbols. These spectators could attest to the fact that when a demon or group of demons abandoned a victim's body, they saw some sort of vapor or, as in the cases of Semenova in 1732 and Irina Ivanova in 1737, a black object akin to a reptile, moustache, or wet crow.[2] As the eighteenth century unfolded, however, possession provoked the ire of Peter the Great (1682–1725) as he began to question whether these individuals were in fact possessed.

Following rationalist practices in Western Europe, Peter I and his spiritual adviser, Feofan Prokopovich—none other than the bishop who investigated Semenova—issued a series of decrees in the early eighteenth century to eradicate those Orthodox believers' practices they perceived to be "superstitious" and potentially seditious in nature. Various religious and political uprisings of the mid-seventeenth and late seventeenth century as well as concerns about the unpopularity of his measures to Westernize Russia led Peter to step up the prosecution of political and religious crimes. Government officials began to arrest, torture, and penalize blasphemers and individuals who falsely claimed religious experiences. Paradoxically, the rationalist state also stepped up the prosecution of witches and sorcerers, charging them with having negative influence on the faithful and threatening the social order, the person of the tsar, or the tsar's family. Peter and his immediate successors believed in the malevolent powers of witches and sorcerers, who, they thought, were capable of causing a variety of ailments, including possession. Possessed individuals also came under greater scrutiny as potential impostors who disturbed the peace or unjustly accused others of hexing or bewitching them. According to a Senate decree of 1716, bishops of the Orthodox Church were required to deliver individuals faking possession to the secular authorities for sentencing. The exact nature of that sentence became clear in spring 1722 when Peter I received memoranda from the Holy Synod, the newly created state religious office, and commented that such persons deserved "eternal banishment to the galleys with [their] nostrils slit."[3]

In writing the Spiritual Regulation of 1721, which transformed the church into a bureaucratic office, Prokopovich defined superstition as "that which is superfluous, not essential to salvation, devised by hypocrites only for their own interest, beguiling the simple people, and like snowdrifts, hindering passage along the right path of truth."[4] He instructed his bishops to be on the watch for not only victims of possession but also false claims of miracles attributed to icons, wells, streams, and supposedly holy but unsanctified corpses. These so-called superstitions, he believed, were undermining the church's authority and increasing the ranks of schismatics who viewed Peter the Great as the anti-Christ. Unfortunately Semenova found herself in the hands of this man who continued to personify the Petrine regime during the reign of Peter's niece, Anna (1730–1740). In the course of Anna's rule, both the persecution of witchcraft and shammed possession intensified. Reacting against what she perceived to be a weak governmental and police apparatus, she ordered officials to prosecute these crimes more systematically.

From the outset, the damning evidence against Semenova derived from the fact that her antics of possession were perceived by various, even prominent, residents of Novgorod to be "some kind of miracle," which they assumed amounted to "the veritable truth." She was becoming a public nuisance who inspired both fear and awe. Had Semenova not attracted so much attention and had she been lucky enough to be outside Archbishop Prokopovich's jurisdiction, Semenova may instead have been given shelter in the monastery and treated with holy water and prayers of exorcism. Such had been the fate of another possessed woman, Anis'ia Fedorova, who found herself in the care of clerics at the Nikolaevskii Radovitskii monastery in Riazan' in the same year of 1732.[5] Determined to carry out the letter of the law and uncover the true reasons behind Semenova's behavior, which he believed to be fraudulent, Prokopovich had her arrested, examined by midwives, and dispatched under guard to his St. Petersburg domicile. In the meantime, he began the investigatory process. Due to the fact that Semenova had been living with a relative who worked at the St. George monastery, Prokopovich immediately wrote to the monastery's abbot.

In his response Archimandrite Andronik provided Prokopovich with damaging information about Semenova.[6] The abbot identified her as a runaway monastic serf who had come to his attention when she had arrived at the monastery in September 1732 on her return from St. Petersburg. At that time she had requested that the abbot issue her a passport, an internal document that she required if she were going to live outside her place of birth within the Russian Empire.[7] The abbot soon learned that Semenova actually belonged to his monastery's village of Syrkovo. Having left the village without the requisite permission twenty years ago, she had thus deprived her owner of valuable labor. Wandering from place to place illegally begging for "crusts of bread in the name of Christ," she finally came to St. Petersburg (located about five hundred kilometers from Novgorod), where she was arrested as a vagrant. Upon her release, Semenova found employment with a foreigner. Once Semenova lost her job, however, she had little choice but to return home to the place of her birth and master; otherwise she risked being arrested again, subjected to corporal punishment, and banished to either a state factory or Siberia, where she would be subjected to hard labor.[8] Archimandrite Andronik denied her the requisite papers for obtaining a passport and presumably ordered her to return to her native village. He ended his report to Prokopovich by saying that Semenova had come to his attention once again, when stories of her fits of demonic possession reached his ear.

Prokopovich, already suspicious of Semenova's claim that she was possessed, would not have been pleased to hear about Semenova's being a runaway serf and vagrant. The system of serfdom, which was officially decreed in 1649 but had been developing since the late sixteenth century, had been designed to tie a substantial population of laborers to the land and their masters. Peter I further solidified that hold by introducing periodic state censuses to ensure that male serfs, free peasants, and lower urban dwellers all paid state taxes and served in the military. He also demanded that individuals seek permission and passports from their overlords or officials to travel anywhere within the empire. In tune with other European rulers, Peter viewed the existence of beggars in cities to be anathema to law and order and their idleness contrary to the needs of the well-oiled military machine he was trying to build. His concern for law and order was certainly not exaggerated. A foreign visitor to Moscow in the early eighteenth century noted that "there were 'such Numbers of Beggars and Rogues, and . . . so many Excesses and Disorders, that after Sun-set no body ventures abroad without sufficient company.'"[9] In an era when all laborers were necessary for the building of a powerful absolutist state and police small in numbers, these measures of social control were meant to account for all human capital. The state regarded runaway serfs as particularly dangerous to the political and economic status quo: these fugitives not only openly defied a system that categorized them as chattel but also deprived their masters of labor. Semenova's crimes, as enumerated by the archimandrite of St. George's monastery, would not have predisposed Archbishop Prokopovich to view the woman sympathetically. As it turned out, however, he was about to discover even more disturbing information about Semenova.

On the night of 23 November, a mere day and a half after the guards brought Semenova to Prokopovich's palace in St. Petersburg, she unexpectedly gave birth to a girl who lived less than two weeks. Four midwives had previously attended to Semenova but could not explain why her belly was swollen. Having heard descriptions of Semenova's demonic fits, it is possible that they were afraid of getting too close to her and becoming infected themselves; claiming ignorance may have been the safer route. Hauled before the angry archbishop to account for her illegal out-of-wedlock pregnancy, Semenova recounted various aspects of her difficult life. She explained that when she was a child she had been bewitched, as a result of which she had developed "the falling sickness," a common premodern term for epilepsy. Anticipating Prokopovich's question about who had bewitched her, she explained that she did not know the identity of the witch or sorcerer who had placed a hex upon her and therefore could not be charged with accusing someone of sorcery unjustly as Petrine law dictated. Semenova also confessed to Prokopovich that she had had a previous pregnancy. Some thirteen years ago, according to her testimony, she had been raped by Fedor Tebnev, a servant at the monastery. At that time she had given an oral deposition against Tebnev to Aaron, the then bishop of Korelsk and Ladozhsk, who sought to punish the rapist. She subsequently gave birth to twin boys, who like their half sister died shortly after birth. Semenova also admitted to being subsequently detained in the Novgorod Provincial Chancery because she had had a seizure connected to the falling sickness on a city street. Trying to gain sympathy from her interlocutor, she showed Prokopovich her damaged left foot. She explained that she had lost her toenails during the torture to which she had been subjected at the hands of the provincial authorities. Due to the ubiquitous practice of torture, Semenova's claim would not have been perceived to be far-fetched. Perhaps feeling unsafe in Novgorod, Semenova had headed off to St. Petersburg, where, she admitted, she was arrested not only for lacking the appropriate passport but also for being possessed by demons. After Semenova was treated at the Kuntskamera's hospital, the Petersburg police released her, and she went to work for Petr Iakovlev, a dealer in flour and meal. While in

Petersburg, she was once again raped. This time, Semenova explained to Prokopovich, she did not tell anyone of her ordeal.

Given the Russian Orthodox Church's disapproval of premarital sex, which could result in eternal damnation if the sin went unrepented, it might appear odd that Semenova readily confessed to the archbishop that she had a history of out-of-wedlock pregnancies. Perhaps she realized that Prokopovich would eventually learn about her past from her father confessor as it was the norm for crime investigators to contact priests about their parishioners' confessional habits. It is also conceivable that Semenova hoped to secure the archbishop's sympathy by portraying herself as having been repeatedly coerced into sexual relations. Unlike early modern Western Europe, Russia had a benevolent attitude toward rape victims. Given the high value that Russians placed on a woman's honor and the purity of male bloodlines, they considered rape a heinous crime. Women of all social classes, including prostitutes, could sue their attackers for damages in ecclesiastical and civil courts. They did not have to produce eyewitnesses or demonstrate that they had resisted the attack. If they became pregnant, rape victims in Russia, unlike their counterparts in Western Europe, were not suspected of giving consent to intercourse.[10] Ecclesiastical judges even took false accusations seriously because of the enhanced honor that women enjoyed in early modern Russian society. What Semenova had not banked on, however, was Prokopovich's reluctance to accept any elements of her story as having veracity. Because he was convinced that demonic possession was a fraudulent behavior, he had sought medical confirmation that she was shamming her seizures.

On the previous day Archbishop Feofan had requested that the Petersburg doctor and professor of anatomy Veitbrekht assess Semenova's condition in order to verify her claims of having both the falling sickness and possession. Unlucky for Semenova, the doctor recognized her from her first visit to the Kuntskamera Hospital (an institution established by Peter I) in April 1731. He informed Prokopovich that at the time of her previous visit, Semenova had been suffering from some sort of ailment, but not the one she now pretended to have; thus he could plausibly conclude, without physically examining her, that she was shamming possession this time as well. After checking with the St. Petersburg Police Department about her vagrancy and with the Novgorod Provincial Chancery about her alleged abuse—which, contrary to Semenova's story, made no mention of having tortured her—Prokopovich decided to have Veitbrekht make another assessment of Semenova's health. This time the physician actually conducted a cursory physical examination and diagnosed her as having "the French disease," or syphilis, because of a chancre he found on her right leg. Finally, Prokopovich learned that Semenova had had sex twice with one of the guards in his own palace. The archbishop expressed his displeasure in his deposition to the Holy Synod by noting that "she did not tell anyone [i.e., any of the other guards] about the rape or did not cry out at the time; it wasn't as if she were kept in some inhabitable place but rather in the entrance hall to a special hut where his other residents" lived. The fact that Semenova was nonetheless a prisoner and vulnerable to a guard's attack did not enter Prokopovich's mind. Moving beyond the Muscovite understanding of rape, the archbishop clearly viewed Semenova as the sexual predator, a temptress of men. And if Semenova was indeed the initiator rather than a victim of the sexual encounter, who could have blamed her? By befriending one of her jailers, she might have been set free from the horrible fate that awaited her.

With the evidence solidly against her, Semenova took her Christian duty seriously by confessing her sins. She admitted to Prokopovich that she had covered up her second shameful pregnancy by pretending to be possessed by demons. Having thought up the ruse about three years ago when she could not find shelter because she did not have the necessary passport, she had experimented with putting two bundles of her hair in her mouth so that it would look as though a demon or a demon in the shape of a reptile was about to emerge from her innards. Semenova also acknowledged her guilt in failing to confess her crimes of shamming possession repeatedly to her priest. As for her fornicating with the guard, she claimed that the man had raped her, but that she did not inform anyone of the incident and had freely engaged in sex with him the second time. Asking for absolution from the bishop for her many transgressions, Semenova even volunteered to take up the veil and live the life of a woman religious as a way of fulfilling the "penance for her impertinence." She noted that she was not suited to hard labor in a monastery, which was the common sentence for her crime.

Semenova's reference to her "impertinence" is an interesting choice of words. As it turns out, according to Prokopovich's deposition, she had insulted both Dr. Veitbrekht and the archbishop himself. She had not only run away from Veitbrekht's care, but upon her return to his hospital pretended to take the medicine he gave her for her syphilis and insulted his honor by hurling obscenities at him. Semenova had also affronted Prokopovich, a public official, by using inappropriate language. Verbal abuse of authority figures ran contrary to the mores of the elite and a centralizing state. Indeed, the Petrine state had "accentuated the Muscovite practice of punishing more harshly insult to public places and officers of the state than insults to private individuals." Semenova's abandonment of the feminine virtues or "meekness and obedience" only underscored her danger to the fragile social order.[11]

The nail that sealed Semenova's coffin came in the form of a letter to Prokopovich and the Holy Synod from the engineer Ivan Beshentsov, who charged Semenova with two new crimes: defecating on a fetus she had miscarried, presumably to hide it, and offering to enchant some salt for Beshentsov so that he would have a love potion that would make women fall madly in love with him and want to marry him. Semenova's dabbling with witchcraft was confirmed by the fact that under arrest in Archbishop Feofan's home, she had taken a cross out of her pocket and hung it from her finger, whispering "God knows what" over it.

Convinced of her guilt, the Holy Synod turned Mar'ia Semenova over to the Novgorod Provincial Office in shackles for sentencing. In so doing, it noted not only Peter I's recommendation that a woman shamming possession be subjected to corporal punishment and exiled to the galleys with split nostrils, but also Empress Anna Ivanovna's 1731 decree that recommended burning at the stake or a lesser punishment, depending on the degree of the crime that had been committed as a result of an engagement in sorcery.[12] Interestingly, the Holy Synod did not mention the punishments for runaways and fornicators, no doubt because the other evidence against Semenova was so overwhelmingly damning, the penalties for shamming possession and indulging in sorcery were so severe, and the crimes with which she was charged presented larger threats to the realm. Unfortunately, the available sources do not tell us what punishment Semenova received at the hands of the civil authorities; as documents that initiated the investigation, they are by nature incomplete. Ultimately, the civil authorities decided the nature of the corporal punishments and at times even made recommendations to the ecclesiastical authorities about the severity of spiritual penances. We can presume from other cases for which penalties were stipulated in the written record that Semenova was probably subjected to a brutal flogging with the knout (the razor sharp tip of which could easily cut the flesh through to the bone) and exiled to a monastery or Siberia. In either place she would have performed in leg irons the hard labor she had so dreaded. In her place of exile, Semenova would also have had to carry out a rigorous penance of daily prayer, full body prostrations, and a minimal diet of bread and water on Wednesdays and Fridays of each week and major religious holidays. In a 1735 case, for example, the authorities had subjected Nastas'ia Iakovleva and Mariia Semenovna Antonova to corporal punishment before exiling them permanently to hard labor in a woman's monastery for lesser crimes (dabbling in witchcraft in the case of Iakovleva and making use of Iakovleva's services in the case of Antonova).[13]

As a shamming possessed woman, sorcerer, runaway, vagrant, fornicator, and insubordinate woman, the outcast Semenova had presented a major challenge to the newly established police state, which "strove to regulate every aspect of people's lives, not so much for their own individual benefit as for the greater good of the state as a whole."[14] The brutal punishments she received

were meant to deter other women from committing the same crimes and ensure their compliance with an exploitative economic, social, and political system that allowed Russia to act as a major player on the European stage. It was
Semenova's great misfortune to have been discovered by the repressive but
simultaneously weak governmental apparatus. She paid the price for those
hundreds of thousands of peasants who had illegally fled their places of residence for the borderlands and cities. Unlike male fugitives, however, who had
a better chance of finding employment or ultimately serving as garrison war-
riors and therefore fulfilling their responsibilities to the state, Semenova had
found herself an outlaw within her own community without any rights. That
situation drove her to indulge in subterfuge, undertake relationships with men
who neglected to take responsibility for the children they sired in spite of
fairly new Petrine laws designed to protect those children, and dabble in love
potions as a way of gaining some authority and respect. Her ultimate refuge
in demonic possession symbolized her best hope of obtaining the social services that she needed. Ultimately, her attempts to survive led to her tragic end.

NOTES

1. Semenova's story and investigation are contained in the *Polnoe sobranie
postanovlenii i rasporiazhenii po vedomstvu pravoslavnago ispovedaniia Rossiiskoi
Imperii*, vol. 8 of 19 (St. Petersburg: V Sinodalnoi tip., 1915), 95–101, no. 2719.

2. Part of the official investigation of Irina Ivanova is included in A. V. Bezrodnyi,
"Proshlyi vek v ego nravakh, obychaiakh i verovaniiakh," *Russkaia starina* 90 (May
1897): 283–87.

3. *Polnoe sobranie zakonov Rossiiskoi Imperii s 1649 goda* (*PSZ*), ser. 1, vol. 2,
no. 532 (1830).

4. Alexander V. Muller, ed. and trans., *The Spiritual Regulation of Peter the Great*
(Seattle: University of Washington Press, 1972), 15.

5. A. S. Lavrov, *Koldovstvo i religiia v Rossii, 1700–1740 gg.* (Moscow:
Drevlekhranilishche, 2000), 391.

6. In the Orthodox Church the title *archimandrite* is reserved for abbots of important monasteries.

7. Internal passports were first introduced in 1719 in order for the state "to keep
track of people liable to conscription and, after 1724, the poll tax." David Moon, *The
Russian Peasantry 1600–1930: The World the Peasants Made* (London: Longman,
1999), 84.

8. For discussion of the Petrine laws against vagrants, see Daniel H. Kaiser, "The
Poor and Disabled in Early Eighteenth-Century Russian Towns," *Journal of Social
History* 32, no. 1 (Fall 1998): 129–31.

9. Quoted in Janet Hartley, *A Social History of the Russian Empire 1600–1825*
(London: Longman, 1999), 103. Hartley notes that in 1744 St. Petersburg had a sub-

stantial number—5,372—of beggars (out of a total population of approximately 95,000) because of famine in the surrounding areas (Hartley, *A Social History*, 104).

10. Eve Levin, *Sex and Society in the World of the Orthodox Slavs, 900–1700* (Ithaca, NY: Cornell University Press, 1989), 221–22.

11. Nancy Shields Kollmann, *By Honor Bound: State and Society in Early Modern Russia* (Ithaca, NY: Cornell University Press, 1999), 239, 249.

12. The law reads,

> If henceforth, someone does not fear the wrath of God and . . . summons sorcerers to his home, or goes to their houses for some kind of magical assistance, or has conversations about magic with them . . . or follows their teaching, or if any sorcerers carry out evil [deeds] for themselves or on behalf of someone else, then these deceivers will be punished by death at the stake; and for those who request their [services] for soul-destroying profit, there will be severe punishment; they will be beaten with the knout, while others, by the seriousness of their guilt, will be sentenced to death. (*PSZ*, ser. 1, vol. 7, no. 2451)

13. *PSZ*, ser. 1, vol. 19, no. 6784.

14. Simon Dixon, *The Modernisation of Russia 1676–1825* (Cambridge: Cambridge University Press, 1999), 80.

SUGGESTED READINGS

Glagoleva, Olga E. "The Illegitimate Children of the Russian Nobility in Law and Practice, 1700–1860." *Kritika* 6, no. 3 (Summer 2005): 461–99.

Kaiser, Daniel H. "The Poor and Disabled in Early Eighteenth-Century Russian Towns." *Journal of Social History* 32, no. 1 (Fall 1998): 125–55.

Kollmann, Nancy Shields. "Women's Honor in Early Modern Russia." Pp. 60–73 in *Russia's Women: Accommodation, Resistance, Transformation*, edited by Barbara Evans Clements, Barbara Alpern Engel, and Christine D. Worobec. Berkeley: University of California Press, 1991.

Levin, Eve. *Sex and Society in the World of the Orthodox Slavs, 900–1700*. Ithaca, NY: Cornell University Press, 1989.

Michels, Georg B. "Ruling without Mercy: Seventeenth-Century Russian Bishops and Their Officials." *Kritika* 4, no. 3 (2003): 515–42.

Ryan, W. F. "The Witchcraft Hysteria in Early Modern Europe: Was Russia an Exception?" *Slavonic and East European Review* 76, no. 1 (January 1998): 49–84.

Worobec, Christine D. *Possessed: Women, Witches, and Demons in Imperial Russia*. DeKalb: Northern Illinois University, 2001.

Chapter Three

Life on the River

The Education of a Merchant Youth

David L. Ransel

*Ivan Tolchenov (pronounced Tal-CHON-aff) represents a handful of mer-
chants in eighteenth-century Russia who faithfully kept a diary. He left behind
three leather-bound volumes of his daily trials and tribulations. The beneficiary of Peter the Great's project to transform Russians into Europeans,
Tolchenov possessed the self-confidence and individualism that propelled him
to aspire to become a member of Russian high society. As David Ransel has
written elsewhere, Tolchenov succeeded in transforming himself from a
parochial businessman to a man of cultivated interests who hobnobbed with
members of the Russian nobility. Financial ruin in the end did not curtail all
of his contacts with high society.*

*In this chapter Ransel introduces us to the young Tolchenov who was home-
schooled and apprenticed in the family's grain business as an adolescent. The
only survivor of nine children, Tolchenov had major responsibilities in the
family business and no option but to continue in that trade. Through his travels we learn about the precariousness of life in late eighteenth-century Russia. Merchants constantly had to battle adverse weather conditions, perilous
rapids, and other obstacles along the waterways. They were not immune to
the ravages of epidemic diseases, of which plague was the most deadly and
terrifying. It is little wonder then that at age nineteen Tolchenov, in the midst
of a dangerous commercial trip to the capital city of St. Petersburg, made a
point of recording the fact that he prayed for guidance in Novgorod's magnificent St. Sophia Cathedral. No doubt he venerated the many icons in the
cathedral, perhaps finding solace in an icon of the Mother of God to whom
sailors and other shipmen had turned for help.*

*At the same time, Tolchenov moved in circles of the high and mighty. His
father had not only been mayor of their provincial town of Dmitrov, but also*

*served as a delegate to the Legislative Commission, which Catherine II
(1762–1796) summoned in 1767 in order to place Russia firmly under the
rule of law by codifying Russia's laws and decrees. Much to Catherine's cha-
grin, the commission's delegates, representing all social estates in Russia
ranging from the nobility to state peasants (agriculturalists who lived on
lands belong to the state and owed obligations to the state rather than to serf
owners), spent much of their time discussing matters that were of concern to
their individual social groupings rather than national issues. She dismissed
that commission a year later, when war broke out against Ottoman Turkey.
Nonetheless, the discussions of Catherine's agenda, her famous "Instructions
to the Legislative Commission," did result in a variety of reform measures in
the 1770s and 1780s. Those reforms included creating better administrative
structures at the town and provincial levels and setting Russia onto the path
of becoming a regulated state in which the government promulgated rules to
serve the common good and establish better order. One of the catalysts for
those reforms was the Pugachev Rebellion of 1773–1774, involving an uprising of Cossacks and recently enserfed peasants on the southeastern frontiers
of the empire against increasing taxes and obligations. Tolchenov's father, as
Ransel points out, allied himself with the local nobility to raise men and arms
against the rebels. In essence, then, the great events of Catherine II's reign
did have an impact on the life of the merchant Tolchenov.*

*What opportunities did Tolchenov have for rising up the social ladder in
Catherinian Russia? What was the relationship between merchants and the
imperial government? What opportunities did St. Petersburg offer members of
the merchant estate?*

When Peter the Great built his new capital city on the shores of the Gulf of
Finland in 1704, he gave a powerful impetus to commerce. The new capital,
St. Petersburg, sited for easy access to Europe, was not well positioned to
supply itself with the necessities of life. The surrounding area was swampy
and cold, unable to produce adequate grain or fuel to feed and warm the rapidly growing population of a major metropolis. Grain, in particular, had to be
brought north to the new capital from distant centers of production in the
south of Russia and in the east far down the Volga River and its tributaries.
Since these waterways ran south, they had to be linked to the northern rivers
running to St. Petersburg by portages and canals. Peter the Great had begun
to build the needed connections in his own time, hiring an engineering firm
to join a tributary of the Volga, the Tvertsa River, to the northern waterways
through a canal at the continental divide at Vyshnii Volochek. Although on the
map the waterways appear to line up neatly and provide broad avenues for
commerce, the journey itself in the eighteenth century was arduous and

fraught with risk to commercial shipments and the persons accompanying them. Before improvements were introduced in the next century, the route from Vyshnii Volochek down the Valdai Hills resembled the white-water rafting of today, but in heavily loaded, rigid vessels, was difficult to maneuver. It is in travels along these waterways that young merchants in eighteenth-century Russia learned their trade. One of these merchants, Ivan Tolchenov, wrote a journal in which we can follow his upbringing and travels.

Ivan was born in October 1754 in the town of Dmitrov north of Moscow. His father was the wealthiest merchant in the city and served for a time as mayor. Many members of the Tolchenov family, including Ivan's uncles on his father's side and his maternal grandfather, made their money primarily in the grain trade to St. Petersburg. Only merchants of considerable wealth could afford to operate this trade. It required heavy investments, and the turnover was slow. A merchant had each year to purchase large consignments of grain and

CENTRAL EUROPEAN RUSSIA

- ◉ Capital city
- • City
- ⌇ Rivers
- ⌒ Canal
- 〰 Body of water

dozens of riverboats and barges; lease flour mills and storage facilities; and hire agents, millers, barge haulers, and pilots. He had to make these outlays long before he could hope to earn a profit by sales in St. Petersburg. Nearly every year a substantial portion of his grain shipments had to overwinter en route, for cold weather closed in early and froze the waterway before all the barges completed the trip. Credit instruments were poorly developed in Russia at this time, and where credit was available it was expensive. In other words, to succeed in the grain trade a merchant had to command sufficient capital to carry his business through many months of delayed compensation.

Formal education for merchant children in the provinces was unknown at the time of Ivan's childhood. Public and private schools of any kind scarcely existed outside the major cities, and, indeed, many merchants questioned the value of a school education for their children even when such an education was available. Empress Catherine II, whose long reign began in 1762 at the time Ivan was seven years old, sought to promote the education of the nobility and the urban dwellers. Among her efforts was the establishment of a Commercial School in Moscow in 1772. To her dismay, scarcely any merchant families cared to send their sons to this school, and its classes were filled by students from other social groups.[1] Merchant families at this time understood that their sons had to know the rudiments of reading, writing, and arithmetic in order to succeed in commerce, but they worried about giving their children a more elaborate schooling lest they acquire pretensions and tastes that would alienate them from their merchant roots and send them seeking employment in government service or other fields.

These attitudes were just beginning to change during the reign of Catherine II. A few prominent merchant families began to provide more education to their children, and some merchant sons could be heard spouting French phrases on the streets of Moscow.[2] In fact, Ivan himself, when he grew up and had children of his own, sent his firstborn son to an expensive private school in Moscow. But these first signs of change were not typical of the commercial classes as a whole at this time. Only about 5 percent of the statements of local need submitted by merchants to Empress Catherine's famous Legislative Commission of 1767–1768 included requests for improved cultural facilities and schools for town dwellers. Most merchants believed that too great an interest in books was an indulgence that would keep their sons from real learning. Real learning, in their view, had to be acquired by experience, by working in the family trade itself. Ivan's father was from this old school. He had achieved great success himself with a modicum of education, and he saw no need to provide more than the basics for Ivan.

Consequently, like most merchant sons of his time, Ivan got his education at home. He writes in his journal that "at age five I was first taught Russian grammar, and I can say that I was a good student, enjoyed learning, and worked hard. Even though I was studying at home without the guidance of a real teacher and was almost self-taught, in less than a year I was able to read any kind of printed text without difficulty."[3] After that, Ivan worked on writing but had to admit that his penmanship was nothing to boast of for want of having a proper instructor. Ivan's father gave him lessons in arithmetic and taught him functions "up to the rule of three" (the method of finding a fourth term in a proportion when three terms are given).[4]

Home study did not last long. A grain merchant was a traveler, and by the time Ivan was eleven years old, he took his first long trip with his father on business. They rode by land north to St. Petersburg, and Ivan got acquainted with the sights of the imperial capital, including the great marketplace for overseas commerce, the Alexander Nevsky monastery, Kazan Cathedral, and the Winter Palace of the tsars. Soon thereafter, we find him in Moscow, the largest commercial center in Russia, where Ivan lived for several months while his father represented his fellow townsmen on the Legislative Commission of Empress Catherine II. By 1768, when Ivan was only thirteen years old, his father sent him to work on the grain traffic through the northern waterways under the supervision of one of the family's agents. He helped to load the barges on the Tvertsa River and then followed them north through the canals and rivers until he reached the city of Novgorod. There Ivan received a message from his father, ordering him to hasten by land to St. Petersburg where his father was participating in a second session of the Legislative Commission. Upon arrival, Ivan learned of his mother's death that week from galloping tuberculosis. This emotionally devastating event ended his apprenticeship for that year. His stay in St. Petersburg extended through much of the rest of the year and gave him an opportunity to continue his book learning. A monk and dean of the St. Petersburg seminary served as his tutor, and it was at this time, Ivan reported, that "I began to occupy myself with books . . . and my eagerness for reading began to grow."[5] Ivan remained an avid reader the rest of his life. At the same time, he was also a writer, setting down in his journal the story of his life.

Moving grain and flour up through the northern waterways was just one side of the family's trade. Ivan also had to learn how to find, purchase, and transport grain to the family's flour mills for processing. Some grain was purchased from the nobility in Ivan's home district, but the largest consignments came from down the great rivers to the south and east. Purchasing occupied the family firm during much of each winter. Ivan's father and his agents went south to the city of Orel on the Oka River and southeast down the Volga and Sura rivers to make purchases at several major grain entrepôts. In late November 1769, at age fifteen, Ivan was introduced to this aspect of the business.

He rode with his father to Orel, where they bought large allotments of wheat, buckwheat, and rye. His father then left to conduct business in Moscow, while young Ivan stayed on with a family agent. In March, they supervised the loading of grain onto large boats and moved them downriver toward the Volga. The transport of grain from the south early in the year faced problems of unpredictable weather, and on this trip Ivan had traveled scarcely twenty-five miles downstream when a cold snap froze the boats into the river for two weeks. Once the weather warmed and the boats could move, Ivan sailed with them to the juncture of the Oka and Moscow rivers, where he left the boats and rode north overland to assist with the barge traffic through the northern canals, again with an agent from the family business. This time he stayed with the barge traffic all the way to St. Petersburg, but not without incident. In the rapids of the Neva River a short distance from the city, two barges in his group collided in a fog with a stranded water boat and sank. Though distressing, such incidents were far from unusual or unexpected. Indeed, it was rare that all the firm's boats and barges arrived undamaged because of the many rapids, shallows, sandbars, and dilapidated locks along the waterway.

Let's take a closer look at this waterway, which at this time was moving 2,400–3,000 boats and barges each year from central Russia to the new northern capital. The traffic passed through the waterway in three large caravans, one each in the spring, summer, and fall. At the high point in the system, the continental divide at Vyshnii Volochek, the main problem, apart from deteriorating wooden canal walls and locks, was water flow. Spring runoff provided more than enough water for the first barge caravan that moved out in April, but flows for the summer and autumn caravans were much less reliable. Because of insufficient reservoir capacity, low water levels often brought the boats and barges to a halt. Downstream the greatest danger was on the Msta River, which was punctuated by stretches of white water, the most treacherous being the Borovichi rapids, where boats had to pass through eleven miles of turbulent, rock-strewn waters. In the 1760s the office in charge of these rapids floated logs attached to mooring lines to guide boats through the rough waters and keep them from smashing into the rocky shoreline, but accidents were frequent as barges broke apart on stones or ran aground. Villagers who lived along the route made good money mounting rescue and repair operations on damaged vessels, a business so profitable that a Senate commission looking into the matter believed that the villagers were replacing obstacles removed from the stream in order to increase their opportunities for earnings.[6]

When the barge caravans exited the Msta into Lake Ilmen, they encountered additional hazards. Not only was Lake Ilmen shallow and silty—barely sixteen feet at its deepest point, putting vessels at risk of stranding—but the open waters of the lake also exposed the boats to high winds and unpredictable storms. Its bottom became the final resting place of countless water-craft. After crossing Ilmen, the boats entered the Volkhov River. More placid than the Msta, the Volkhov nevertheless contained a number of rapids as well, the worst requiring portages, except during the high water flow in the spring. Merchants appealed again and again for the authorities to clear the rapids, but no lasting solution was found until late in the century when the government began building canals in the streambed through the rapids, a project only completed well after the turn of the century. The barges completed their journey by traveling down the Ladoga canal to the Neva River and from there into the northern capital. The reason for the Ladoga canal was the turbulence of Lake Ladoga itself. Early in the century, the barges had used the lake route, but so many of them sank that the government quickly realized the need to cut a canal along the south shore of the lake.

The condition of this waterway had another unfortunate feature: goods moved almost exclusively in one direction. The difficulties and expense of transporting goods downstream from central Russia to St. Petersburg were compounded in moving goods back up the shallow and rocky watercourses. Indeed, shipments from St. Petersburg back up the waterway were so unprofitable that nearly all the boats and barges entering the city were broken up at their destination and sold for firewood. This practice brought complaints from people in central Russia about deforestation along the waterway and the increasing cost of wood locally. The government responded to these complaints in the 1780s with an inducement to merchants to run their barges back upstream. The authorities offered a dividend of fifty rubles for each boat taken back to the Borovichi rapids. The effort failed. It cost at least two hundred rubles to haul a barge back to Novgorod, still some distance from the Borovichi rapids, whereas a trader could purchase a barge at Novgorod for eighty to one hundred rubles.[7]

Ivan's education on the river continued. In 1771, for the first time he ran the barges himself downriver from Novgorod. An agent of the family firm had accompanied him through the more hazardous segments of the waterway above Novgorod, but from there Ivan took charge and guided the family's boats into St. Petersburg. He was sixteen years old. Lucky for him, too, that he was in the north that summer, far from Moscow. That ancient capital had been hit by the last great outbreak in Europe of the bubonic plague. The scourge carried away a quarter of Moscow's population in a short time and led to riots against the authorities, including the brutal murder of the archbishop by a mob enraged at his prohibitions of religious assemblies (intended to reduce the spread of the disease). In Ivan's own hometown of Dmitrov only about forty persons died of the plague. Ivan consoled himself with the thought that the dead were people who had received personal goods or visitors from

Moscow without taking the proper precautions, by which he probably meant quarantining and fumigation, the methods then in use to contain the spread of the disease.[8] Precautions such as these and fear of the plague hindered the grain business for a time. The following year, when Ivan was accompanying the family's barges north, he was held up for many days in the Volkhov River, waiting out a quarantine, and when the grain shipments finally reached St. Petersburg, sale of the rye flour they had hauled from Moscow proved difficult, evidently because of fears that it might contain plague contamination. By contrast, sales of their grain from the central Volga were brisk.

The year 1773 marked a major turning point in Ivan's personal and working life. In January his father arranged a marriage for him with the daughter of a merchant family from Moscow. Evidently, the first time Ivan saw his future wife and lifelong companion was a week before the wedding, when his father introduced him to the young woman and then conducted negotiations with her family. Russian marriages involved economic and personal commitments between families that required detailed definition. Ivan was eighteen years old and apparently satisfied to let his elders manage these matters, as was customary. In fact, he was marrying younger than most merchant sons. Because marriage implied an economic alliance, most merchant sons were not in a strong enough financial position to make an advantageous match at a young age.[9] The business success of Ivan's family and Ivan's own position as the sole surviving child gave his marriage proposal exceptional appeal.

During the first half of the year following his marriage, Ivan was permitted to spend most of his time with his young wife either at home in Dmitrov or with his father and stepmother at one of their mills near the Volga. Life in the grain business, the need to be on the road much of the year in bad weather and good, gave Ivan a keen appreciation of the pleasures of home life. In Dmitrov he enjoyed all the conveniences of the family's large, two-story timber home (featuring an addition of guest apartments recently completed in masonry), a staff of servants, and the respect of his fellow citizens as the leading family of the city. Ivan found it hard to give up these pleasures and go on the road where he often lodged in post stations, on barges, and even in open fields. Some days he had to work and ride through the night with no rest. At the end of each year he remarked wearily in his diary the number of miles he had traveled that year and the exact number of days he had been separated from his wife. After his father died and Ivan inherited the business, he abruptly ended his life on the road and turned this arduous side of the business over to agents in his employ. But this change was some time off; the years following his marriage found him on the road more than ever.

Ivan's marriage signaled the end of his apprenticeship in the family business. While he remained a junior partner in an enterprise dominated by his energetic father, Ivan was now regarded as capable of directing transport and trading operations on his own, including the hazardous passage down the northern waterways from Vyshnii Volochek. In September 1773, his father for the first time entrusted him fully with one of the family's grain shipments from central Russia. He dispatched Ivan to the family's grain barges that were waiting near Vyshnii Volochek to set out on the third and final shipping caravan of the year. Ivan's notes from this trip reflect his new level of responsibility and also provide a vivid picture of the difficulties that merchants encountered in moving their goods to market.

The fall caravan was moving through the locks in a series of columns. The first with 139 barges started through on 14 September. The next day another 236 moved out in two columns, one in the morning and one in the afternoon. Ivan had 13 barges divided between these two. The following day, still more barge columns departed, placing Ivan's barges in the middle of a lengthy, tightly packed string of vessels. The real test began when the columns slid through the locks leading from Lake Mstino into the Msta River. From here until the river emptied into Lake Ilmen the barges had to pass through eighteen rapids, including the feared Borovichi rapids, plus nine treacherous shoals, not to mention other obstacles such as enormous rocks (each bearing a colorful name) and occasional narrows. Ivan worked out of his barges in the front column but often rode ahead in a government boat to judge the hazards and hire river pilots locally to guide the barges through difficult stretches. He also moved backward to check on his barges in the trailing column.

On 24 September Ivan reached the Opechenskii wharf just above the Borovichi rapids. He hired a pilot to run his barges through the rapids and rode on ahead in a government boat to the town of Borovichi to await their arrival. Luckily, all of the barges in this column came through unharmed. The trailing column was, however, stalled in heavy traffic above the rapids. Ivan rode back by land and found that a knot of boats was going to delay entry of his seven trailing barges into the rapids until late in the day. What was he to do? Should he send them on their way at last light? Nervously, he decided to dispatch five of them and hold the last two back until morning. The five got through, but one of them so filled with water that it had to be pumped out all night. Even then, it proved unseaworthy, and Ivan transferred its contents to his other vessels. The remaining two barges arrived safely the next morning, but probably only because their crews had shifted sixty sacks of flour from them to a third craft known as a lighter (a low-draft boat used in shallow waters). The lighter, however, sank, and this mishap further delayed Ivan while his men reloaded the flour from the disabled lighter onto other barges.

The rest of the way down the Msta, low water and fog made the remaining rapids and shoals exceptionally dangerous. The barge carrying Ivan was again and again stranded on rocks and ran aground in sandbars, each time having to be pulled free by other boats and slowing the column's overall progress. When Ivan's first barges finally reached the town of Bronnitsy, a few miles above Lake Ilmen, Ivan rode forward to the estuary and discovered that haulers were having to drag barges through the shallows with great effort, managing to pull no more than ten or twenty barges a day into the lake. Riding back to find his barges in the trailing column, he located them about four miles above Bronnitsy where a government boat was aground at midriver. It quickly became clear that his trailing barges could go no farther. He hired stevedores and unloaded the cargo on the riverbank for overwintering. Ivan then went downstream and was able to get some of his barges from the first column down to the estuary, but strong winds off the lake and heavy rains sank nine nearby barges (fortunately, not his own). Ivan faced a dilemma. The weather was unsettled. Winter was closing in. Should he risk going farther or give up and fail to get any of the family's fall shipments to market? A big decision for a young man just turning nineteen years old. On 14 October, he shifted some bags from three barges onto a fourth empty one to make the vessels more seaworthy, evidently expecting to proceed into the lake. However, the next day, his birthday, Ivan decided to trudge through miles of swamps to the ancient city of Novgorod and pray for guidance at its famous St. Sophia Cathedral. When he returned to the boats, he decided to call it quits. A wise decision. Later the same day, as he moved back upriver, Ivan ran into strong winds and blinding snow that trapped him on the water at night and nearly prevented him from reaching the safety of his upstream barges. He had halted his shipments none too soon.

Although the family firm had ended the year with barges stranded all along the waterway (Ivan's on the Msta and others on the Tvertsa), this was not unusual. When the ice broke up the next spring and the high water from the melt lifted the boats and sped them to St. Petersburg, Ivan found their cargo in great demand, and brisk sales fetched a handsome profit. With his commercial work finished quickly in this early summer of 1774, Ivan had time free to enjoy some pleasures of the imperial capital. He joined a great promenade on Pentecost Sunday at the imperial summer residence, Catherine's Palace, where the empress and her son and heir, Grand Duke Paul, were in attendance. Three weeks later he went to the other suburban palace of the tsars, Peterhof, the guest of a relative, Pavel Tolchenov, a purveyor to the court. There Ivan attended a masquerade that occupied the palace and its surrounding gardens and included, in his enthusiastic report, "a magnificent decoration of many-colored lights."[10] This young man of nineteen obviously enjoyed these opportunities to witness the splendors of imperial rule and to rub shoulders with the wellborn and the powerful.

Another opportunity to connect with the nobility awaited Ivan on his return to Dmitrov soon after. Fears sparked by a popular upheaval on the Volga had brought the local nobility and merchants into an alliance. The upheaval was a murderous rebellion of Cossacks and serfs led by a man named Emelian Pugachev, who was posing as Empress Catherine's husband, the assassinated Peter III. Pugachev's army of the angry and dispossessed asserted that Peter III had miraculously escaped death and was returning to claim his rightful throne. The Pugachev forces conquered much of the lower and middle Volga region, taking over landlord estates and executing any nobles who failed to flee in time. Fears that Pugachev might move toward the Moscow region caused the nobles there to join with the leading merchants to form a united front in the face of this challenge. It was then that Ivan went for the first time with his family to dine with the most prominent noble of their city, Prince Ivan Golitsyn. Ivan's father and Golitsyn were evidently consulting on specific actions. Soon after, Golitsyn gathered the entire nobility of the district together, and they decided to form a militia from their serving men, donating one man per one hundred serfs. Golitsyn went directly from this meeting to Ivan's home to report this matter to Ivan's father, the leading merchant of the city. The merchants then gathered at city hall and agreed to contribute to the cause in the same measure as the nobles. Although the government was able to stamp out the rebellion later that year without the help of this militia, the scare seemed to build a bond between the local elites. From this time onward, Ivan spent more and more time socializing with local nobles.

We see another example of the influence of the commercial elite in two events that touched Ivan the following year, 1775. Again, he was on the road early in the year in the south of the country, buying grain at major depots such as Orel and Promzino Gorodishche. When spring arrived and the ice on the northern waterway broke up, he rode north to join the first barge caravan, which was lining up at the Vyshnii Volochek locks for the journey to St. Petersburg. This time, however, Ivan found the caravan at a standstill in front of the locks because of a labor dispute. Migrant workers, who arrived each spring from all over central Russia to work the barge traffic, were demanding higher wages than the merchants were willing to pay, and nothing was moving. This situation prompted the energetic, young governor-general of the province, Jakob Sievers, to take action, and he deployed a couple of stratagems to defeat the workers. He first ordered the merchants not to pay workers any more than a certain set wage, well below what the workers were asking. Then he told the merchants in the front column to hire only workers from the surrounding Vyshnii Volochek district and to hire them only for the first portion of the trip. This united front of government and merchants, plus the threat to exclude the migrant laborers altogether, quickly broke the resistance of the workers, and they agreed to sign on for the wage set by the governor-general. Ivan was very impressed with Sievers's fast and effective action and called him "a staunch defender of merchants in the waterborne trade to St. Petersburg."[11] When the grain shipments reached St. Petersburg three weeks later, Ivan saw a different face of government. The day after the barges arrived, he and the other grain merchants were summoned to the central police headquarters of the city and asked to sell their rye flour at a price no higher than three rubles, fifty kopecks a sack. The police in Russian cities, I should point out, were responsible not just for criminal matters but for urban security more generally, including the maintenance of grain reserves. Since St. Petersburg was a very expensive city, the police were under pressure to keep bread prices down. Rye bread was the dietary staple of the less-wealthy city dwellers. The merchants, however, stood their ground and refused to sell their flour at anything less than three rubles, eighty kopecks per sack. A week later, Ivan and the other merchants received a second summons, this time to a more splendid and intimidating venue: the Winter Palace of the imperial family. Although the court was away at the time, the merchants were greeted by the highest-ranking military officer in the country, General Field Marshal Alexander Golitsyn, commander in chief of the capital-city garrison. He, too, did his best to persuade the merchants to reduce the price on rye flour. And he, too, failed. Ivan reported that the other merchants again refused to budge, pointing out that the price requested by the government would deprive them of their profit.

We could well designate this as Ivan's graduation day, the end of his education, as at age twenty he stood together with his fellow merchants in the Winter Palace, rejecting the entreaties of the leading tsarist military official.

To sum up, what do Ivan's upbringing and experience in business tell us about the life of the commercial elite of eighteenth-century Russia?

First, children were family assets who were trained and put to work in the family business very early. Indeed, this was true of peasants and ordinary town dwellers as well as wealthy merchant families like Ivan's. Only the children of the nobility, and then only children of affluent noble families, received an extended education before entering adult life. For a merchant son, formal education was brief, and life on the road began young. Ivan was working the barge traffic under adult supervision at age thirteen. Two years later, his father was already delegating responsibility to him for some tasks. By age eighteen Ivan was in charge of an entire season's grain shipments and thereafter apparently represented the family enterprises in St. Petersburg and elsewhere with full authority.

Second, despite what history textbooks say about social hierarchy and class division in Russia, merchants actually enjoyed a cozy relationship with government officials and the local nobility, especially so when authority was under challenge. Petty merchants sometimes complained about competition from peasant traders owned by the nobiliy or about competing enterprises on noble estates, but the leading commercial families cooperated closely with the nobility, bought and sold goods produced on noble estates, and even socialized with the nobility.

Finally, as was true elsewhere in Europe, the government and commercial elites were more often in league than in conflict. The government understood that the wealth of the nation depended on the health of its commerce and protected merchants against the demands of workers for higher pay. Moreover, as Ivan's story about the summons to the Winter Palace demonstrates, Russian merchants were not the cringing servants of government power that they have often been portrayed to be. They were quite prepared to defend their private interests. By the same token, the monarchy, however absolutist it claimed to be, was not so foolish as to assault the laws of supply and demand. The relationship between government and the commercial classes was one of negotiation and accommodation, and in this period it worked to bring Russia to the height of its power and prestige in the modern era.

NOTES

David L. Ransel's chapter and accompanying map are part of his *A Russian Merchant's Tale: The Life and Adventures of Ivan Alekseevich Tolchënov, Based on His Diary* (Bloomington: Indiana University Press, 2008). They are being reprinted here with permission of Indiana University Press.

1. P. M. Maikov, *Ivan Ivanovich Betskoi: Opyt ego biografii* (St. Petersburg: Tip. Obshchestvennaia pol'za, 1904), 412–15.
2. M. V. Briantsev, *Kul'tura russkogo kupechestva. Vospitanie i obrazovanie* (Briansk, Russia: Kursiv, 1999), chapter 2.
3. I. A. Tolchenov, *Zhurnal ili zapiska zhizni i prikliuchenii Ivana Alekseevicha Tolchenova.* Rukopisnyi otdel Biblioteki Akademii Nauk, shifr 34.8.15 (kn. 1–3), kn. 1, l. 2.
4. Tolchenov, *Zhurnal*, kn. 1, l. 2.
5. Tolchenov, *Zhurnal*, kn. 1, l. 5.
6. E. G. Istomina, "Vyshnevolotskii vodnyi put' vo vtoroi polovine XVIII–nachale XIX v.," pp. 193–95 in *Istoricheskaia geografiia Rossii XII–nachalo XX v.: Sbornik statei k 70-letiiu professora Liubomira Grigor'evicha Beskrovnogo* (Moscow: Nauka, 1975).
7. Istomina, "Vyshnevolotskii vodnyi put'," 197–98.
8. Tolchenov, *Zhurnal*, kn. 1, l. 12. People of this time did not understand the ratflea vector of the plague infection, but they did know through observation that the

plague moved from one locale to another, and they devised measures to keep persons and goods from moving freely from plague-infested regions. For a detailed understanding of the plague in Russia, see John T. Alexander, *Bubonic Plague in Early Modern Russia: Public Health & Urban Disaster* (Baltimore: Johns Hopkins University Press, 1980).

9. A. I. Aksenov, *Ocherki genealogii uezdnogo kupechestva XVIII v.* (Moscow: Nauka, 1993), 76.

10. Tolchenov, *Zhurnal*, kn. 1, l. 29.

11. Tolchenov, *Zhurnal*, kn. 1, l. 40.

SUGGESTED READINGS

The English-language literature on Russian merchants and their history is rather limited. I have included in this list a few books that will allow students to deepen their knowledge of this subject, plus three excellent works on related topics: a general study of Catherine the Great's reign, a specialized study of the bubonic plague in Russia at the time Ivan Tolchenov encountered and luckily avoided contracting it, and an economic history of eighteenth-century Russia.

Alexander, John T. *Bubonic Plague in Early Modern Russia: Public Health & Urban Disaster*. Baltimore: Johns Hopkins University Press, 1980.

De Madariaga, Isabel. *Catherine the Great: A Short History*. New Haven, CT: Yale University Press, 1990.

Hittle, J. Michael. *The Service City: State and Townsmen in Russia, 1600–1800*. Cambridge, MA: Harvard University Press, 1979.

Jones, Robert E. *Provincial Development in Russia: Catherine II and Jakob Sievers*. New Brunswick, NJ: Rutgers University Press, 1984.

Kahan, Arcadius. *The Plow, the Hammer, and the Knout: An Economic History of Eighteenth-Century Russia*. With the editorial assistance of Richard Hellie. Chicago: University of Chicago Press, 1985.

Mironov, Boris N. "The Nobility and the Urban Estates." Pp. 371–424 in *The Social History of Russia, 1700–1917,* edited by Ben Eklof. Boulder, CO: Westview Press, 2000.

Ransel, David L. "The Diary of a Merchant: Insights into Eighteenth-Century Plebeian Life." *Russian Review* 63, no. 4 (October 2004): 594–608.

——. "An Eighteenth-Century Russian Merchant Family in Prosperity and Decline." Pp. 256–80 in *Imperial Russia: New Histories for the Empire*, edited by Jane Burbank and David L. Ransel. Bloomington: Indiana University Press, 1998.

——. "Enlightenment and Tradition: The Aestheticized Life of an Eighteenth-Century Provincial Merchant." Pp. 305–29 in *Self and Story in Russian History*, edited by Laura Engelstein and Stephanie Sandler. Ithaca, NY: Cornell University Press, 2000.

———. *A Russian Merchant's Tale: The Life and Adventures of Ivan Tolchënov, Based on His Diary.* Bloomington: Indiana University Press, 2008.

Rieber, Alfred J. *Merchants and Entrepreneurs in Imperial Russia.* Chapel Hill: University of North Carolina Press, 1982.

Ruckman, Jo Ann. *The Moscow Business Elite: A Social and Cultural Portrait of Two Generations, 1840–1905.* DeKalb: Northern Illinois University Press, 1984.

Chapter Four

The Good Society of Russian Enlightenment Theater

Elise Kimerling Wirtschafter

In his quest to modernize the Russian state and turn it into a well-ordered state in which the rule of law prevailed and the government promoted "the common good" through a variety of reforms, Peter I demanded that government and military officials be well educated. Expanding upon and reforming the Muscovite service state in which noblemen were expected to serve the tsar in a variety of capacities, in return for which they received rewards of property and titles, he created a regularized Table of Ranks (1722) for military officers, civil servants, and court officials that elevated expertise over birthright and tied these officials' obligations firmly to the state. Peter's intent was not to provide equal opportunity for all servitors, regardless of birth, but rather to ensure that his noblemen were qualified for their positions as natural leaders of society. To achieve that end, he set up a variety of schools and for the first time made formal education a requirement for full-time state service.

At first resistant to the demands that Peter made upon them, noblemen by the middle of the eighteenth century viewed the acquisition of education to be a noble prerogative. Education abroad, especially in Prussia, became common for these noblemen's sons, who brought back with them a treasure trove of Enlightenment ideas. Governing the continuously expanding Russian Empire and serving the monarchy, the small but significant educated elite advocated civic engagement. Not having political bodies such as diets, provincial estates, and parliaments or a developed periodical press, they turned to theatrical drama as a genre particularly suited to the discussion of civic issues. They were particularly encouraged in such endeavors by Catherine II (1762–1796), who was a poet and playwright in her own right. In the hands of Catherine and Princess Catherine Dashkova (1744–1810), whom the empress appointed as president of the Academy for the Russian Language, plays

served, according to Elise Wirtschafter, as "vehicles of moral and social ed-
ucation." "Virtue" ironically became an important watchword just as noble-
men earned the exclusive privilege to own serfs in 1785.

How did the playwrights of the Enlightenment in Russia define virtue? Why
were they concerned about social mobility? What did these dramas say about
their attitudes toward authority and hierarchy? How did the educated elite
understand Russian society and their place in it? Were society and polity in-
tegrated at this time?

> Theater is always a sensitive seismograph of an era, perhaps the most sen-
> sitive one there is; it's a sponge that quickly soaks up important ingredi-
> ents in the atmosphere around it.
>
> —Václav Havel (1986)[1]

> A true poet does not avoid influences or continuities but frequently nur-
> tures them, and emphasizes them in every possible way. . . . Fear of influ-
> ence, fear of dependence, is the fear—the affliction—of a savage, but not
> of culture, which is all continuity, all echo.
>
> —Joseph Brodsky (1992)[2]

How did subjects of the Russian Empire understand the social relationships
that shaped their lives? Historians seeking to answer that question face a major challenge. Decades of archival research have given scholars a relatively
well-documented understanding of the legal-administrative categories that
defined social relationships. Petitions, lawsuits, and instructions to legislative
commissions offer important information. But the people who speak in these
sources must do so in a framework provided by the state. Beginning in the
eighteenth century, the expansion and consolidation of a Russian (and broadly
European) print culture produced additional forms of social expression—correspondence, memoirs, literature, history, and the periodical press—that em-
anated directly from the minds of a reading and writing public. At the center
of this process was the creation of permanent public theater, a place where educated Russians self-consciously imagined themselves as members of a collective social body.[3] Through an examination of the texts produced for that
theater, historians can begin to reconstruct the ways in which Russians understood their society. How Russians came to conceptualize a "society," or a
social way of life, beyond the immediate spheres of kinship and locality explains much about Russian political culture, particularly the resilience of absolute monarchy and its ability to integrate the imperial Russian polity.[4]

Because theatrical plays articulate problems that derive from the self-defi-
nitions and perceptions of various groups and individuals in a society, they

can serve as tools with which to reconstruct social thinking in the past. In eighteenth-century Russia, where constituted political bodies did not exist and where the periodical press was in its infancy, theater provided a unique forum for public discussion. While it may seem an intrinsically elite phenomenon, theater reached a broader range of social groups than one might expect: performers and audiences were drawn from all ages and social statuses, including serfs and monarchs. Because plays were staged at court, in private homes and sheds, in seminaries and schools, and in commercial and state-sponsored settings, they were accessible to a socially diverse public. Plays were written not only by professional men of letters but also by amateurs whose main vocations were as policymakers, courtiers, state officials, military officers, serf owners, churchmen, professors, private tutors, or actors.[5] Lacking pretensions to the status of poet, such amateur authors wrote to educate children, honor patrons, entertain family and friends, influence society, be useful to the fatherland, promote knowledge, and express feelings. In their works, the strains of social and political life found vivid expression.

Like many recent works by historians of society, politics, and culture, this chapter is concerned with the relationship between power and ideas—or systems of interrelated ideas, whether dubbed ideology, discourse, or language. But it departs from the conventional alternatives in which such studies have been couched. Most assume that ideas should either be seen as emanations or opaque defenses of existing power and privilege (in the tradition of Karl Marx and Michel Foucault), or as forms of resistance by subordinate groups (as suggested by James Scott), or as some combination of the two, usually labeled "negotiation." Social control from above versus resistance from below; the effort by the powerful within government to maintain authority, hierarchy, and privilege versus the struggles of people in society for greater autonomy and equality—these are the alternatives with which many recent historians operate, explicitly or implicitly. Others point to the role of culture in raising consciousness about the gap between idea and reality and hence providing a stimulus to governmental reform or social change. While I, too, began with these implicit alternatives, my research has led me to conclude that what the plays actually document falls outside these conventional categories. The plays present a complex and sometimes heart-wrenching portrait of conflicts and tensions in the relationship of various social groups to the government and to social institutions such as the family and serfdom. Yet by and large, among educated Russians of diverse origins, an acute awareness of these strains led not to revolt but to reconciliation, not to a desire to overthrow flawed institutions but to live within them despite a recognition of their costs.

That the social thinking of the eighteenth-century educated public almost always produced reconciliation is well known, and in the case of theater, literary convention also required dramatic resolution. Censorship provides another possible explanation, though Russian intellectuals do not seem to have experienced significant fear of repression before the 1790s. Still, even if dramatists practiced self-censorship—and any person who identifies with a kinship group or immediate community does so to some extent—their published plays articulate ideas that could be debated in public. Unless one assumes that in a monarchy or dictatorship the only effective instrument of social control is coercion, the terms of public debate explain much about how society and polity are integrated. Thus, in an effort to explore the moral and philosophical ideas that educated Russians employed in order to achieve reconciliation with hierarchy and authority, I analyze theatrical treatments of social mobility. The four comedies to be discussed express the characteristic eighteenth-century tension between Enlightenment notions of linear progress and open-ended change, on the one hand, and more traditional social attitudes that assumed a preexisting, but by no means static, divine or natural order, on the other. In these and the scores of other plays I have examined, the more traditional way of thinking clearly prevailed.[6]

Theatrical treatments of noble-merchant marriages sent a particularly strong message to those who would aspire to rise in the social hierarchy. Osip Cherniavskoi's comedy *In the Company of Merchants* describes a merchant girl whose parents have chosen a noble groom so that their daughter can become wellborn.[7] Social pretensions have led them astray, however, for the groom is a complete scoundrel, a carouser and gambler, who uses his post in the city magistracy to enrich himself at the expense of others. The girl is saved from the unhappy match when a relative returns from a business trip financially ruined. The relative had gone to purchase grain from a landowner who persuaded him to sign a letter of credit that subsequently was used to deprive him of thirty thousand rubles.[8] The parents likewise have jeopardized their property in questionable dealings with nobles. They acquired a serf woman as payment for a debt; however, because it is illegal for nonnobles to possess serfs, they can lose their human property and hence also the payment on the debt. As a friend explains, merchants who think they can own villages in the name of a son-in-law risk the loss of everything. The parents recognize the parallel between their relative's ruin and their own potential ruin at the hands of the noble groom. They postpone the wedding for a year, the groom understands the hint, and catastrophe is avoided. The chastened father remembers that "God provides for us" and reminds his family "that a noble person is not one who possesses a noble rank, but one who has a noble spirit and lives virtuously." Lured by the prospect of social mobility, the merchants find solace in the hierarchy of moral virtue.

Because formal social status was inherited from the father or transmitted from husband to wife, only women could achieve upward mobility through marriage. A man in search of social eminence could either enter service or cultivate prestigious personal relationships. In theatrical depictions, the merchants who chose this route tended to associate with dishonorable nobles, thereby revealing their inability to understand the noble way of life. In *The Wedding of Mr. Voldyrev,* a comic opera by V. A. Levshin (1746–1826), extravagant living has brought a noble widow and her lover to the brink of ruin.[9] The widow's creditor, the merchant Mr. Voldyrev, is threatening to have her house placed under distraint. Her solution is to marry him on the assumption that she can then live freely in the French manner. The ruse is successful, and Voldyrev falls for the noblewoman. Not only does he allow her promissory notes to be destroyed, but he also signs over to her his property. Blinded by the noblewoman's rank, Voldyrev's social pretensions are no match for her moral corruption. The ease with which she robs him provides a clear warning. *The Wedding of Mr. Voldyrev* assumes that in noble-merchant marriages, merchants seek to rise above their natural social station, and nobles seek unsavory economic gain. Neither motive corresponds to virtue, and the possibility of romantic love does not even enter the picture.

A second approach to the question of social mobility appeared in plays about wealthy merchants who ruined themselves trying to live like nobles. In *Merchant Becoming a Noble* by V. P. Kolychev (1736–1794), an imitation of Molière's *Le bourgeois gentilhomme* (1670), the young merchant Razmotaev (Squanderer) is falling into ruin.[10] His creditors are hounding him, his credibility is being undermined, and his business deals are failing. Instead of tending to trade, Razmotaev sleeps late; maintains an elaborate toilet with servants; entertains nobles; and attends theater, assemblies, and masquerades. He utterly disdains the merchant way of life yet foolishly plays cards with dishonorable nobles. To escape merchant baseness, Razmotaev hopes to sell his factories and shops, enter service, obtain a rank, purchase an estate, and visit Paris. Filled with illusions of grandeur, he cannot see that while his noble friends pretend to teach him refined behavior during card games, their real goal is to rob him. Most recently, Razmotaev has squandered money that was supposed to pay customs duties, losing half of it at cards and lending the rest to a count.

Can Razmotaev become a real noble? In his discussion of Molière's comedy, Kolychev suggests not, and Razmotaev himself appears to accept his merchant destiny as he is being escorted to the magistracy to face his creditors. The young spendthrift's financial recovery is assured thanks to a sensible family friend, who also has the last word on merchants becoming nobles. In his view, all social groups can be happy if they live according to their status and do not try to leave it. Nobles and merchants are "equal citizens and equally useful" to the state. Nobles defend the fatherland with their lives and administer affairs of state; for this labor they receive ranks and villages. Merchants possess the right of trade, which is useful to the state and protected by the government. Merchants and nobles have different privileges, "but all the parts of the people are so connected that one [part] cannot manage without another. Not everybody can be a noble, a merchant, or a farmer but all are equally useful and important." This vision of the good society was fully consistent with the Catherinian "constitutional" structure, which sought not to prevent social mobility but to ensure that it served the common good and preserved rightful order.

Praise for useful merchants and warnings about the dangers of social pretension did not condemn mobility as a matter of principle. In *Merchant Becoming a Noble* Razmotaev's aspirations are laid to rest; however, in the anonymous comedy *Change of Morals*, a similar plotline produces a more ambiguous result.[11] *Change of Morals* is the story of Bogatov (Rich-Man), the son of a wealthy merchant, who has become an officer and is preparing to petition for ennoblement. Bogatov disdains his merchant origins, ignores the advice of his enlightened uncle, and leads a frivolous Frenchified life in the company of nobles interested only in his money. Although Bogatov has squandered his property and fallen into debt, he continues to gamble, attends parties into the early morning hours, thinks about how to order fashionable buttons from Paris, and sees no reason to obtain a service appointment. Eventually, when Bogatov is rejected by his self-serving friends and faces incarceration for debt, he experiences feelings of shame, recognizes his errors, and repents. His uncle, Dobronrav (Good-Morals), who all along has blamed "faulty education and pernicious acquaintances" for his nephew's behavior, eagerly reconciles and accepts Bogatov as his own child. Generosity and obedience abound: Dobronrav's daughter and future son-in-law agree to share their inheritance, so that Bogatov's debts can be paid, while Bogatov decides to obey his uncle's injunction that he enter the sovereign's service.

Throughout the play, the moral corruption of *le grand monde*, represented by the willful depravity of Bogatov, is contrasted to rightful social order, represented by the "healthy reason" of Dobronrav. Dobronrav's thinking defines society as it should be organized whereas the behavior of Bogatov illustrates the threat to social order. Through Bogatov's moral transformation this threat is removed, and a vision of social harmony emerges—a vision that extends from the patriarchal household to the harsh realities of serfdom to the promise of divine providence.

"Oh parents, parents! You are the cause of all his calamities! With poor education, you made a boy of good morals and qualities completely empty-headed." Thus does Dobronrav condemn the upbringing of Bogatov, who had a French tutor to teach him foreign languages and accompany him abroad. The result was an education that instilled neither good morality nor the desire to be useful. Like so many others, Bogatov's parents entrusted their son to a teacher whose character they did not know and then carelessly sent him abroad before he had acquired an adequate moral and educational foundation. In condemning elite educational practices, and particularly foreign travel, Dobronrav does not express proto-Slavophile or proto-nationalist notions of Russian superiority. He dismisses nationality as a basis for the selection of teachers, emphasizing instead the need for good morality and a mind enlightened by knowledge and the sciences. Nor does he deny the utility of travel abroad, as long as Russian youths are prepared for it: thus they first must acquire an understanding of the sciences and learn to appreciate "the benefits of their fatherland." Consistent with the educational policy of the Petrine service state, the purpose of their travel should be to gain knowledge of the administration, laws, customs, commerce, science, and arts found in other states, so that upon returning home, these young Russians can be useful to the fatherland.

Bogatov and his friend the count have an entirely different understanding of education and foreign travel. They view travel as an opportunity to see the world of high society, to stroll along promenades and engage in merrymaking, to imitate foreign fashions, and perhaps even to catch a distinguished bride and dowry. As the count explains matters, travel abroad teaches a young man how to live in "better society," which requires that he furnish his home lavishly, dress fashionably, maintain French servants, and invite guests to balls and concerts. To meet the expenses of this lifestyle, the young man can increase the quitrent of his peasants or, if they become too poor, sell them. In addition, he can borrow money against his parents' villages, buy goods on credit for purposes of resale, and pass out promissory notes. When his creditors try to collect, he need only skip town. In the words of the count, "To live in *le grand monde*, it is not necessary to wear the attire of shame and conscience."

Spendthrifts such as Bogatov and the count, teetering on the brink of absolute ruin, appear frequently in eighteenth-century plays, where also it is the duty of enlightened characters such as Dobronrav to help return them to a life of virtue. The first step toward successful rehabilitation is explicit condemnation and the ability to watch a loved one suffer the consequences of his actions. As Dobronrav explains matters, when a young man such as the count (and by implication Bogatov) retires from service, he does not strive to observe economy or enhance agriculture. Instead, he squanders his estate on cards, lovers, and foppishness. Both his peasants, who are ruined, and his parents, who exerted such effort to leave their son an inheritance, become victims of his luxury. Dobronrav's judgment is clear; however, in the manner of enlightened thinking, his social critique is tempered by the assumption that young fops are innately good; that they have been corrupted by a bad education, for which their parents are to blame; and that they can in fact reform themselves. Bogatov's eventual repentance, including his new willingness to obey the instructions of Dobronrav, ensures that he can become both morally virtuous and socially useful. If, as Dobronrav suggests, we find the sudden change in Bogatov's "thoughts and heart" to be strange—an admission that reform through enlightenment has its limits—we should remember that the change is attributable to "Divine providence." The deus ex machina of providential intervention, a dramaturgical technique traceable to Greek tragedy, equates Bogatov's change of morals with the restoration of rightful order, which has been violated by poor education and unbridled profligacy.[12]

If enlightenment and virtue ultimately derive from God and if bad education and pernicious social influences account for Bogatov's fall from natural goodness, can morality extend beyond familial relations into the larger arena of civic society? Dobronrav describes society as a place where people denigrate themselves to the point of utter baselessness, if they hope to receive some benefit or think that somebody is in a position to help them. Likewise, once people realize that the person from whom they expected a favor no longer can serve their needs, they abandon him, all because of ambition. Even praiseworthy deeds can be motivated by vanity rather than sincerity. Clearly, society is a source of moral danger and social uncertainty. Yet as Dobronrav's understanding of hierarchy and equality reveals, it also is a place where moral virtue can be realized and where each individual can find happiness, security, and freedom in his or her God-given place. In keeping with this vision of the good society, Dobronrav leads a well-ordered life: he rises early, tends to his commercial affairs, and provides for his family. In contrast to Bogatov, who has used his inheritance to join the army and obtain a rank only so that he can quickly retire and live quietly, Dobronrav regards nobility as a title granted by the sovereign for important services to the fatherland. Dobronrav recognizes that commerce is useful to society yet has no desire to become a noble or take up the military calling. His nephew's desire to obtain nobility without striving to serve is nothing short of unforgivable, laughable, and foolhardy. Thus while Bogatov pursues happiness in eminence and wealth, Dobronrav finds it in the love and respect of honorable people, in virtue and justness, and in a tranquil spirit. Bogatov also is wrong, in Dobronrav's opinion, to regard merchants and peasants as base. Nobles do indeed enjoy privileges before these groups, but the latter are equally necessary for the fatherland. The only real scoundrels are the people who are useless to society.

When Dobronrav rejects the idea that his commercial contribution to society merits social elevation, he also assumes the absence of a correspondence between the hierarchy of social status and the hierarchy of appropriate social postures based on moral worth. Dobronrav's understanding of social propriety is quite different from the justification of social hierarchy. Setting aside legal, economic, and social distinctions, Dobronrav believes that one should behave humbly before those exalted by spiritual worth, courteously with one's equals, and tolerantly toward the unfortunate. To the poor, one should offer assistance. The character of Dobronrav belongs to a sizable group of enlightened patriarchs assigned by eighteenth-century playwrights to be the voice of moral virtue. Dobronrav is unusual, however, in being a merchant rather than a noble. By assigning the role of enlightened *raisonneur* to a merchant, our anonymous author not only reinforces social hierarchy—Dobronrav is happy with his merchant status—but shows that the voice of enlightenment and moral authority actually transcends it. The hierarchy of social status and the hierarchy of moral virtue occupy two separate realms, with preference clearly given to the latter. Thus, Bogatov's moral regeneration does not require that he abandon his noble aspirations, only that he become useful to society. *Change of Morals* does not reject social mobility outright; it simply shows that the desire to move beyond one's original social station can lead to moral disaster. This is not because moral virtue depends on social hierarchy, but because in the arena of civic society, beyond the patriarchal household, individuals easily lose their moral bearings. The good "society" of Russian Enlightenment theater is best understood in terms of moral rather than social relationships.

As suggested above, the evidence from theater reveals a characteristically eighteenth-century tension in the way Russians thought about social relationships. The more traditional attitude assumed the existence of a transcendent natural order created by God (in classical literature also represented by the gods and fate) and protected on earth by church and monarch. The natural order, which—absent the laws of physics and modern scientific knowledge—was completely consistent with the Judeo-Christian divine order, represented right and justice, so that concrete social relationships and historical events were understood as the unfolding of natural/divine laws. This view of social relationships did not allow for open-ended linear change but neither was it static, immutable, or inevitably religious. Rather, the God-given natural order continually was being reenacted through human history. Through rational inquiry and scientific discovery of nature's physical laws, it became discernible to human beings. The more traditional understanding of social relationships also recognized challenges to and violations of the natural order that had to be overcome through divine or human intervention. In its entirety, the natural order was right and known only to God; however, through the justice of God's vicar on earth, the sovereign monarch, it provided the framework for human relationships. Thus justice and legitimate social relationships corresponded to the natural order, whereas injustice and social conflict signaled its violation. The path to justice and legitimacy lay in the restoration of the natural order, change being circular, not in the open-ended linear transformation of established social relationships.

In contrast to the more traditional attitude toward social relationships, a newer form of social thinking, associated with the Enlightenment, assumed open-ended transformation through human agency. In this conception, there was no assumption of a preexisting rightful order that had to be preserved or, when violated, restored. Instead history and concrete experience provided the standard by which to measure human progress. According to the more recent understanding, human beings, armed with rational thought and free will, consciously could improve themselves and the conditions in which they lived. Human judgment replaced the God-given natural order as the basis for evaluating social relationships. The individual's social identity—how he defined himself and was defined by others in social terms—no longer was divided between transcendent idea and historical reality. Rather, idea and reality were expected to correspond. Yet precisely because complete correspondence rarely could be found—what people thought they were or wanted to be often was at odds with what historical conditions allowed them to be—cognitive reconciliation with concrete social relationships became more difficult to achieve. The molding of social relationships to promote justice and virtue became an end in itself rather than an expression of the transcendent natural order. The possibility of infinite change superseded the exercise of free will within a natural order that while fully created was not yet fully realized.

It is important to distinguish attitudes toward social relationships from political ideology and administrative practice in eighteenth-century Russia. The reform of administration, the effective mobilization of resources, and the ability of Russian subjects to find protection in judicial institutions did not translate into modern social consciousness. There was a contradiction between the goals of absolutist monarchy, which by actively pursuing resource mobilization gave prominence to ideas of social transformation and progress, and the educated public's understanding of social relationships, which by overcoming the tension between enlightened ideas and historical realities consistently upheld the hierarchy and authority of a preexisting natural order. Throughout the eighteenth century and well into the nineteenth, the reformist policies of the government and the social consciousness of the educated public were sufficiently elastic to permit a reconciliation of the two. Binary categories of opposition and otherness were muted, and in neither government nor educated society was there significant awareness of a need for fundamental change. Even if an enlightened monarch such as

Catherine II (1762–1796) believed that the abolition of serfdom was desirable, she certainly did not think it was immediately possible. Similarly, the pursuit of political reform implied change in the institutional projection of monarchical authority, not in its essential nature. Educated Russians, in official and unofficial capacities, subordinated their commitment to progress and human agency to the assumed stability of a natural order. Given the institutional fragmentation of eighteenth-century Russian society, the physical hardships of everyday life, and the insecurity of social and legal status, it is no surprise that the traditional aspects of enlightened thought took precedence over its more modern elements.

NOTES

Sections of Elise Kimerling Wirtschafter's chapter first appeared in her *The Play of Ideas in Russian Enlightenment Theater* (DeKalb: Northern Illinois University Press, 2003). They are being reprinted here with the permission of Northern Illinois University Press.

1. Václav Havel, *Disturbing the Peace: A Conversation with Karel Hvíždala*, trans. Paul Wilson (New York: Knopf, 1991), 51.
2. Joseph Brodsky, "A Hidden Duet: The Intimate Connection between the 'Magdalene' Poems of Boris Pasternak and Marina Tsvetaeva," *TLS: The Times Literary Supplement*, no. 5030 (27 August 1999): 13–16.
3. Nancy Kollmann notes that "Muscovites did not reflect self-consciously on the collective body in which they lived." See Nancy Shields Kollmann, *By Honor Bound: State and Society in Early Modern Russia* (Ithaca, NY: Cornell University Press, 1999), 59.
4. Keith Baker defines "political culture" as "the set of discourses and symbolic practices" by which "individuals and groups in any society articulate, negotiate, implement, and enforce the competing claims that they make upon one another and upon the whole." Consequently, political authority becomes "essentially a matter of linguistic authority" in that (1) "political functions are defined and allocated within the framework of a given political discourse" and (2) "their exercise takes the form of upholding authoritative definitions of the terms within that discourse." Because such a broad definition potentially treats "political culture" as the sum of the economic, social, and institutional relationships situated in public society, Baker also stresses the role of multiple and infinitely changeable "language games" played by human agents. For purposes of concrete research, and in order to understand the dynamics and interactions of specific language games, it is necessary to identify distinct discursive fields. Eighteenth-century Russian theater can be viewed as a discursive field expressing the language games not of a particular socioeconomic or legal class but of a sociocultural environment populated by the enlightened educated public, whose

members formulated policy and governed the country. Keith Michael Baker, *Inventing the French Revolution: Essays on French Political Culture in the Eighteenth Century* (New York: Cambridge University Press, 1990), 4–7.

5. The assumption of amateur status by authors also could represent literary convention, as in French autobiographical and epistolary novels of the eighteenth century. The fact remains, however, that educated Russians who had no professional literary pretensions wrote plays.

6. I began my research with a "database" of more than 650 plays, published or performed in Russia between 1672 (the year of the first theatrical performance at court) and 1825 (the year of the Decembrist uprising, the first attempt to overthrow the monarchy by members of the educated public). Subsequently, I focused on 259 secular literary plays (tragedy, comedy, opera, comic opera, and drama) written, and for the most part also published, from the 1740s to the 1790s, the period when original Russian theater achieved national self-consciousness and European recognition. A. P. Sumarokov's earliest published play, *Khorev*, a five-act tragedy in verse, appeared in 1747; it was performed at the Noble Cadet Corps in St. Petersburg in 1749, at court in 1750, and by the Volkov troupe in Iaroslavl at about the same time. The late 1790s provide a logical terminus because before the reign of Paul (1796–1801), there was little effort to impose systematic censorship on literature or the periodical press. In terms of literary movements, this was a time of neoclassical ascendancy, with the incorporation of sentimentalism and preromanticism in the last third of the century and the eventual rise of romanticism proper in the first decades of the nineteenth century.

7. Osip Cherniavskoi, *Kupetskaia kompaniia. Komediia v odnom deistvii* in *Rossiiskii teatr, ili polnoe sobranie vsekh Rossiiskikh teatral'nykh sochinenii* (*RF*), 43 vols. (St. Petersburg: Imperatorskaia akademiia nauk, 1786–1794), 27:149–208. *In the Company of Merchants* was first published in Moscow in 1780. I have no record of performances or biographical information about the author available.

8. The landowner was in debt to another noble, and the letter of credit was supposed to allow him to pay his creditor with the money the merchant would owe for the grain. The landowner died, all his property went to settle debts owed to the treasury, and the merchant was made liable, because of the letter of credit he had signed to pay the noble creditor, who also happened to be the father of the prospective groom.

9. Vasilii Levshin, *Svad'ba g. Voldyreva. Opera komicheskaia v odnom deistvii* in *RF*, 42:109–56. Set to music by I. F. Kertselli, *The Wedding of Mr. Voldyrev* received one Moscow performance in 1803. Born in Tula province, the son of a modest landowner and army colonel, Levshin joined the Novotroitsk Cuirassier Regiment in 1765 and served in the Russo-Turkish War of 1768–1774. Illness forced him to retire from service in 1772 with the rank of lieutenant and return to the family estate. In 1779 Levshin was elected to a four-year term as district judge and in 1803 became special official to State Secretary A. A. Vitovtov in St. Petersburg. He retired from state service with the rank of state councillor in 1818. Throughout his career Levshin's activities as author, translator, and compiler supplemented his salary and the meager income from his estate. *Slovar' russkikh pisatelei XVIII veka* (*SRP*), 2 vols. (Leningrad: Nauka, 1988; St. Petersburg: Nauka, 1999), 2:198–201.

10. V. P. Kolychev, *Dvorianiushcheisia kupets. Komediia v trekh deistviiakh* in *Teatr V. K.,* vol. 1 (Moscow: V Senatskoi tipografii, 1781), 107–65. *Merchant Becoming a Noble* was performed once in St. Petersburg in 1780. Kolychev was born to aristocratic parents, received his early education at home, and entered the Noble Infantry Cadet Corps in 1752. After serving in the Vyborg Infantry Regiment and the Seven Years' War, he left military service with the rank of lieutenant. Kolychev then entered civil service in Moscow, which allowed him to spend summers at his Tula estate. Until his death he remained an active estate manager. *SRP*, 2:109–10.

11. *Peremena v nravakh. Komediia v dvukh deistviiakh* in *RF*, 38:37–128. *Change of Morals* was to my knowledge never staged.

12. On deus ex machina, see Patrice Pavis, *Dictionary of the Theatre: Terms, Concepts, and Analysis*, trans. Christine Shantz (Toronto: University of Toronto Press, 1998), 95.

SUGGESTED READINGS

Baker, Keith Michael. *Inventing the French Revolution: Essays on French Political Culture in the Eighteenth Century.* New York: Cambridge University Press, 1990.

Cracraft, James. *The Petrine Revolution in Russian Imagery.* Chicago: University of Chicago Press, 1997.

Dixon, Simon. *The Modernisation of Russia 1676–1825.* Cambridge: Cambridge University Press, 1999.

Karlinsky, Simon. *Russian Drama from Its Beginnings to the Age of Pushkin.* Berkeley: University of California Press, 1985.

Leach, Robert, and Victor Borovsky, eds. *A History of Russian Theatre.* Cambridge: Cambridge University Press, 1999.

Madariaga, Isabel de. *Catherine the Great: A Short History.* New Haven, CT: Yale University Press, 1990.

Marker, Gary. *Publishing, Printing, and the Origins of Intellectual Life in Russia, 1700–1800.* Princeton, NJ: Princeton University Press, 1985.

O'Malley, Lurana Donnels, trans. and ed. *Two Comedies by Catherine the Great, Empress of Russia: "Oh, These Times!" and "The Siberian Shaman."* Amsterdam: Gordon and Breach/Harwood, 1998.

Pavis, Patrice. *Dictionary of the Theatre: Terms, Concepts, and Analysis.* Translated by Christine Shantz. Toronto: University of Toronto Press, 1998.

Raeff, Marc. *The Well-Ordered Police State: Social and Institutional Change through Law in the Germanies and Russia, 1600–1800.* New Haven, CT: Yale University Press, 1983.

Rogger, Hans. *National Consciousness in Eighteenth-Century Russia.* Cambridge, MA: Harvard University Press, 1960.

Roosevelt, Priscilla. *Life on the Russian Country Estate: A Social and Cultural History.* New Haven, CT: Yale University Press, 1995.

Shcherbatov, Prince M. M. *On the Corruption of Morals in Russia.* Edited and translated by A. Lentin. London: Cambridge University Press, 1969.

Smith, Douglas. *Working the Rough Stone: Freemasonry and Society in Eighteenth-Century Russia*. DeKalb: Northern Illinois University Press, 1999.

Wirtschafter, Elise Kimerling. *The Play of Ideas in Russian Enlightenment Theater*. DeKalb: Northern Illinois University Press, 2003.

———. *Social Identity in Imperial Russia*. DeKalb: Northern Illinois University Press, 1997.

Chapter Five

The 1827 Peasant Uprising at Bernovo

Rodney D. Bohac

Serfdom, an exploitative system of unfree labor, lasted over two centuries in early modern and modern Russia. Growing out of the need in the late sixteenth century to provide necessary labor on the estates of Russia's aristocratic and gentry military servitors and promulgated into law in 1649, serfdom ironically paid for Russia's Westernization and development as a major European power with ever-expanding borders. Seigneurial serfs owed their masters either labor or rent dues, or a combination thereof. Unless they were household serfs, they had indirect control over some lands that they farmed for themselves. Serfs also owed taxes to the state and, after the introduction of regular conscription in the mid-seventeenth century, military service. Beginning in 1699 that military service amounted to a life sentence and then, as of 1793, twenty-five years. Subject to their owners' administrative and juridical authority, serfs were at the mercy of these nobles' whims. They could be flogged repeatedly, exiled to Siberia, sold, or gambled away. A few reforms in the early nineteenth century, including protecting serfs from extremely abusive owners, mitigated some of the harshest features of the system.

One of the distinct features of peasant life under serfdom was the existence of the village commune, or mir, an institution of local government. Every household was represented by a male head in the commune, usually its most senior member. Household heads in turn elected elders. These representatives served as mediators between the households, on the one hand, and the serf owner and his or her bailiff, on the other. They were also responsible for dividing the responsibilities that owners and the state exacted on the peasants. Furthermore, the commune managed land redistribution and crop rotations, and adjudicated disputes among peasants. Naturally, tensions within communes were common as peasants did not always agree with the decisions made at this level.

During the course of serfdom's history, there were only four major rebellions of serfs against their exploitation, the most famous being the Pugachev Rebellion in 1773–1774 during the reign of Catherine the Great. In all four cases, Cossacks led the revolts that united serfs from various locations along the peripheries of the empire and challenged central authority. Revolts such as the Bernovo uprising of 1827 tended instead to be isolated, localized phenomena that could be easily put down by military force. They erupted in response to new exactions against serfs, which often resulted from the hiring of a new bailiff or the accession of a new heir to an estate, and to periodic crises such as harvest failures, which could lead to famine conditions if those failures occurred in consecutive years. Peasants expected their masters not only to feed them in times of need but also to waive their responsibilities until the crises were over.

The number of harvest failures in various regions of Russia escalated in the first half of the nineteenth century, causing tensions between masters and their peasants that sometimes exploded in rebellion. It is estimated that during the reign of Alexander I (1801–1825) there were about 280 localized disorders and about double that number under his successor, Nicholas I (1825–1855); in the second quarter of the nineteenth century rumors of emancipation helped to raise their frequency. Other tensions between seigneurs and serfs simmered just below the surface as peasants continued to protest the unfree labor system through everyday small deeds such as showing up for work late, being careless in and slow to complete their work, stealing grain or timber from their lords' property, and grazing animals on their owners' pasture.

What does the Bernovo uprising that Rodney Dean Bohac reconstructs for us reveal about the system of serfdom, the authority of serf owners and the state, and the nature of serfs' exploitation? Why did peasants bother to protest, if the odds were against them, and what were their objectives? What forms did their protest take, and why did serfs refrain from using violence? Why was it difficult for peasants to unite themselves around an issue? Why were women not present in the Bernovo uprising? Ultimately, why might passive resistance, the everyday small deeds described above, have been the most successful type of rebellion in which serfs could engage?

The T'ma River moves slowly through the rolling, tree-covered hills of central Tver province. Its waters run through lands settled almost nine centuries ago but still covered with virgin forest interspersed with meadows and cultivated fields. Along its banks villages nestle close to the water. At one such village, Bernovo, the river quietly passes near peasant homes and a stone church built in the early nineteenth century, giving the settlement a feeling of tranquility and timelessness. The river's solemnity can also be funereal.

In the spring of 1827 the sleepiness of Bernovo was shattered as the ice on the T'ma thawed early and quickly, and the river overflowed its banks, threatening the village. An overseer ordered its peasants upstream to cut timber and use the flood to float the logs down to their village. The peasants instead went home, and an uprising began that lasted almost two months. During its course, Bernovo peasants refused to sow their master's fields, held clandestine meetings in the forest at night, sent men to petition the tsar, and demonstrated at the entrance of the county jail. Their efforts came to naught, but the story of the rebellion illustrates the tactics of peasant resistance and government suppression. It also hauntingly reveals the limits of peasant resistance to serfdom.

The 30th of March 1827 did not turn out to be a good day for nobleman Ivan Ivanovich Vul'f. Sometime around mid-morning Vul'f's manager told him the peasants had refused to follow his orders to cut timber. The overseer had then tried to get them to work in Vul'f's fields, but the peasants would not do that either. While Vul'f mulled over what to do next, his peasants gathered in the village and marched up to the manor house. Vul'f tells us in a petition that they came to his house "without any order from me."[1]

Who were these defiant peasants? As serfs, they belonged to I. I. Vul'f and were obligated to work in his fields, carry out other agricultural tasks, and pay money rent as well. As serf owner, Vul'f served as their judge, commanding the right to try petty crimes and settle civil suits. He could even force his serfs to marry. Bernovo peasants also could not leave the estate without his permission. In return, the peasants received land to grow crops for themselves and had at least nominal assurance of help at times of crisis. They were registered as living in two villages, and the inability to move from these villages defined them as serfs. According to the 1816 revision, 248 peasants lived in Bernovo's forty-one households, and 163 peasants lived in the sixteen households of the second village, Voropun, four miles to the north.

The manor house before which these rebellious peasants gathered sits heavily on the top of a hill that gradually slopes downward toward the river, the church spire rising next to it, and the village. Built at the turn of the nineteenth century, the large, two-storied stone palace contains over thirty rooms. The second floor has not only spacious dining areas, sitting rooms, and bedrooms, but a large ballroom as well. In addition to Vul'f, his wife, and frequent guests, the manor house and the surrounding outbuildings were filled with dozens of servants, clerks, and coachmen.

The Bernovo peasants probably approached the back entrance, which faced the village. They moved past the man-made pond, which by summer was covered with lily pads, and then came down an alleyway framed by two lines of trees. Once they arrived, the peasants greeted their master with obscenities and informed him they would not do any kind of work for him. When a servant tried to carry water into the house, the crowd shouted at him to stop. Later Vul'f proudly remarked that the servant continued on into the house. That was Vul'f's only triumph, as he did not get the other peasants to obey him. Needing help, he promptly sent a missive to the local sheriff, explaining he did not have "the necessary means" to compel his peasants' obedience.

Luckily for Vul'f, the sheriff was his brother-in-law, I. D. Vel'iashev. In early nineteenth-century Russia in-laws were sometimes more important to please than blood relatives, and Vel'iashev was in a position to help his wife's brother. As the sheriff, he was in charge of law enforcement for Staritsa county in which the Vul'f estate was located. The sheriff, elected for a three-year term by county nobility, conducted criminal investigations, chased down runaways, supervised the county jail, and headed the lower land court, which decided whether the accused would be indicted.

The next day Vel'iashev headed off to the estate with the county's marshal of the nobility, two army officers, and maybe sixty soldiers. On their way they rounded up twenty-six peasants from two neighboring villages to serve as witnesses. Once in Bernovo the officials gathered about fifty-five male peasants, all most likely household heads. The peasants complained about the burdensome demands placed on them, to which Vul'f retorted they had to work so often because on assigned workdays they started late and left early. Sheriff Vel'iashev decided that circumstances warranted quick action. He first warned the assembled peasants about the laws they had broken and the punishments they might suffer if they did not carry out their work diligently. Then he summoned the priest to cajole them to obey the authorities. The peasants evidently were not persuaded, for Vel'iashev turned to the use of force. He dispersed the soldiers among the peasant households. Living in the midst of peasant families, the soldiers could, Vel'iashev reasoned, monitor "down to the last detail" whether the peasants carried out orders. In a final warning the sheriff told the peasants that "if they did not stay within the limits of their own power then there would be dire consequences."

Despite the threats and the soldiers stationed in their homes, the peasants took four long days to capitulate. "With one voice" they finally proclaimed their obedience to Vul'f and asked him for his "Christian forgiveness." Three days later Vul'f sent a message to Staritsa authorities, telling them he no longer needed the soldiers' aid. The peasants' mutiny seemed to be over as a result of the quick action of local authorities. As it turned out, however, the serfs' capitulation was only temporary. The peasants may have submitted in public, but in private they were still seething.

Sometime in early April to mid-April, evidently soon after Vul'f's letter announcing the crisis was over, a peasant from another of the county's estates visited the Bernovo household of Vasilii Antonov.[2] Nothing in the records even remotely hints how the visitor, Gurian Akinfiev, ended up in Antonov's house. But once there Gurian told the peasants that when he had been mistreated by his owner, he had sent two petitions to the tsar and, as a result, had been given his freedom. The sheriff's office later discovered Gurian had been accused of insubordination to his master, but the county court decided he had indeed been mistreated and freed him, not from serfdom, but from the county jail. Gurian was sent back to his estate and, fearing retribution from his owner, immediately fled. For over a year he had evidently been hiding in forests near his village. He made this short visit to Bernovo and then left, never to be seen again, at least by the authorities.

What the Bernovo peasants got from his story is unclear, except perhaps the motivation to launch their own petition. Rumor played an integral part in peasant lives and shaped their reaction to national as well as local events. One advantage of rumor rested in its ambiguities and possibilities for a wide variety of interpretations. Gurian, for example, mentioned petitions to the tsar, but Bernovo peasants decided to present their petition to the provincial marshal of the nobility. Whether the peasants believed that the petitioning would result in their community's freedom from serfdom or less ambitious achievement of some relief is open to question. They themselves were probably not certain of the outcome, but thought it was worth taking a chance.

Gurian had told his story of freedom to a handful of men with evidently some political clout among the peasants. One man, Stepan Larionov, who had recently served as a village head, probably brought Gurian to Antonov's home. It is further likely that Larionov, with the others' aid, took the initiative to convene a secret, nighttime meeting of the mir assembly somewhere on the grounds of the manor house. Peasant mir assemblies generally consisted of male heads of household. Women could present petitions and often stood on the sidelines shouting out their opinions. Because the secret meeting occurred at night, few women, if any, probably attended. At the meeting Gurian's story was told, and the peasants decided to send three men to the provincial capital of Tver to compile and present a petition to the provincial marshal of the nobility. The mir leaders collected sixty kopecks per head for expenses, and the three men, Stepan Larionov, Nil Afanasev, and Filip Fedorov, headed off on the fifty-mile journey to Tver. There in a tavern they found someone to write up their long, detailed petition for a cost of nine rubles. When the three took the petition to the marshal's residence, they found out he was on his estate down in Rzhev county. Traveling another forty miles to the marshal's estate, they presented him with the petition. The marshal took it, but made no promises. Upon returning to the estate, the three men reported that further action was needed.

The peasants again met at nighttime, this time in Voropun. Since the petition to the marshal was not going to bring results, they decided to petition the tsar. To do so was risky, as petitions to the tsar were forbidden. Such a step required unanimous, fervent agreement. To ensure loyalty, one peasant brought an icon to the meeting. After agreeing to the idea of the petition, each peasant came forward and kissed the icon, pledging "to stand strongly one for another." More money was then collected to pay for expenses, and Stepan Larionov and another peasant, Timofei Ivanov, set out for Staritsa. There they found a retired government official to write the petition. On their way home, they were arrested.

Despite the oath taking, someone had informed Vul'f about the men's absence, and Vul'f immediately asked Staritsa authorities to find the "runaways." In his request Vul'f also admitted that most of his peasants, up to ninety of them, again refused to work and that his fields had not yet been planted. Without a crop, he complained, he would not be able to make the payments for the mortgage he had taken out on his estate. He urged the authorities to take decisive action.

Vul'f sent his petition on 22 April, and five days later the two men were arrested carrying copies of both petitions with them. They were taken to the sheriff's headquarters and interrogated. According to the purloined documents, the peasants felt compelled to send the petition due to a wealth of burdensome rents and imposts. Peasants had to pay thirty rubles per married couple, and every year they had to provide the lord's household with set quantities of beef, rams, chickens, eggs, linen, mushrooms, and berries.

In addition to rents in money and in kind, the peasants had to labor four days a week in the lord's fields. This duty exceeded the maximum of three days set by tsarist legislation. The peasants worked in the fields all the way up to St. Peter's Day (24 June) with little time to prepare their own fields. On holidays they often had to work on the fencing surrounding Vul'f's fields, and in the summers they had to cut his hay. Finally, they had to use their own horses and carts to carry Vul'f's grain the sixteen miles to markets in Staritsa and the thirty miles to Torzhok.

Such duties undoubtedly seemed onerous to the peasants, but the deciding blow came when the overseer announced an additional tax on boys. Every peasant household would have to send their boys between the ages of ten and fifteen to work in the lord's fields for two days a week and pay fifteen rubles of money rent for each one as well. The overseer further declared that for each boy under age ten, households would have to pay thirty rubles per year. As Larionov said in his deposition, "We have come to such destruction that we barely have any horses or cattle." The marshal of the nobility, commenting on the petition presented to him, called the duties "burdensome."

The marshal called for an investigation of the Bernovo rebellion's circumstances, work to be done "without publicity." Even though sending petitions to the tsar was a crime, so, too, was unusually cruel treatment of serfs by their owners. Tsar Nicholas I in several speeches in 1826 had decried exorbitant burdens on the serfs, and often local authorities took his words seriously. These officials, sometimes with few or no serfs of their own and perhaps influenced by growing sentiment against serfdom, felt obligated to investigate claims of maltreatment. In a case a few years later in the same county, a nobleman was accused of raping young maidens on his estate. The authorities, on the basis of the girls' stories, placed the nobleman under house arrest in a neighboring county seat and put his estate under guardianship. They even examined his genitalia. In the end, though, the peasants seldom won; in this case the nobleman was acquitted and the female peasants accused of lying.

Not surprisingly, in the Bernovo case the peasants' claims were found to be exaggerated. The day after Stepan Larionov and Timofei Ivanov were captured with the petitions, the sheriff interrogated them. Their depositions, as was the case for all depositions taken by the sheriff's office, were not transcriptions but paraphrases composed by the clerk listening to the interrogation. In the depositions both Larionov and Ivanov admitted that Bernovo peasants only worked for Vul'f three days a week rather than the four days stated in the petition. This important admission immediately turned the case against the peasants. In order to get the attention of the marshal and the tsar, the peasants had deliberately exaggerated their plight. In the depositions the two men also conceded that although the overseer had announced the new burdens on the estate's boys, the peasants had not confirmed this announcement with Vul'f himself. They accordingly implied that the peasants had not yet fulfilled the new obligations.

Vul'f denied the serfs' allegations. The new duties on young boys were entirely voluntary, he claimed, as peasants wishing another half *tiaglo* worth of field land to sow could do so in return for taking on the extra rent assessed on a boy.[3] Many of the other imposts, he asserted, had been started by his parents decades earlier. He went on to minimize the amount of work the peasants did on such projects as fencing and blamed the peasants' poor work habits for much of their troubles.

In defending his policies Vul'f also inadvertently explained much of the peasants' anger. The peasants' poverty, he noted, came not from his actions but from several years of crop failures. These crop failures plagued much of the province, and many peasants faced dwindling grain reserves and growing arrears. The economic strains created political tensions. Sometimes these tensions erupted into intense intra-community factionalism, as in one community about thirty-five miles to the south where a faction burned down the house of their rivals' leader. While Vul'f's peasants were defying him, Tver's governor was dealing with another uprising in nearby Ostashkov county. Pressures resulting from the crop failures coupled with some kind of additional demand from Vul'f created the climate for action. The runaway Gurian's words about freedom perhaps further energized the peasants by sparking hope for emancipation.

One other intriguing fact may have solidified peasant resistance. Vul'f's nephew, A. N. Vul'f, claimed in his memoirs that the Bernovo serf owner had his own harem of serf women and that a number of illegitimate children roamed the manor house. Bernovo peasants brought up no such accusation; it would have been difficult to prove, as well as dangerous to mention. If true, it added to a climate of mistrust, which combined with agricultural failures and Vul'f's intensifying demands, gave the peasants enough reason to continue resisting their owner.

And continue to resist they did. The same day the sheriff had arrested the two petitioners, the Bernovo peasants decided that each household should send one man to Staritsa to free the prisoners. The next day, 8 May, as many as fifty to sixty men traveled the sixteen miles to the county seat and gathered at the entrance of the sheriff's office. The sources say almost nothing about this dramatic moment, but it must have frightened county officials. The crowd shouted obscenities at the sheriff and his deputies and demanded their comrades' release. They would not leave, the angry peasants threatened, until the men were set free. But the officials held their ground and the peasants eventually gave up. Or so it seemed to the officials.

Sensing their demonstration was leading nowhere, the peasants dispatched the villager Filip Fedorov to get yet another petition to the tsar. On the same day as the demonstration, he set out for Tver where in a tavern he found a scribe to write the petition. Then he carried the petition almost fifty miles south to Zubtsov county. There at the village stagecoach station he caught up to the tsar and, according to Fedorov, "gave the petition to His Imperial Majesty." Whether he did or did not remains unclear; the Staritsa court did not want to know and did not try to find out.

Sheriff Vel'iashev and the county marshal, unaware of Fedorov's trip, wanted to get Vul'f's peasants back to work. Almost a week after the Staritsa demonstrations, authorities went back to the estate and interrogated fifty-eight peasants and a few of Vul'f's officials. The sheriff primarily wanted to know whether each peasant had agreed to sending the first two petitions, had given money for having them written, had sworn the oath on the icon, and, having done all that, was now willing to obey Vul'f. In the first wave of questioning a little over 70 percent of the serfs admitted to having committed at least two of three illegal acts and asserted that they were not ready to obey Vul'f. Most claimed they would not carry out their master's orders without the agreement of the mir assembly. "As the mir [does], so [do] I," said one peasant.

Not every peasant displayed such loyalty. Aleksandr Ivanov claimed that when he refused to go Staritsa due to illness, members of the mir beat him; two others confirmed his story. Eleven more admitted to participating in some way in the uprising but now wanted to ask for forgiveness. Two of these said they only participated because other peasants had intimidated them. After these eleven recanted, six more peasants changed their minds and declared they would now obey Vul'f. The apparently united front began to crumble.

The Bernovo peasants may never have been strongly united, and the unanimity in their resistance to Vul'f was undoubtedly based to some degree on intimidation. Throughout Russia most difficult decisions made by mir assemblies involved long, often heated debates. The vote, if a count was taken, was sometimes very close. Subsequently, all participants often agreed to make the decision unanimous, even though many still opposed it. In fact, not long after many unanimous resolutions, the same issue would reemerge and again have to be debated. In making risky decisions, as in the Bernovo case, having everyone agree meant no one had to take responsibility. Peasants could and did say they were only following the will of the mir. Of course, the peasants were the mir.

Despite the defections, not enough Bernovo peasants broke ranks to suit the authorities. Then on 20 May they found out that Filip Fedorov had presented the third petition to the tsar. The next day four imprisoned peasants added the final piece to the puzzle. Imprisoned for almost three weeks, the peasants evidently thought a guarded confession might improve their position. The four men told the county lawyer that they had decided to send the first petition upon the advice of the runaway Gurian.

The discovery of this outsider's role probably both upset and relieved the authorities. Knowing a runaway was spreading rumors that had already led to one uprising raised the specter of further troubles. On the other hand, believing an outsider instigated the Bernovo uprising allowed authorities to consider the peasants' actions a temporary aberration and to reason that serfdom was not at fault.

But for now, too many lies had been told by Bernovo peasants; too much information had been withheld; and too many still disobeyed authority. Due to the new information, county authorities on 28 May received permission to convene a military court on the estate. Such courts had been instituted by Tsar Nicholas I in August 1826 in response to rebellions allegedly caused by the Decembrist uprising. While assembling the court, the sheriff interrogated Vasilii Antonov and the other peasants who had reputedly conversed with the alleged instigator Gurian. After hearing all four deny they had directly talked to Gurian, the authorities sent them home to await the military court.

Soon after they arrived back at the estate, Vasilii Antonov hanged himself. The next day his distraught widow went to see Vul'f and told him that her husband had confessed his crime to her. Antonov had told her that he and the other three men arrested for talking to Gurian had agreed to deny everything during the interrogation. She then acknowledged she had seen all of them in the house with Gurian, although her husband had not come in until the conversation was over.

The pall cast by the suicide made the military court hearing on 7 June an even more somber event. The Bernovo court consisted of six judges—the county court's three judges and three army officers. The officers had brought with them sixty soldiers who once again were quartered in peasant homes. On the first day the six judges informed the peasants of the nature of the proceedings and took their oaths to tell the truth. The next two days they interrogated the ten main suspects: the four who had gotten the petitions written, the three who had been designated as additional ringleaders by Vul'f, and the three who had been in the hut with Gurian. The rest of the peasants sent a petition asking for their lord's forgiveness and promising to obey him in the future.

At a break in the proceedings, Vul'f petitioned the court to show his peasants mercy and asked for clemency for all but the ringleaders. The serf owner needed the peasants' obedient labor, not harsh punishments. So in his petition he no longer characterized the peasants as duplicitous; now they were just "gullible" in "thoughtlessly" listening to the words of the "vagrant" Gurian and committing acts of "stupidity." Vul'f played the role of the forgiving father, treating his serfs as children who, though failing to act wisely, did not deserve harsh punishment.

The military court did not immediately choose to play the forgiving father. Regarding Vasilii Antonov's suicide, the court coldly noted his act "served the cause of justice" by confirming his guilt. Then the judges proceeded to investigate evidence of yet more duplicity on the part of the peasants. They had discovered that at least ten peasants had hidden livestock with a peasant in a neighboring village. The judges surmised the peasants wanted to convince authorities they had indeed been driven into poverty. The peasants and their confederate, however, argued that some of the livestock were transferred through sales and as collateral on loans. The rest had been handed over so the soldiers quartered in peasant homes would not use the animals. The court could not crack the peasants' stories, but got the livestock returned.

Not all the peasants had given up their resistance. Two peasants, who had never been interviewed before, adamantly refused to obey Vul'f. Grigorii Merkulov, a twenty-seven-year-old household head, refused to ask forgiveness, because he had sworn a sacred oath and could not break it. His younger brother, age sixteen, told the judges he would do whatever his brother did:

"As my brother [does], so [do] I." Four of the eleven originally interrogated because of their active participation in the rebellion still insisted they had due cause for participating. One declared that the serf owner's labor obligations placed a great burden on him, and a second asserted he had "felt oppression," as he "had no grain." He and a third peasant said they would continue to follow the mir's wishes. A fourth, Filip Fedorov, who had carried the petition to the tsar, simply said, "I will not obey."

A final peasant, Nil Afanasev, had already been remanded for punishment. Not only had he gone to Tver to have the first petition written, but he had also committed sacrilege. Four weeks earlier, on 12 May, the sheriff summoned the peasants to the parish church where at the end of the service the priest read the 1826 law on uprisings. He emphasized the provisions outlining when the military courts might be used and the possible punishments. When the priest read the law, Afanasev laughed. When church leaders asked him why he was laughing, he simply continued doing so until he left the church. The court's judges believed reverence toward the God and the Orthodox Church led to obedience toward tsar and serf owner as well. Afanasev's laughter displayed the highest level of disrespect. The perceived link between religious observance and obedient subjects was confirmed by the fact that thirty-nine of the peasants interrogated since the beginning of the rebellion had not been to confession or communion for anywhere from two to ten years. One of the military court's last acts was to draw up a list of these men, so that the diocesan church leadership could determine appropriate disciplinary action.

For most Bernovo peasants, church reprimands comprised their only punishment. Eight men considered instigators, voluntarily active in the uprising, or unrepentant were punished more harshly. On 28 June, Prokofei Ivanov and Stepan Merkulov, who were not activists but had refused to ask forgiveness, received fifty and thirty blows, respectively. The three men who had met with the runaway Gurian ran a gauntlet of 250 men. The belligerently recalcitrant Grigorii Merkulov and the two probable leaders, Stepan Larionov and Filip Fedorov, ran a gauntlet of 500 men. After the punishment Grigorii Merkulov and Filip Fedorov had to be sent to the Staritsa jail for medical treatment. When they recovered, they were to be sent into Siberian exile, joining Nil Afanasev, who for sending the petitions and laughing in church had already been whipped and exiled.

The authorities had suppressed the uprising. Motivated by fears of widespread rebellion and upset with peasant intransigence, officials severely punished the ringleaders as an example to the other peasants. Conversely, a paternalism that demanded serfdom not be excessively burdensome fostered moments of caution and hesitancy. That paternalism, coupled with the need to maintain a sufficient number of laborers, also led to leniency for most of the Bernovo peasants. At the beginning of the rebellion, the peasants had tried to take advantage of this paternalism. They hoped descriptions of excessive burdens would lead to improved conditions or even freedom. The peasant activists further attempted to create, through persuasion and intimidation, a community united enough to stand up resolutely against injustice and withstand threats of punishment. Then they held secret meetings, dispatched peasants to present petitions, refused to work, hid property from inspection, and withstood interrogations. In the end one man committed suicide and eight were severely beaten; three of the latter were subsequently exiled to Siberia.

And what did they achieve? An 1858 description of the estate listed labor and quitrent obligations that closely resembled, except for rent imposed on boys, those described in the first petition to the tsar. Students sometimes ask why serfs rebelled so infrequently. The results of this uprising suggest that they should instead be asking why peasants, given the risks, rebelled as often as they did.

NOTES

1. All quotes come from "Materials Concerning the 1827 Insurrection of I. I. Vul'f Serfs, Bernovo Village," Tver Regional Archive, *Fond* 673. Staritsa County Court, *delo* 2601. This work was inspired by M. A. Il'in's "Bunt krepostnykh v sele Bernovo v 1827 [The 1827 Serf Uprising in Bernovo Village]," pp. 125–36 in *Voprosy biografii i tvorchestva A. S. Pushkina*, ed. Viktor Aleksandrovich Nikol'skii (Kalinin, Russia: Kalininskii gosudarstvennyi universitet, 1979). Il'in, a good friend and respected colleague who died in 1999, took me to visit Bernovo in 1989 and 1994. Head of the Tver archive, he did much to preserve the Bernovo manor house and other historical sites in Tver province.

2. In the first half of the nineteenth century, most peasants did not have surnames. Antonov, then, is Vasilii's patronymic, not his surname. In speech, peasants evidently used the patronymic as we would use a surname. So they would say, "Antonov invited the stranger."

3. Under serfdom, a *tiaglo* was a labor unit that usually consisted of a married couple. Landowners apportioned allotments of land to serf households based upon the number of labor units they contained. Thus, a half *tiaglo* allotment was half the regular amount.

SUGGESTED READINGS

Blum, Jerome. *Lord and Peasant in Russia from the Ninth to the Nineteenth Century*. Princeton, NJ: Princeton University Press, 1961.

Bohac, Rodney. "Everyday Forms of Resistance: Serf Opposition to Gentry Exactions, 1800–1861." Pp. 236–60 in *Peasant Economy, Culture, and Politics of European Russia, 1800–1921*, edited by Esther Kingston-Mann and Timothy Mixter. Princeton, NJ: Princeton University Press, 1991.

Hoch, Steven. *Serfdom and Social Control in Russia: Petrovskoe, a Village in Tambov*. Chicago: Chicago University Press, 1986.

Kolchin, Peter. *Unfree Labor: American Slavery and Russian Serfdom*. Cambridge, MA: Harvard University Press, 1987.

Melton, Edgar. "Household Economies and Communal Conflicts on a Russian Serf Estate, 1800–1817." *Journal of Social History* 26, no. 3 (Spring 1993): 559–85.

Mironov, Boris, with Ben Eklof. *A Social History of Imperial Russia, 1700–1917*. 2 vols. Boulder, CO: Westview, 1999.

Moon, David. *The Russian Peasantry, 1600–1930: The World the Peasants Made*. London: Longman, 1999.

Chapter Six

Reframing Public and Private Space in Mid-Nineteenth-Century Russia

The Triumvirate of Anna Filosofova, Nadezhda Stasova, and Mariia Trubnikova

Rochelle G. Ruthchild

Much ink has been spilled on the history of feminist movements in Europe and the United States in the modern period, but comparatively little on the Russian feminist movement, which arose in the mid-nineteenth century and climaxed during the heady months following the overthrow of the tsar in February–March 1917 when it achieved full women's suffrage. Historians are often partial to the victors of revolutionary change, and in the case of Russian history that distinction fell to the Bolsheviks and members of the working class who toppled the weak Provisional Government in October 1917 and instituted a socialist system that was supposed to privilege the proletariat, or working class. The attempt to create an egalitarian social and economic system and destroy capitalism initiated major changes having to do with women's positions, including the legalization of divorce and abortion and the right to labor alongside men. Bolshevik feminists also promised women liberation from the constraints of marriage through free love and from the drudgery of housework through the creation of communal kitchens. Indeed, by the early 1930s the Bolsheviks had proclaimed the achievement of women's emancipation, even though women continued to receive lower wages than men and were expected to toil in both the home and the factory. Paradoxically, a pro-natalist policy championing the reproductive functions of women existed alongside a policy touting women's labor obligations to the state.

The socialist and particularly Bolshevik variant of the women's issue, which promised women total equality once the capitalist system had been overthrown, has overshadowed the broader prerevolutionary feminist movement, which sought advancements for women of all classes and ultimately their equality by way of education, self-help, economic independence, suffrage, and civic engagement. Rochelle Ruthchild challenges the dominant paradigm by looking at the beginnings of the women's movement in Russia through the lens of three aristocratic women who were instrumental in challenging the subordination of women in a patriarchal society. Remarkably, they were able to do so within the confines of an autocratic system that did not permit political representation of any kind but was not immune to the stirrings of a civil society that sought greater engagement in the political and social arenas.

Already by the mid-eighteenth century, Russian upper-class, merchant, and urban-estate women, in contrast to their European counterparts, enjoyed inalienable rights as property owners, regardless of their marital status. That change had come as a result of Peter the Great's failed attempt to introduce single inheritance and the nobility's efforts to shore up the corporate privileges that Peter's reforms gave them and to infuse Russia with a legal order. Management of property gave women, especially of the upper classes, some independence from their husbands and ability to participate in the legal system in their own names.

That independence in turn spurred a growth in women's literacy, although their literacy rates lagged well behind those for women in other European countries. In pre-Petrine Russia literacy rates for both men and women were abysmally low because of the lack of a formal system of primary education: by the late seventeenth century less than 10 percent of the entire population was literate. Peter I's promotion of literacy among his servitors spurred noblemen to introduce their daughters to informal education within the home. By the mid-eighteenth century women of the upper classes had tutoring in reading, writing, and foreign languages; by the end of the century most elite women were literate.

With the exception of Catherine II's 1764 founding of the Smolnyi Institute for Noble Girls, formal schooling for women at the private and state levels was not introduced until the first quarter of the nineteenth century. Nevertheless, a number of well-educated women made their mark in the early nineteenth century as salon hostesses. They cultivated the talents of male intellectuals and writers and encouraged debates over leading questions of the day, including the injustices of serfdom, Russia's place in the world, and Russian identity. The public role of these women was critical for the emergence of the "woman question" as it was known at the time. As university education and professional opportunities outside the bureaucracy expanded for men and the emancipation of the bulk of the population, the peasantry, became imminent, women began to clamor for access to higher education.

Why was education so critical for women's liberation in Russia and elsewhere? How were the elite women Rochelle Ruthchild describes able to step out of their traditional roles as wives and mothers? At the same time, what constraints on their activities still existed?

In 1859 three women of the aristocracy, called "the triumvirate," banded together to launch a remarkable series of philanthropic and educational services for women, including cheap lodgings for divorced and abandoned women, work cooperatives, higher education courses, and soup kitchens. Their activities have been discussed in studies of the Russian women's movement by Linda Edmondson, Barbara Engel, Richard Stites, and Grigorii Tishkin, but since the 1980s no more detailed studies have ensued. Discussion of the woman question in mid-nineteenth century Russia has focused mostly on the men who wrote about it, such as the physician and educator Nikolai Pirogov, who in 1856 called for educating women to be better wives and mothers; the radical publicist M. L. Mikhailov, who used the arguments of the French feminist Jenny d'Héricourt against Michelet and Proudhon in a series of articles for the radical journal *The Contemporary* between 1858 and 1861; and the revolutionary Nikolai Chernyshevskii, in his highly influential 1863 utopian novel about the woman question, *What Is to Be Done?* While these men were important in helping to raise Russian educated society's consciousness of women's issues, the attention scholars have given them obscures the roles that women like Anna Filosofova (1835–1912), Nadezhda Stasova (1822–1895), and Mariia Trubnikova (1835–1897), who comprised the triumvirate, played in the early stages of Russia's women's movement.

In discussing the lives and work of Filosofova, Stasova, and Trubnikova, I will focus on how these three activists redefined their lives in the public and private spheres to empower their feminist activity and examine the interconnections between those spheres. Russian society in the reign of Alexander II was sufficiently permeable to allow these early feminists to reframe spaces and institutions in their milieu and use them to advance the larger cause of promoting women's equality.

First a note on terminology and sources is necessary. In Russia the word *feminist* was not widely used until the turn of the twentieth century; rather the phrase *woman question* referred to discussions of the role of women in society. Nevertheless, the kind of activity engaged in by the three women discussed here, advocating and creating organizations aimed at attaining equal rights and economic self-sufficiency for women, was a key element of the progressive agenda of Russian society at the time, and by any contemporary understanding would fit the label *feminist*. In mid-nineteenth- to late nineteenth-century Russia, the woman question was an integral part of the understanding of social change. Ann Hibner Koblitz notes that a confluence of interests in "science popularization, feminism, and social activism" marked the Russian intelligentsia in the 1860s and 1870s.[1]

I chose Filosofova, Stasova, and Trubnikova because each made feminism their primary public commitment for much of the period from 1859 to 1881, and as a group they have left the most detailed biographical sources of any Russian feminists. Since they were women inclined to deeds more than the written word, none wrote an autobiography. Two were the subjects of biographies written by family members. Stasova's brother, the prodigiously prolific historian and art and music critic V. V. Stasov, wrote a 508-page memoir of his sister that was published in 1899, four years after her death. The writer, feminist, and Kadet[2] activist Ariadna Tyrkova-Williams published a 488-page biography of Filosofova in 1915, three years after Filosofova's death, along with a second volume containing several hundred more pages of testimony and remembrances from a variety of sources. Finally, Olga Bulanova-Trubnikova, Mariia Trubnikova's daughter, wrote a biographical sketch of herself, her mother, and her grandfather that appeared in print in 1928, eleven years after the Russian revolutions and thirty-one years after Trubnikova's death in 1897.

Nadezhda Stasova, the godchild of Tsar Alexander I; Anna Filosofova, a society "butterfly" married to a high-ranking bureaucrat; and Mariia Trubnikova, the wife of the publisher of the *Stock Exchange News*, seem like unlikely feminist activists. Yet the lives of the three women were marked by personal transformation and subversion of traditional female roles. These changes occurred in two of the chief public arenas, the salon and the ball, in which there were opportunities for women and men of the small educated class to mingle socially. And they also took place in the private arena, namely, the family, in which women and men have historically interacted. To understand how the three women reframed areas of their lives to enable them to embrace feminist activities, the social and political context within which they lived and worked requires examination.

The late 1850s, with the advent of a new and reformist tsar, Alexander II, and anticipation of the emancipation of the serfs, were a time of ferment within Russian society. Comparisons between the plight of serfs and that of women were common. Some women writers and editors urged upper-class women to lead the campaign to free the serfs, much as U.S. women crusaded for the abolition of slavery. In the *Journal for Education*, for example, Madame X argued that Russian women could provide a moral example for humankind by emulating such women as Harriet Beecher Stowe, the author of *Uncle Tom's Cabin*. The year 1859 marked the appearance of *Rassvet*, the first thick journal specifically for women. The editors noted in the first issue their hope to jolt their readers, who had "still not awakened from a prolonged sleep, and could not understand what they mean when they say that she must be a citizen."[3] The ferment about and among upper-class women was heightened by uncertainties about the social and economic impacts of the serf emancipation, fueling aspirations for more formal education. In 1859 Nataliia Korsinia also became the first woman auditor at St. Petersburg University. She was soon followed by others at the university and the Medical Academy; female auditors became so numerous that in some classes they outnumbered the official male students. It is thus little wonder that in the magical year of 1859, amidst the challenges presented to women by the possibility of emancipation of the peasants and themselves, Mariia Trubnikova's salon also came into being.

Held in her home, Trubnikova's was a salon within a salon. The larger salon appears to have followed the traditional pattern, with women establishing a supportive atmosphere for creative and in this case politically active men. It was a gathering place for liberals, government officials, and young radicals such as the brothers Serno-Solovevich, founders of the secret revolutionary society Land and Freedom in 1862.[4] Women who led traditional salons appear to have been isolated from each other; they were often idealized as muses inspiring male creativity. By recruiting other women such as Anna Filosofova and Nadezhda Stasova to her smaller women's salon for the express purpose of educating them about the woman question, Trubnikova, however, redefined her salon as a venue for empowering and uniting women.

Trubnikova, daughter of the Decembrist[5] V. P. Ivashev and his French wife, Camille LeDantieux, could be said to have had rebellion in her blood. Born in 1835 in the Decembrist exile community in Siberia, Trubnikova lost her father and mother at an early age, in 1839 and 1840, respectively. Raised by a wealthy aristocratic aunt, Princess Khovanskaia, she grew up in an atmosphere in which her father was revered as a "saint" and the Decembrist revolt idealized. By the time she was twenty Trubnikova had married a young bureaucrat, K. V. Trubnikov, who impressed her by his liberalism and quotations from the socialist Alexander Herzen. In the first years of her marriage, pregnancy-related illnesses kept Trubnikova home a great deal, but they also provided her the free time to indulge her penchant for reading, including feminist literature.[6] By 1859 she was ready to act, promoting the ideals of feminism through the venue of the salon.

Trubnikova played the role of mentor to the women who attended her gatherings. Both Filosofova and Stasova described themselves as "empty-headed" before they met Trubnikova. In Russian intellectual life, as elsewhere in the West, it was common for men to help educate and transform women, as in the Pygmalion legend. In her salon, Trubnikova usurped that traditional male role by choosing to play Pygmalion herself. Like most women of her class, she was fluent in several languages. She corresponded with several foreign feminists, including Jenny d'Héricourt, the feminist who influenced Mikhailov, and Josephine Butler, the English crusader against legalized prostitution. Trubnikova also kept abreast of the progress of the U.S. women's movement.

An indefatigable proselytizer, she sought recruits for the cause of women in all kinds of settings. During a doctor's appointment, for example, Trubnikova persuaded the doctor to send his wife to her salon and declared to Varvara Tarnovskaia herself, "My dear, you can't live and do nothing. There is too much to do. Do you want to work with me?" In this way she found one of the best feminist workers. Men also recruited women for Trubnikova's cause. A mutual friend, F. S. Unkovskii, telling Filosofova that "you are bored with nothing to do," introduced Filosofova to Trubnikova. Filosofova in turn described Trubnikova as "an angel, gentle and patient. She developed me, read with me. This was hard, since I didn't understand anything."[7]

Filosofova and Stasova were attracted to Trubnikova's salon, not only because of Trubnikova's engaging personality and mentorship, but also because of experiences in their own lives that led them to question their traditional social roles. Anna Filosofova, born into the venerable Diaghilev family and married at eighteen to a man seventeen years her senior, quickly discovered that the commonplace life of a woman of her class, that of a social "butterfly," did not satisfy her. She confided later to Tyrkova, her biographer, "I didn't understand what was wrong," and compared herself to Polinka Saks, the main character in a popular story by Alexander Druzhinin, who discovered the folly of her ways when it was too late. Filosofova's husband considered himself enlightened and was also very concerned about his wife's education. But Filosofov, a man "of exceptional goodwill," had limited goals as far as Anna was concerned; initially she did not understand why he "wanted to make me into an educated society woman."[8]

Filosofova may have thought her mind empty, but her early adult life was in other ways full and marked by a growing degree of social consciousness. In 1858, two years after her marriage, she had her first child, Vladimir. Like the wives of other bureaucrats of the time, Filosofova was left with the responsibility for a growing family, a home in the capital, and a country estate. By the time she was twenty, Nonochka (Filosofova's nickname) was spending summers without her husband at the Filosofovs' ancestral estate. It was here that Filosofova, like many U.S. feminists who initially fought against the injustices of slavery before making the connection to their own oppression, claimed first to have seen the brutality of serfdom. Her father-in-law, Dmitrii Nikolaevich, particularly abused serf women, forcing them to be sexually available in his personal harem. Filosofova's awakening to both class and gender inequalities in Russia shaped her political philosophy and commitment to social change. Her correspondence with her husband reveals her developing perspective. Viewing changes in society and in herself as transcending the earthly realm of patriarchal power, either political or familial, she hailed the emancipation of the serfs in 1861 as "a holy day, a day of moral renewal." In claiming her right to independent action, she invoked a force outside herself and her husband: "To yield to you is beyond my power, I yield to a mysterious force, I see it everywhere."[9]

Nadezhda Stasova's characterization of herself as empty-headed belies the events in her life that also led her to Trubnikova's salon. Thirteen years older than Trubnikova and Filosofova, godchild of Tsar Alexander I, and daughter of an architect close to the royal family, Stasova was born in Tsarskoe Selo in 1822. One of seven children (five brothers and one sister), she was nine when her mother died in the cholera epidemic of 1831. At an early age she became aware of the unequal treatment of members of her sex. "My father," she wrote, "although he was an intelligent man, still thought (as they all did then), that we did not have the same needs as our brothers." Stasova's brothers were indoctrinated to think the same way. One brother once returned from a piano lesson and teasingly repeated the teacher's admonition against playing like a girl, that "teaching girls was a waste of money," and that girls were empty-headed. Like Filosofova, Stasova recalled how she was raised to fit the stereotype of the empty-headed girl: "my youth was extraordinarily light-hearted and without seriousness, all my thoughts inclined to entertainment."[10]

A comparison between Stasova's early life experience and that of her brother and biographer, V. V. Stasov, illustrates the difference in possible opportunities for women and men at the highest levels of Russian society at that time. By 1859, Stasov, two years younger than his sister, had finished law courses, worked in several government ministries, lived in Florence and Rome, and written a series of biographical essays about Tsar Nicholas I.[11] Stasova, on the other hand, had not yet left home.

Before meeting Trubnikova and Filosofova, Stasova nonetheless had two life-transforming experiences that revealed her strong will and her ability to transform adversity into a positive impetus for change in her life. In her late twenties, already old by the standards of the day, Stasova became engaged to a guards officer with whom she was madly in love. At the last moment he broke the engagement and immediately married another woman, apparently acceding to paternal threats of disinheritance. Devastated, Stasova had a nervous breakdown. Her doctors, despairing when no traditional treatment worked, tried hypnosis. By her brother's account, Stasova miraculously recovered, dictated her own prescriptions in Latin (which she had never studied), and completely recuperated by the following summer.[12]

Her health regained, Stasova vowed never to marry and to begin an entirely new life, refusing to take the role of the abandoned woman. Turning to the terrain of the imagination, she read voraciously. Her reading list reflected the popular authors favored by enlightened Russians of her day: George Sand, Voltaire, Jean-Jacques Rousseau, Walter Scott, Byron, Heinrich Heine, and

Nicholas Karamzin, among others. At first she directed her energies and emotions toward her family, particularly her sister, Sofia. Depressed by the death of her son, Sofia contracted consumption and died in Stasova's arms in 1858. The death of her only sister, the person to whom she was closest, deeply affected Stasova. Returning to St. Petersburg, she felt that "my fascination with my family, with my own, disappeared. I felt a love for a universal family; this would be my cause to the end of my days."[13] Thus, by the time she joined Trubnikova's salon, Stasova had rejected two traditional female roles for those in her situation, that of abandoned woman and that of maiden aunt enmeshed in and dependent upon her family.

While Trubnikova's salon brought the triumvirate together, Trubnikova, Filosofova, and Stasova did not act alone. Vera Ivasheva, Trubnikova's sister; N. A. Belozerskaia; and the Baronesses Korff and Shtakel'berg also frequented the salon. In discussing ways in which they might help women, the salon attendees specifically focused on the economic plight of women. The group's first project, however, immediately sparked conflict, portrayed by biographer V. V. Stasov as being divided along national lines. The baronesses, soon dubbed the German party, insisted on a traditional philanthropic model with close supervision of the recipients of their largesse. The triumvirate and their allies, labeled the Russian party, rejected the notion of controlling poor women's lives; they advocated helping poor women improve their living situations. The traditionalists left Trubnikova's salon to set up their own project elsewhere. Unfazed by the conflict, Stasova thrilled at the prospects for collective action, noting that "up to this time we had acted and helped those we could on our own, not contacting anyone else. Now . . . we decided to unite, to collect a general sum and help together."[14]

At first the women triumvirate and their supporters worked through informal channels. The first beneficiary of the group's largesse was the wife of an artisan, deserted and left with six children. But as word soon spread about the new services, many others sought aid. To continue their work, the group had to move into the public realm, seeking government approval for their activities by drafting a charter and applying for legal recognition, calling themselves the Society for Cheap Lodging and Other Aid to the Needy Residents of St. Petersburg. Emphasizing self-help rather than charity and seeking to address the plight of women abandoned or divorced by their husbands, the triumvirate and their allies won approval of their charter in 1861, on Filosofova's name day and sixteen days before the emancipation decree.

Although Trubnikova was the society's first president, Filosofova was the moving force behind its growth. President of the society for most of the twenty years between 1859 and 1879, she used her connections to help increase the organization's assets from five hundred to seventy thousand rubles.

She also expanded its service institutions to include a school, dormitories, cafeterias, a child-care center, a store, and a clothing workshop supplying uniforms to the War Ministry.[15]

Trubnikova's salon served to empower the women who were part of it and provide a base of support for their various ventures. Overall, the feminist projects did not seek dramatic structural change in society. Rather, the feminists of the triumvirate sought to make incremental change, subverting and undermining the foundations of the social system but not, like the younger *nigilistki* (nihilist, or radical women), attempting a frontal assault against the status quo. The feminists' politics was that of the possible. This can be seen in the clothes they wore.

Traditional dress, which Filosofova particularly used effectively, gave the feminist philanthropists entry to social occasions in which they could plead their cause. Wearing formal and fancy dress marked the older feminists from many of the younger women they sought to help. Shtakenshneider describes the former as wearing "fashionable silk dresses and hats," and the latter as dressing in "black wool dresses, with short hair and no hats."[16] Such dress often engendered hostility from the younger women. Once, two nihilists were at Trubnikova's when Filosofova came in, formally dressed to go to a party afterward. One of the nihilists commented nastily, "If she comes dressed like a doll to a serious meeting like this, it must mean she has nothing to do," to which Filosofova replied, "Clothes do not make the woman."[17] The revolutionary Petr Kropotkin described the strategy of the older feminists well: "They seemed to say to the younger and more democratic people: 'We shall wear our velvet dresses and chignons, because we have to deal with fools who see in a velvet dress and chignon the tokens of "political reliability"; but you, girls, remain free in your tastes and actions.'"[18]

With their fashionable clothes Filosofova, Stasova, and Trubnikova all used their high-society connections to further the cause of women's rights. The world of government was closed to women; the places in which women and men interacted were with their families inside the home and outside, primarily in the salon and at the ball. If the salon was the place where the small educated class of Russians met to exchange ideas, the ball was where informal contacts with government officials were most possible. Filosofova in particular continued to host and attend society balls, using them to lobby for women's education. The jurist A. F. Koni described how Filosofova came up to him at a masked ball to lobby for women's education.

Filosofova's controversial activities made her notorious within court circles. Some called her "red" as much for her tendency to blush with anger as for her politics. After one argument with her at a ball at the Winter Palace, Alexander II's very conservative minister of education, Dmitri Tolstoi, sent

Filosofova a portrait of the French revolutionary Madame Roland, with whom she was often compared. Once, at a court ball, she overheard an "important person" say, "Trubnikova and Stasova have done much damage to Russia."[19] Despite such social disapproval and ridicule, Filosofova continued her lobbying efforts and met significant success.

In 1869 a petition campaign initiated by the journalist Evgeniia Konradi and actively supported by the triumvirate, resulted in government approval for a series of coed public lectures in the humanities and natural sciences. Refused space at St. Petersburg University for the lectures, Filosofova persuaded Minister Tolstoi to house them temporarily in his private apartment. Of course, this venue also allowed Tolstoi personally to supervise the content of the lectures. In general, Tolstoi singled out Filosofova as his go-between to those agitating for women's higher education. And finally, in 1878, women's higher education courses opened in St. Petersburg, with government approval. Paying a sardonic tribute to the persistence of women like Filosofova, Tolstoi said at the time, "What women want, God wants."[20]

Although the feminists were able to establish new types of philanthropic enterprises and win government concessions in regards to women's higher education during the reign of Alexander II, all did not always go smoothly both in their public activity and in the private sphere. Another project aimed at encouraging women's economic self-sufficiency, the women's publishing *artel*, met stronger government resistance. The *artel*, again hewing to the model of encouraging women's self-sufficiency, concentrated on publishing books in translation, as knowledge of foreign languages was one skill shared by most educated women. At Trubnikova's suggestion, the group decided to have all its work done by women, including printing, artwork, binding, and selling the books. The *artel* was a shareholding society, with each member agreeing to pay fifteen rubles in annual dues or an equivalent amount in work. In its sixteen years of existence (1863–1879), the *artel* published fourteen books, including children's books such as *The Tales of Hans Christian Anderson*, two short stories by Louisa May Alcott, and scientific works by Charles Darwin, among others. In all, twenty-seven women earned their living from this venture. For years after the *artel* closed, shareholders received royalties from the sale of its books.

The ultimate collapse of the publishing effort can be attributed to several factors, both political and personal. The *artel*'s charter was never approved by the government; no reason is listed even in the official records, and innumerable appeals to high officials by Filosofova failed to reverse this decision.[21] But there were additional problems. Two of the group's most active members, Trubnikova and Stasova, withdrew. Trubnikova had begun to show the signs of mental illness, while Stasova had to depart Russia in 1872 to care for two fatally ill nieces, leaving Filosofova to manage the *artel* on her own. Finally, the bankruptcy of the bookselling firm that had carried much of the *artel*'s inventory contributed mightily to the *artel*'s financial woes.

The personal issues that surfaced in the *artel* exemplify the ways in which the personal and public spheres intersected for the women of the triumvirate. Indeed, the activism of these women affected their roles in the family, in one case with tragic results. Trubnikova's initial infatuation with her husband and his quotations from Herzen soon faded. The man who enchanted her by his erudition and ideals proved to be threatened by, and then openly hostile to, her feminist ideals and erudition. Trubnikov undermined not only his wife's intellectual but also her material and physical well-being. He completely mismanaged Mariia's inheritance money through bad investments and diverting resources to his second family. Trubnikova's fiscal woes were combined with deteriorating health. Like most married women of her day, Trubnikova was almost constantly pregnant. Trubnikova bore seven children, practically in succession, after her marriage in 1854. Four, all daughters, survived. For Trubnikova, the constant pregnancies took a heavy physical toll. They also brought back memories of her mother, who died in childbirth when Mariia was four years old. By the late 1860s, Trubnikova began to show signs of the mental illness that was to cause her complete withdrawal from feminist activity. Seeking a cure, she left the country in 1869. When she and her husband finally separated in 1876, Trubnikova, already sick and fatigued, was forced to find work as a writer to support herself and her children. Thus, Trubnikova became like the women she, Stasova, and Filosofova sought to aid with their early self-help societies.

Despite her serious difficulties throughout this period, Trubnikova defied the social and political status quo and encouraged rebellion among her female offspring. Trubnikova and her daughters often donned male clothing when on their country estate. Although she disagreed with their tactics, Trubnikova gave direct support to radical women. When her daughter Olga joined the revolutionary groups Black Repartition in 1879 and then People's Will in 1881, she held meetings and stored illegal literature at her house.[22] At one point Sofiia Perovskaia, leader of the group that assassinated Tsar Alexander II, hid in Trubnikova's house.[23] With time however, Trubnikova's condition worsened, and in a reversal of roles, her daughters nursed their mother until her death in 1897.

Filosofova was more fortunate than Trubnikova, appearing to have successfully balanced her multiple roles in and outside the family. Her wealth enabled her to be helped by servants, although no one else could carry and give birth to her children. Between 1858 and 1872, while she championed the feminist cause, Filosofova was almost constantly pregnant. She had six children, several miscarriages, and possibly one or two stillbirths, but her health does not seem to have been affected, although she did blame a fight with nihilists in Peter Lavrov's Society for Women's Work for one miscarriage.[24] Filosofova was by all accounts a concerned mother. Her third child and namesake, Nonochka, was sick and hunchbacked, requiring Filosofova to travel outside the country for her treatment in the mid-1860s and to care for her until she died in 1865.

Unlike Trubnikova, Filosofova was able to reach a modus vivendi with her husband. Although their relationship may have influenced Filosofova to believe that reform could work and that change was possible within the system, the brunt of government displeasure about her feminist activity fell on her husband. Vladimir Filosofov was a key aide to Dmitri Miliutin in the War Ministry and was active in the drafting and implementation of the emancipation decree and subsequent reforms. His work kept him away from home for long periods of time. Miliutin once confided to Filosofov that his wife's activities had cost him the post of minister of justice. If he was bitter, Filosofov seems to have kept these thoughts to himself. There is no evidence that he reproached his wife for her activities or was openly hostile, as was Konstantin Trubnikov. Indeed an 1869 letter chiding his wife for her opposition to capital punishment indicates his "live and let live" attitude. Vladimir Filosofov wrote, "I don't agree with your ideas. But to each their own. My work involves the most unfavorable side of public activity—punishment. As a result I have special information, and since you cannot deny the necessity of criminal law, someone must implement it."[25]

Despite her vow to devote herself single-mindedly to her "universal family," in reality Stasova balanced her feminist activism with family concerns, sometimes to the detriment of those in the larger world she had vowed to help. Her decision to leave Russia in 1872, spending the next five years tending her nieces, affected the survival of the women's publishing *artel*. Nevertheless, Stasova achieved almost saintlike status among those who knew her, as they noted with awe her unquenchable fervor. In her diary, Elena Shtakenshneider described Stasova as tireless for the cause: "In a feverish state, with flaming cheeks, with hands like ice, so feeble she could hardly move her legs; almost hoarse from weakness, she toils, works, bustles about all day long."[26]

By taking advantage of a society in flux, the triumvirate, three women of the Russian privileged class, answered the woman question in their own lives. The process transformed them, and this transformation informed the ways in which they acted out their ideals in the public and private spheres of their lives. Mariia Trubnikova reframed the salon to be a women's and feminists' discussion group into which she recruited Filosofova and Stasova, thus providing a base for the feminist activity of the triumvirate. Nadezhda Stasova rejected the roles of the abandoned woman and the maiden aunt devoted solely to serving her family, instead redefining a significant portion of her life as one of service to other women. Anna Filosofova, her consciousness raised, went into an arena familiar and pleasurable to her, the ball, no longer as an empty-headed society butterfly but as a champion of women's rights. This reframing enabled her to continue to enjoy the social life of the balls and also use it effectively to lobby for women's rights. In such fashion did the daughter of the Decembrist spark feminist action, the godchild of the tsar become a feminist saint, and the society belle become a "beautiful lady" and a "red lady."

NOTES

1. Ann Hibner Koblitz, "Spreading the Gospel of Science," p. 84 in *Science, Women, and Revolution in Russia* (Amsterdam: Harwood, 2000).

2. The Kadet, or Constitutional Democratic, Party emerged in 1905 out of the liberal 1904 Union of Liberation to champion constitutional rights in autocratic Russia. The Kadet Party hoped to gain more concessions from the tsarist government than were granted in the October Manifesto of 1905.

3. The quote is from Elena Likhacheva, *Materialy dlia istorii zhenskogo obrazovaniia v Rossii*, 2 vols. (St. Petersburg: Tip. M. M. Stasiulevicha, 1899–1901), 2:458–59.

4. Land and Freedom emerged in opposition to the reforms of Alexander II. Believing that the emancipation provisions were inadequate, these radicals erroneously expected former serfs to mount a revolution. Scattered rebellions among peasants did protest the temporary obligations that they continued to owe their former owners as well as the fact that once that period of obligation came to an end, they had to purchase the land they had come to believe was rightly theirs.

5. Mythologized as the first Russian revolutionaries, the Decembrists led an unsuccessful revolt against the Russian autocracy in 1825 by refusing to swear the oath of allegiance to the new tsar, Nicholas I.

6. O. K. Bulanova-Trubnikova, "Doch' dekabrista" (part 2), *Byloe* 6, 34 (1925): 20–37, 23–24.

7. O. K. Bulanova-Trubnikova, *Tri pokoleniia* (Moscow: Gosudarstvennoe izdatel'stvo, 1928), 170.

8. Ariadna V. Tyrkova, "Anna Pavlovna Filosofova i eia vremia," in *Sbornik pamiati Anny Pavlovny Filosofovoi*, 2 vols. (Petrograd: P. Golike i A. Vil'borg, 1915), 1:109.

9. Anna Miliukova, "Obshchestvennoe nastroenie 60-kh godov i Anna Pavlovna Filosofova: Po perepiske eia s muzhem," in *Sbornik pamiati Anny Pavlovny Filosofovoi*, 2:35–46, 41, 43.

10. V. V. Stasov, *Nadezhda Vasil'evna Stasova: Vospominaniia i ocherki* (St. Petersburg: Tip. M. Merkusheva, 1899), 10, 21, 20.

11. *Entsiklopedicheskii slovar' Brokgauz-Efron* (St. Petersburg: I. A. Efron, 1900), 61:466–68.

12. Stasov, *Stasova*, 25–26.

13. Stasov, *Stasova*, 61.

14. Stasov, *Stasova*, 65.

15. Tyrkova, *Sbornik pamiati Anny Pavlovny Filosofovoi*, 1:123.

16. Elena A. Shtakenshneider, *Dnevniki i zapiski (1854–1886)*, ed. I. N. Rozanov (Moscow: Academia, 1934), 352.

17. Tyrkova, *Sbornik pamiati Anny Pavlovny Filosofovoi*, 1:123.

18. Petr Kropotkin, *Memoirs of a Revolutionist* (New York: Grove, 1970), 262.

19. A. F. Koni, "Pamiati A. P. Filosofovoi," in *Sbornik pamiati Anny Pavlovny Filosofovoi*, 2:1–10, 3–5. The quote is from Bulanova-Trubnikova, *Tri*, 181. Information about the Madame Roland portrait is from Tyrkova, *Sbornik pamiati Anny Pavlovny Filosofovoi*, 1:181. See also L. D. Filippova, "Iz istorii zhenskogo obrazovaniia v Rossii," *Voprosy istorii* (February 1963): 209–18.

20. Quoted in Tyrkova, *Sbornik pamiati Anny Pavlovny Filosofovoi*, 1:298.

21. I am indebted to Rhonda Clark for this information.

22. The Black Repartition, in advocating the redistribution of all land, including private property, among the peasants, sought change through propaganda and gradualist methods, while the People's Will embraced terrorism as a way of challenging the autocracy. Members of the People's Will masterminded the 1881 assassination of Alexander II.

23. Z. A. Evteeva, ed., *Vysshie zhenskie (Bestuzhevskie) kursy: Bibliograficheskii ukazatel'* (Moscow: Izd-vo Kniga, 1966), 143.

24. Tyrkova, *Sbornik pamiati Anny Pavlovny Filosofovoi*, 1:486–87. On the miscarriage, see Shtakenshneider, *Dnevniki*, 350.

25. Miliukova, "Obshchestvennoe nastroenie," 45.

26. Shtakenshneider, *Dnevniki*, 400.

SUGGESTED READINGS

Bisha, Robin, Jehanne M. Gheith, Christine Holden, and William G. Wagner, comps. *Russian Women, 1698–1917: Experience and Expression, an Anthology of Sources.* Bloomington: Indiana University Press, 2002.

Edmondson, Linda. *Feminism in Russia, 1900–1917.* Stanford, CA: Stanford University Press, 1984.

Engel, Barbara Alpern. *Mothers and Daughters: Women of the Intelligentsia in Nineteenth-Century Russia.* Cambridge: Cambridge University Press, 1983.

Heldt, Barbara. *Terrible Perfection: Women and Russian Literature.* Bloomington: Indiana University Press, 1987.

Johanson, Christine. *Women's Struggle for Higher Education in Russia, 1855–1900.* Kingston, ON: McGill-Queen's University Press, 1987.

Koblitz, Ann Hibner. "Science, Women and the Russian Intelligentsia: The Generation of the 1860s." *Isis* 79 (June 1988): 208–26.

Stites, Richard. *The Women's Liberation Movement in Russia.* 2nd exp. ed. Princeton, NJ: Princeton University Press, 1991.

Tishkin, G. A. *Zhenskii vopros v Rossii, 50-60e gody XIX v.* Leningrad: Leningradskii universitet, 1984.

Chapter Seven

Happy Birthday, Siberia!

Reform and Public Opinion in Russia's "Colony," 1881–1882

William B. Husband

In the aftermath of Russia's resounding defeat in the Crimean War (1853–1856), which exposed the backwardness of the empire's economy and military in comparison to those of England and France, Alexander II (1855–1881) and enlightened bureaucrats began to propose a series of reforms to bring Russia into the modern world. In order to facilitate discussion among educated society as to the precise nature of these changes, the government loosened its censorship laws. The abolition of serfdom on 19 February 1861 amounted to the most monumental reform, but other reforms were significant as the autocratic government created new institutions at the local level. The 1864 introduction of the zemstvo at the provincial level constituted a significant shift away from centralized administration to local self-government, whose officials were elected indirectly by local residents. Through self-taxation the zemstvo had responsibilities for social welfare, the maintenance of roads and bridges, and the provisioning of newly emancipated peasants with food supplies in the wake of harvest disasters, veterinary and agricultural advice, and fire insurance. More important, the zemstvos were charged with setting up public schools to teach peasants basic literacy and hospitals in provincial towns to provide professional medical care to the rural populations. Other reforms endowed universities (1863) with rights of self-regulation, introduced the jury system (1864) to nonpeasant subjects of the realm, created municipal councils (1870), and made military conscription (1874) universal (with years of service reduced considerably).

Leery of providing regions inhabited by diverse ethnic groups with institutions that could be used for separatist national movements, however, imperial bureaucrats limited the introduction of the zemstvos and municipal councils to thirty-four provinces of European Russia, not including Siberia. In the privileged areas the populations were overwhelmingly Russian (including Orthodox Belarusians and Ukrainians, which the autocracy did not recognize as separate ethnic groups) and therefore considered to be "loyal citizens" of the realm. As if on cue, the 1863 Polish uprising in Warsaw had served as a warning bell about the dangers of non-Russian nationalism. The fact that Siberia lay outside the safe zone of so-called Russian territories became contested in 1881–1882 with the tercentenary of Siberia's annexation, the subject of William Husband's chapter.

By the mid-nineteenth century Russia had become a huge empire, stretching for thousands of miles from Polish lands in the west to Kamchatka in the east and significant stretches of Central Asia to the southeast. This multinational empire had been created by a combination of economic and military conquests and spontaneous colonization of new areas by peasant settlers constantly searching for virgin lands. Akin to the Canadian frontier, Siberia had attracted fur trappers in the sixteenth century, who levied heavy exactions on Siberian native peoples, exploiting them both for their furs and women. With the explorers came cartographers who began to map the area and turn it from a dark wilderness into an earthly paradise dotted with monasteries and their Christian crosses. That utopian vision, however, could not entirely hide the conquest of tribal peoples by way of violence and disease. It was as if the early violence of conquest begat further violence as the vast open spaces of Siberia quickly emerged as the dumping grounds for the empire's convicts and political prisoners. At the same time, this colony or frontier developed prosperous towns and settlements of free labor as a result of voluntary migration.

On the eve of the tercentenary of Siberia's annexation, Siberia had seized the attention of educated society. Why did Siberia emerge as a focus of interest on the part of the educated subjects of the empire, both local and nonlocal, official and nonofficial? What did Siberia personify in the educated worldview? Why was the reconstruction of its founding so contested? At the same time, why was the history of this frontier region far less important than its future? And what does this contested celebration of Siberia's conquest reveal about the emergence of a civil society in the empire by the 1880s?

On 26 October 1881, Siberia turned three hundred years old. This, in any event, was how much of Russian society chose to characterize the tricentennial anniversary of the annexation of the vast territory that extends eastward from the Ural Mountains to the Pacific Ocean and southward from the Arctic Sea to China. The occasion attracted such significant interest on both sides of the Urals that what was initially planned as a one-day holiday did not conclude until the end of the following year. But this commemoration did not extend over fourteen months because it generated unanticipated levels of good-will. On the contrary, even in its organizational stages the tricentennial created controversy. And by the time the final speech, toast, and shout of *"Urá!"* faded away in December 1882, the birthday had exacerbated contentious political and social issues whose importance extended far beyond the borders of Russia's eastern "colony." To make matters worse from the perspective of the central government, when regional officials petulantly attempted to alter the timing of the event, they unintentionally created an opportunity for national and Siberian periodicals to comment legally on what Emperor Alexander III's course of action ought to be. As it ran its course, therefore, the anniversary brought broad public attention to a diversity and intensity of views on the future of reform and importance of public opinion, not only in Siberia, but in the empire as a whole.

Little friction, of course, was openly evident at the actual anniversary events, which were outwardly characterized by high spirits and cheer as well as the excesses of rhetoric and alcohol consumption common to such occasions in any society. Because it took place in the nation's capital and involved important dignitaries, the celebration that received the greatest attention in the press—even though it was privately organized and the date of the official commemoration had not yet been decided—was a banquet held on 26 October 1881 at the Hotel Demut in St. Petersburg. Two hundred distinguished state and military leaders, scientists, doctors, professors, students, and society women gathered in its large hall beneath an electric sun (the Demut's electric lights were still a novelty) that shone on a gold wreath above the caption "26 October 1581–1881." Adjutant General Sofiano, former chairman of the Imperial Geographic Society in Siberia, raised a toast to the health of the emperor, which caused the audience to break into patriotic songs and repeated shouts of *"Urá!"* A deeply personal speech by B. A. Miliutin, scion of one of Russia's most accomplished families, that concluded with a dramatic toast "To Siberia!" then raised the mood even higher.

But the gathering at the Demut focused more on the future than the past, and speakers pointedly eschewed simply commemorating the annexation of Siberia in the sixteenth century. Instead, they questioned the value of the natural wealth of the *krai*[1] in light of its abysmal schools and preponderance of illiteracy; recommended abolishing the practice of exiling criminals to the region; advocated the development of industry, introduction of new courts and zemstvo institutions, settlement of unoccupied land, and extension of freedom of the press; proposed the establishment of the first Siberian university; and outlined the problems faced by non-Russian nationalities. In the midst of these speeches and toasts, the group opened a large number of messages of congratulation from throughout Russia and composed its own telegram, which it sent to similar events being held that night in Moscow and a dozen Siberian towns. At the end of the scheduled program, revelers remained in their seats to hear extemporaneous talks by other audience members, and festivities continued well into the night.[2]

The ninety people who attended the parallel celebration that night at the Slavianskii Bazar Hotel in Moscow expressed their opinions no less frankly. Following the requisite toasts to the emperor and Siberia, speakers chastised the remainder of Russia for thinking of the region only as a "gold mine" for three hundred years, exiling criminals there, and giving little attention to the quality of its governing officials. The master of ceremonies, one Chukmaldin, asserted that Siberia had made intellectual and moral advances *in spite of* state policy and largely because of its success in assimilating its political and criminal exiles, an accomplishment he called unique in the world. Another Siberian, Mr. Basnin, stressed the need for new courts, zemstvos, and a more free and open press. But the key address of the evening came in the form of an extended toast to the proposed founding of a Siberian university. Speaking in the name of his generation, the student Efimov, who attended the Petrov Agricultural Academy in Moscow, asserted that ending the annual exodus of bright young Siberians who left in pursuit of higher education—frequently never to return—required not only words, but deeds. As if on cue, one of the masters of ceremonies immediately announced that a fund for needy students at the future Siberian university had been created from private donations and another for Siberians at Moscow University. Then followed toasts to the printed word, Siberian women (who were lauded as mothers, wives, and sisters and favorably compared to American frontier women), toiling immigrants and colonists, travelers, and a proposed trans-Siberian railroad. The writer Moskvin concluded the evening with a poem he composed especially for the occasion.[3]

The celebrations held throughout Siberia on 6 December 1882, the date state administrators ultimately selected for official ceremonies, evinced much the same spirit. Although these followed a common format, in more than one locale observances began even before the designated holiday. On 4 December in Omsk, students of the boys' and girls' gymnasia acted scenes from *Ermak Timofeevich*, Nikolai Polevoi's play on the conquest of Siberia: dressed as Muscovites they delighted that "God has sent Russia a new kingdom" as Cossacks bestowed the region on Tsar Ivan IV; dressed as natives of Siberia they greeted the approach of the conquering Russians with trumpets and cheers; and in a final tableau Russia and Siberia, represented as two women, walked off hand in hand. The streets of Irkutsk, Tomsk, and Tobol'sk, draped in flags and garlands, took on a holiday air; at night the towns were brightly illuminated. The Holy Synod of the Russian Orthodox Church ordered that prayers of thanks be offered in all cathedrals, parish churches, and monasteries from the Urals to Kamchatka. Accordingly, on 6 December in every region of Siberia celebrations began with a liturgy in the local cathedral attended by leading dignitaries, and schools and government offices closed. Following the religious service, there were public toasts to the health of the emperor and heir (6 December is the winter feast of St. Nicholas the Miracle Worker and consequently the name day of the future Tsar Nicholas II). Then came repeated singing of the national anthem, a speech by the governor, and a dress parade by the local reserve regiment. The general population, despite attempts to characterize these as "public" commemorations, largely participated only as spectators at parades, lectures, and speeches; designated representatives of their social class at official ceremonies; and the audience of performances of Polevoi's *Ermak Timofeevich*. A partial exception was Irkutsk, where an array of local organizations—the missionary society, geographic society, society of doctors, Red Cross, society of Siberian hunters, charity society, society of aid to the students of eastern Siberia, musical society, and the fire brigade—was included in an afternoon program. The events everywhere concluded with a ball and dinner that only invited dignitaries attended.

Within this limited format, however, the three regional governors in Siberia pressed for many of the same reforms that the self-appointed representatives of public opinion had advocated on 26 October 1881. Lieutenant General Anuchin, governor-general of eastern Siberia, dispatched a telegram to Alexander III in which—following obligatory words of loyalty to the emperor and praise for the Orthodox faith—he harshly denounced the system of exile and hard labor and the weakness of local state and social institutions in the *krai*. In Tobol'sk, Governor V. A. Lysogorskii praised *voluntary* migration as the engine of Siberia's internal growth and attainment of civic maturity. Social activism, the development of industry and trade, a rise in the level of education, and the founding of a university, he said, would all improve Siberia in ways beneficial to the future of the entire Russian state. Although the mood of the day was more hopeful than defiant, local government representatives voted overwhelmingly to forward the governor's address to the minister of internal affairs with the recommendation that he bring it to the attention of the emperor. And in Omsk, the steppe governor, Lieutenant General Kolpakovskii, supported remarks delivered by I. A. Kozlov of the Imperial Russian Geographic Society that advocated improving public initiative and education in the *krai*.[4]

Not all press coverage, however, celebrated Siberia or sympathized with the aspirations of reformists. *News and Stock Market Gazette* reacted to the dinners of 26 October 1881 with claims that sympathizers in the press had inflated the importance of the Siberian anniversary, saying it had passed almost unnoticed by the general public. In the *Gazette*'s view, St. Petersburg and provincial periodicals had seized upon issues such as the proposed Siberian university to disguise the region's problems and champion reformist programs. It disagreed with papers such as the *Odessa Leaflet*, which contended that Siberia's present governors were not the unscrupulous individuals of the past who capriciously sent their enemies to prison or Canada (*sic*) for some minor transgression. And, according to the *Odessa Leaflet*, the horrific drunkenness—when Siberians counted their alcoholic intake by the barrel and then often rioted, killed one another, or raped women—had now significantly decreased. In this view, education among Siberians was improving, the local press was exercising a positive influence, and Siberia was generally changing for the better. But the *News and Stock Market Gazette* said it was "not so naive" as to accept the *Odessa Leaflet*'s "self-deception" at face value. It belittled the fact that so many different dates had been proposed for the celebration of Siberia's birthday and characterized the region as a wilderness similar to "an African Sahara" that, despite its riches, lacked proper modes of communication, schools, "and generally speaking any kind of thoughtful, intellectual life." The continuation of drunkenness, capricious imprisonment, and government corruption at alarming levels in Siberia was "not a secret to anyone." Skeptical of the preparedness of such a place for reform, the *News and Stock Market Gazette* asked how a university could solve the problems of a region that lacked adequate elementary schools and where women and officials feared crossing public squares even in daylight.[5]

Expressing a different mode of criticism, periodicals that supported the private reform initiatives of October 1881 found fault with the state-organized events of December 1882. In contrast to more favorable government coverage, the *Siberian Newspaper* said that 6 December was celebrated in Tomsk "imperceptibly." Reforms had been awaited there since 26 October 1881, and the fact that they had not materialized by the end of 1882 bred indifference to the holiday.[6] The *Eastern Review*, which did not yet exist in October 1881, voiced an additional criticism of state administration. In the past, it asserted, Siberians had always commemorated 26 October 1581, and the official decision to shift the celebrations to December 1882 cast a tense and strained mood over the preparations. Yet the main issue, the paper continued, was what the officially designated anniversary of 6 December signified for the future of Russian social consciousness. It lamented that there were no special observances of the anniversary in St. Petersburg, but seized the opportunity to mention that on 5 December Nikolai M. Iadrintsev, publisher of the *Eastern Review*, had addressed a meeting of the Society of Russian Industry and Trade in the capital on the contemporary economic position of Siberia. Iadrintsev, who had long supported the independent development of Siberia and rejected its status as an economic colony of European Russia, hoped "that exploitative economics would end" and that the Russian Far East would even become the cultural center of Asia.[7]

The extended birthday of Siberia in 1881–1882 turned out to be, in short, a unique opportunity for the public expression of preexisting issues, most of which had little directly to do with celebrating the conquest of the region three centuries earlier. First, the anniversary demonstrated definitively that educated Siberians at home and in European Russia considered themselves to be the representatives of present "public opinion" in the *krai* as well as the best qualified architects of its future. The recent emergence of a Siberian press in conjunction with increased coverage of Siberia in central publications made it possible for them to articulate their agenda, and in practice newspaper and journal writers regularly identified with the views and aspirations of social progressives. They spoke for Siberian society not as it presently existed but for the one they hoped to create. Second, although private and government events marked the beginning and end of this extended commemoration, respectively, the reformist agendas expressed at both were remarkably similar. Private proponents of the region championed a specific socioeconomic ideal while multiple motivations moved state officials to advance Siberian interests, but both tacitly agreed on which improvements they deemed necessary.

Third, the similarity of the reforms advocated on so many different occasions indicated that common concerns had started taking shape well in advance of 1881. Although all sides in the discussion chose to characterize the annexation in the sixteenth century as the acquisition of a "colony" rather than the conquest of an area occupied by indigenous peoples, the advocates of Siberia's reformed future felt that the region should no longer serve primarily as a source of wealth for the rest of the empire. Siberia, they argued, should experience its own rational economic development and voluntary agricultural settlement, all of which would be facilitated by a railroad. The zemstvo, court, and press reforms that Tsar Alexander II had enacted for the rest of Russia during the 1860s needed to be extended to Siberia, and her manifold educational deficiencies required correction. Having reduced government corruption significantly and attained a higher level of civic maturity, the argument ran, Siberia had earned these concessions.

But to begin in 1881–1882 is to run ahead of the story, because it did not take contrived anniversary commemorations to focus Russian attention on Siberia. Those who lived west of the Urals had long viewed Siberia with an ambivalence comprised equally of fascination and fear. The region's very size, mixture of cultures, and extremes of climate regularly excited flights of imagination among outsiders, and during the nineteenth century the connection of Siberia with adventure became a leitmotif in Russian popular fiction. The exile of the revolutionary Decembrists and of common criminals there, the bravado Siberians displayed before nonresidents, and the habitation of the region by a myriad of non-Russian ethnic groups all reinforced its image as a place both forbidding and forbidden. The state itself was by no means immune to Siberia's spell. From the time of Siberia's annexation, tsarist officials period-ically conceived grandiose—but mostly unrealized—plans for its economic development.

This vast area thus intrigued outsiders on a number of levels. It appeared as a place of imprisonment and hard labor; a refuge for runaway serfs, religious dissidents, and bandits; the site of one of the largest gold discoveries in his-tory; and a magnet for hunters, traders, explorers, and rootless adventurers. Siberia became the destination of choice for entrepreneurs attracted by the possibility of amassing huge fortunes with little state regulation; people will-ing to endure privation in order to distance themselves from the constraints of mainstream civilization; and, in the case of those who migrated with the per-mission and even encouragement of the state, peasants seeking to elude serf-dom legally. And if such a mixture of images and influences made it impossi-ble to identify a single Siberian personality concretely, this only made it easier for the fanciful to project onto the region whatever they hoped to find there.

The roots of this mystique long predated the nineteenth century. The first serious entry of Russians into Siberia occurred when Novgorodians came to the area during the eleventh century, but they sought trade, not occupation. Expansionist Moscow was different. Muscovite missionaries entered western Siberia in 1383, in 1465 Vasilii Skriaba led subjects of Ivan III across the Urals, and by 1488 the tsar claimed sovereignty over the region by adding it to his list of titles. Actual annexation began during the reign of Ivan IV. On 23 October 1581, the Cossack Ermak, a mercenary in the employ of the pow-erful Stroganov family, decisively defeated Kuchum, the Tatar leader who ruled the region, at the Irtysh River. Three days later Ermak occupied the Tatar capital, Isker. He then dispatched Ivan Kol'tso to Moscow to present the region to Tsar Ivan IV, which this emissary accomplished sometime between 16 November 1582 and 1 March 1583. The first *voevoda*, as Muscovite re-gional administrators were known, accompanied Kol'tso back to western Siberia, and within seventy years the Russian Empire reached the Pacific Ocean, Bering Straits, and Amur River. By the reign of Peter the Great, Siberia was fully part of the Russian Empire, and in 1707 Peter appointed Matvei Gagarin as the region's first governor-general.

Against this backdrop, interest in the three-hundred-year anniversary be-gan to surface slowly and largely inconspicuously during the mid-1870s, yet by spring 1881 the birthday had become sharply politicized. Initially Siberians had nothing in mind beyond a few dinners and the traditional holiday illuminations of their towns.[8] Organizers needed only to determine the correct day to celebrate. The two-hundred-year anniversary had been observed in Tobol'sk, site of the ancient capital, on 26 October 1784. This commemorated the day of Ermak's entry into the Tatar capital in 1581 but had also caused confusion by memorializing the year 1584. In so doing, the two-hundred-year anniversary paid tribute to the year of Ermak's death or, in a competing explanation of its significance, the year of the full administrative annexation of Siberia.[9] As the anniversary drew closer, Ermak became a symbol of initiative in Siberia, even though papers were generally reporting widespread public indifference toward "Siberian questions" at the same time. In early 1881, the newspaper *Siberia* felt it had to challenge its readers to prove such assertions false.[10]

But there were also small harbingers of the controversy that lay ahead. At the beginning of 1880, the activist journalist Iadrintsev had proposed making the anniversary an event of greater substance. He advocated holding a congress so that people and the press could express their preferences, perhaps including an exhibit of local products and the founding of a museum in Tomsk or Irkutsk.[11] Others took up the same suggestions.[12] A significant moment then came on 2 April 1881 when the city council in Enisei unanimously passed a proposal to link the upcoming anniversary with the introduction in Siberia of zemstvos, open courts, freedom of speech and of the press, freedom of the person and the inviolability of property, "freedom of public productivity and industry," freedom of movement, and an end to the exile system. The Enisei proposal to link reform with commemoration quickly gained the support of public opinion throughout Siberia.[13]

At this juncture the legend of the conquest by Ermak and subsequent consolidation of state power assumed proportions that, despite the serious issues at stake, appeared comic even to some contemporaries. In 1880 opponents of Siberian initiative began trying to discredit its most powerful symbol, Ermak. Simultaneously, they attempted to shift the emphasis in the legend from his military victory to the establishment of administrative hegemony that followed—that is, to rank the existence of the Russian state above acts of initiative from below. In this they faced a serious obstacle. The date Ermak entered the town of Isker was well known, but no documentation existed to determine the precise date on which Ivan Kol'tso gave the region to Ivan IV.

But if the attempt to affirm the primacy of the state at the expense of social initiative was undermined by an inability to determine the exact date when Ivan IV met with Kol'tso, this did not prevent some spirited attempts. Late in 1880, a member of the Imperial Geographic Society, one Balkashin, argued that Ermak did not merit the title of prince and should be reduced in future references to the Cossack rank of ataman. The prestigious Moscow Archaeological Society took up the issue in even greater detail at its meeting of 15 May 1881. Members researched in vain for evidence to determine precisely when in 1582 Ivan IV received Ermak's emissary (although only the *News and Stock Market Gazette* seriously questioned the absence of documentation for so significant an event). By way of compensation, the society felt it could at least improve Ermak's non-Christian name, which appeared in some sources as the Christian name German and in others as Vasilii. The gathering solemnly decided to rename him Vasilii Timofeev Povol'skii. As the *Week* reported with gleeful amusement, "There was a new christening in Moscow 296 years after Ermak's death." But the *Week* found the motivations behind such machinations far less amusing, attributing them to non-Siberians, especially newly arrived bureaucrats and the attitudes of their superiors, who wanted to stifle local initiative and reduce the region to submissiveness.[14]

As the debate over the relative importance of the victory and annexation broadened in the press, the appearance of other issues and personalities complicated any possible resolution. Siberians did not themselves always present a united front. Prevailing private opinion was in favor of celebrating the exploits of Ermak rather than the arrival of state administrators in Siberia, but a vocal minority championed celebrating the victory on 23 October instead of the 26th, the date of the occupation of the Tatar capital.[15] The *Moscow Telegraph* might have called the victory one of the most renowned days in Russian history,[16] yet *New Time*, after reviewing the lengthy arguments, played down Ermak's exploits in 1581 as but a single episode in what it considered the natural and systematic striving of the Russian population to the northeast.[17] The events of 6 December 1882 once again brought the debate to prominence; defenders, critics, and aspiring peacemakers all had their say.[18]

And how did the state choose to celebrate Siberia's anniversary on the name day of the tsar's heir, when protocol would demand that the heir be honored in any celebration? One explanation—that the period of mourning following the assassination of Alexander II in 1881 prevented any official celebration on 26 October—was not fully convincing,[19] and the suggestion that in the absence of any documentation, 6 December "might have been the very day" was even less helpful.[20] *Country* added little by stating that people should still celebrate 6 December even though nothing actually happened on that day in 1581.[21] In the end, the press did not directly question the motives of state administrators in selecting the name day of the heir, but one must certainly speculate that the choice of Nicholas's name day was a ploy on the part of the state to divert attention from the significance of Siberia on that day.

The most detailed interpretation came from the irrepressible Iadrintsev. Writing in the *European Herald*, he reviewed in detail all points of view but attempted no resolution. Instead, he characterized the conquest of Siberia as an accomplished fact that had produced its own historical ramifications. In Iadrintsev's view, Ermak's victory was not accidental but "the first step of popular colonization which, renewed by new waves of movement, created Siberia and subsequently consolidated her civic life." But if the pressure of voluntary migration and not conquest were the key, the real hero was "neither Ermak nor the *voevoda*, but the Russian people in general . . . who continue the great cultural conquest in the East." In fact, Iadrintsev held, Siberia's manifold problems could be traced to the arrival of the *voevodas*, who ruled more arbitrarily there than elsewhere. Iadrintsev noted that the Tomsk and Irkutsk councils had followed Enisei in petitioning for reforms, whose value he felt lay largely as protection from the capriciousness of state officials. The introduction of the rule of law and of reforms presently enjoyed in European Russia would aid Siberian development and take maximum advantage of her location in Asia. This, argued Iadrintsev, was in the interest of the whole empire.[22]

Neither private reformers nor those within Siberian administration achieved what they desired. In the months following October 1881, literally every issue of pro-reform periodicals carried material that either directly advocated reform or promoted it indirectly by discussing the general merits of individual changes. Opponents principally responded not by opposing reform directly but by questioning the readiness of Siberia for any new responsibilities or talking past the issue entirely. A speech delivered by Professor Zamyslovskii on 3 June 1882 at the Historical-Philological Institute, and reprinted in many papers, encapsulated this strategy. Zamyslovskii ignored reform and social questions, concentrated on Siberia as a physical entity with industrial and agricultural potential to be developed, and in a seemingly dry, academic discussion put forward what amounted to an argument in favor of continued "colonization."[23]

Thus matters stood until the three governors-general as well as lesser organizations and personages sent their respectful but reformist messages to the tsar in December 1882. But once the *Government Herald* published Alexander III's replies and other periodicals gave this material wide dissemination, it was clear that the emperor did not intend to expand reform or alter Siberia's subordinate status. On 7 December 1882, Alexander countered the overtures of the Governor-General Anuchin in Irkutsk with his own vision. Siberia was close to his heart and in his prayers, the tsar said, and he was particularly concerned with the development of its natural riches and correct administration.

He called upon God to keep Russia and Siberia inseparable for their "mutual benefit and the glory of our dear Fatherland." In a similarly worded communication to the governor-general in Omsk, the emperor also stressed the inseparability of Russia from Siberia and the need to develop her wealth, which he gave his assurance would be used for the consolidation of the power of the empire.[24] In neither case did Alexander III directly address the request that his father's great reforms be extended east of the Urals.[25]

These responses, which communicated clearly that the emperor did not intend to bow to reformist opinion or alter Siberia's subordinate status, frustrated reformers, but it did not silence them. Intellectuals continued to gather annually in Siberia on 26 October to reiterate their reformist agenda: the plight of the peasants, the problems caused by criminal exile, and the expansion of education. By the mid-1880s, some changes did appear—preparations for a university that would open in Tomsk in 1888, work on a trans-Siberian railroad to be completed in the 1890s, court reforms—but reformers continued to work for the full slate of reforms that existed in European Russia but not Siberia.[26] But, even as Alexander III instituted changes, the state rather than society provided the impetus. While he worked for the economic development of his empire, on the one hand, his government launched a comprehensive program to undo his father's social reforms and to bring regional and local power more firmly under central direction, on the other. This philosophy led to the energetic repression of dissent. State censors twice warned the *Eastern Review* that it was publishing materials designed to undermine the legitimacy of public officials in the eyes of the public before they suspended its publication for two weeks in 1885. The paper managed to operate until January 1906, when local authorities in Irkutsk closed it.[27]

In the short term the anniversary of Siberia provided an early test of the intentions and temperament of Alexander III, but the issues it raised would reverberate until 1917 and thereafter. As he followed his reformist father to the throne in 1881, the new emperor inherited a legacy of unfulfilled progressivism as well as a crisis of state authority. This anniversary, which had only symbolic national significance, therefore assumed a visibility in 1881–1882 far out of proportion to its actual importance. But beyond the scope of the press coverage it generated and the opportunity it provided for the legal, public discussion of reform, the birthday of Siberia highlighted the meaning of political and social currents no educated Russian of the period could ignore. Above all, it defined the existence and nature of "public opinion." In late nineteenth-century Russia this was not a mass phenomenon as much as a reflection of the convictions and aspirations of the educated elite on both sides of the Urals. The fact that these battles were waged largely through newspapers and journals illustrated that journalists, public officials, and civic intellectuals assumed the largest voices. The nature of these discussions also showed that these self-appointed representatives of the public conscience used print media, not primarily to reflect society as it existed, but to advocate a social ideal they felt was more meaningful. In their hands, the juncture of politics and journalism was not reportage or even editorial comment on what had transpired as much as the attainment of a level of consciousness that could then be conveyed to others. Nor was reformist sentiment confined to progressives or Siberian intellectuals. As we have seen, state administrators with responsibility for the development and administration of Siberia championed many of the same changes advocated by their liberal counterparts outside government. Under Alexander III, Siberia would therefore remain European Russia's political and economic colony, but during the friction of 1881–1882 it briefly became a metaphorical colony through which filtered all reformist sentiment in the Russian Empire.

NOTES

The following periodicals and newspapers were consulted in the compilation of this article: *Akmolinskie oblastnie vedomosti* (Omsk), 1882; *Bessarabskie gubernskie vedomosti* (Kishinev), 1882; *Delo* (St. Petersburg), 1882; *Ekho gazet* (St. Petersburg), 1881; *Gazeta ezhedel'noe illiustrirovannoe pribavlenie k Krestnomu Kalandariu* (later *Gazeta A. Gattsuka*) (Moscow), 1875, 1882; *Golos* (St. Petersburg), 1882; *Irkutskie gubernskie vedomosti* (Irkutsk), 1882; *Istoricheskii vestnik* (St. Petersburg), 1881–1883; *Minuta* (St. Petersburg), 1881; *Moskovskie vedomosti* (Moscow), 1878, 1881; *Moskovskii telegraf* (Moscow), 1881; *Nedelia* (St. Petersburg), 1881; *Novoe vremia* (St. Petersburg), 1881–1882; *Novosti i birzhevaia gazeta* (St. Petersburg), 1881–1882; *Olonetskie gubernskie vedomosti* (Petrozavodsk), 1882; *Poriadok* (St. Petersburg), 1881; *Pravitel'stvennyi vestnik* (St. Petersburg), 1881–1882; *Russkaia mysl'* (Moscow), 1881, 1883, 1890; *Russkie vedomosti* (Moscow), 1881; *Samarskie gubernskie vedomosti* (Samara), 1882; *Sibir'* (Irkutsk), 1876–1882, 1886; *Sibirskaia gazeta* (Tomsk), 1881–1882; *Strana* (St. Petersburg), 1881–1882; *Tambovskie gubernskie vedomosti* (Tambov), 1882; *Tobol'skie gubernskie vedomosti* (Tobol'sk), 1882–1883; *Tomskie gubernskiia vedomosti* (Tomsk), 1882; *Vedomosti odesskogo gradonachal'stva* (Odessa), 1882; *Vestnik Evropy* (St. Petersburg), 1881; *Volga* (Saratov), 1881; *Vostochnoe obozrenie* (St. Petersburg and Irkutsk), 1882, 1884–1885.

1. A *krai* was a prerevolutionary administrative unit that consisted of several provinces. At the time of the anniversary, Siberia consisted of three areas ruled by governors-general, and the press commonly used the term *krai* to refer to the region as a whole.

2. *Ekho gazet*, 27 October 1881, 1; *Moskovskii telegraf*, 27 October 1881, 1; *Nedelia*, 8 November 1881, 1492–94; *Novoe vremia*, 26 October 1881, 1; *Poriadok*,

27 October 1881, 2; *Sibirskaia gazeta*, 22 November 1881, 1086; 29 November 1881, 1113–14; *Volga*, 28 October 1881, 102.

3. *Nedelia*, 8 November 1881, 1492–96; *Sibirskaia gazeta*, 29 November 1881, 1113–16.

4. *Akmolinskie oblastnie vedomosti*, 14 December 1882, 3–4 (quotation is on p. 3), and 21 December 1882, 4–7; *Istoricheskii vestnik* 11, no. 2 (February 1883): 473; *Sibir'*, 5 December 1882, 1–3, and 12 December 1882, 1; *Olonetskie gubernskie vedomosti*, 15 December 1882, 1025; *Samarskie gubernskie vedomosti*, 11 December 1882, 5; *Sibirskaia gazeta*, 12 December 1882, 1283–84; *Tomskie gubernskiia vedomosti*, 9 December 1882, 1010–14; *Tobol'skie gubernskie vedomosti*, 25 December 1882, 1–3, and 1 January 1883, 1–3.

5. *Novosti i birzhevaia gazeta*, 2 November 1881, 2.

6. *Sibirskaia gazeta*, 12 December 1882, 1283–84.

7. *Vostochnoe obozrenie*, 9 December 1882, 1–2.

8. *Gazeta ezhedel'noe illiustrirovannoe pribavlenie k Krestnomu Kalandariu*, 8 February 1875, 81–82; *Sibir'*, 9 October 1877, 1.

9. *Sibir'*, 22 October 1878, 2; *Moskovskie vedomosti*, 13 December 1878, 5; *Samarskie gubernskie vedomosti*, 11 December 1882, 5.

10. *Sibir'*, 15 February 1881, 1.

11. *Sibir'*, 2 February 1880, 1.

12. *Istoricheskii vestnik* 9 (September 1881): 209–10.

13. *Sibir'*, 3 May 1881, 2; *Nedelia*, 14 June 1881, 818; *Sibir'*, 16 August 1881, 4–5; *Istoricheskii vestnik* 9 (September 1881): 208–10.

14. *Moskovskie vedomosti*, 22 May 1881, 3; *Nedelia*, 14 June 1881, 816–18 (quotation is on p. 816); *Novosti i birzhevaia gazeta*, 6 December 1882, 1.

15. *Sibirskaia gazeta*, 8 March 1881, 60–64, and 7 June 1881, 462–63; *Sibir'*, 3 May 1881, 4–5; *Moskovskie vedomosti*, 12 October 1881, 3; *Pravitel'stvennyi vestnik*, 22 October 1881, 2, and 5 December 1882, 2.

16. *Moskovskii telegraf*, 25 October 1881, 3.

17. *Novoe vremia*, 26 October 1881, 1.

18. *Novosti i birzhevaia gazeta*, 6 December 1882, 1; *Golos*, 6 December 1882, 1; *Vostochnoe obozrenie*, 9 December 1882, 1–2; *Bessarabskie gubernskie vedomosti*, 22 December 1882, 509. See also *Vostochnoe obozrenie*, 8 April 1882, 6–8.

19. *Samarskie gubernskie vedomosti*, 11 December 1882, 5.

20. *Gazeta A.Gattsuka*, 11 December 1882, 876.

21. *Strana*, 7 December 1882, 1.

22. *Vestnik Evropy* (December 1882): 834–49.

23. *Pravitel'stvennyi vestnik*, 5 December 1882, 3; *Bessarabskie gubernskie vedomosti*, 29 December 1882, 516.

24. *Pravitel'stvennyi vestnik*, 8 December 1882, 1; *Akmolinskie oblastnie vedomosti*, 14 December 1882, 4. See also *Golos*, 9 December 1882, 2; *Novosti i birzhevaia gazeta*, 9 December 1882, 1.

25. *Novosti i birzhevaia gazeta*, 10 December 1882, 2; *Sibir'*, 12 December 1882, 1; *Istoricheskii vestnik* 2 (February 1883): 473.

26. *Vostochnoe obozrenie*, 14 February 1885, 10; *Sibir'*, 2 November 1886, 2–3.
27. *Vostochnoe obozrenie*, 4 November 1882, 1; 14 June 1884, 1; and 10 October 1885, 1.

SUGGESTED READINGS

Bassin, Mark. "Inventing Siberia: Visions of the Russian East in the Early Nineteenth Century." *American Historical Review* 96 (June 1991): 763–94.

Dallin, David. *The Rise of Russia in Asia*. New Haven, CT: Yale University Press, 1949.

Diment, Galya, and Yuri Slezkine. *Between Heaven and Hell: The Myth of Siberia in Russian Culture*. New York: St. Martin's Press, 1993.

Dmytryshyn, Basil, E. A. P. Crownhart-Vaughn, and Thomas Vaughn, eds. and trans. *To Siberia and Russian America: Three Centuries of Russian Eastward Expansion, A Documentary Record*. Vol. 1: *Russia's Conquest of Siberia, 1558–1700*. Portland: Oregon Historical Society, 1985.

Forsyth, James. *A History of the Peoples of Siberia: Russia's North Asian Colony, 1550–1990*. Cambridge: Cambridge University Press, 1992.

Kotkin, Stephen, and David Wolff, eds. *Rediscovering Russia in Asia: Siberia and the Far East*. Armonk, NY: M. E. Sharpe, 1995.

Marks, Steven G. *Road to Power: The Trans-Siberian Railroad and the Colonization of Asian Russia, 1850–1917*. Ithaca, NY: Cornell University Press, 1991.

Treadgold, Donald. *The Great Siberian Migration*. Princeton, NJ: Princeton University Press, 1957.

Wood, Alan, and R. A. French. *The Development of Siberia: Peoples and Resources*. New York: St. Martin's Press, 1989.

Chapter Eight

Life in the Big City

Migrants Cope with "Daily Events"

Laura L. Phillips

Migration from the countryside to Russia's two major capitals, Moscow and St. Petersburg, had already begun under serfdom, but with the 1861 emancipation and industrialization, greater employment opportunities in the cities opened up first for men and then, by the end of the nineteenth century, for women. As the Russian Empire embarked upon industrialization in order to recover from the debacle of the Crimean War (1853–1856), the tsarist government was intent upon insuring that the country would avoid the pitfalls of Western industrialization, which had brought about worker unrest and revolution in European countries in the 1830s and 1848. Consequently, Russia's emancipation decree purposely limited migration to the cities by enforcing communal land tenure and requiring communes and their various households to purchase the lands that they received from former serf owners. According to the decree, a peasant family could not abandon its communal lands unless the head of household made provisions for paying taxes and redemption payments on that land. Anyone wishing to work outside the village had to have the permission of the household head for the government-mandated internal passport. Given these restrictions and the lack of affordable housing in a major city, a migrant laborer usually left his wife and children behind in his father's household to farm the communal land allotments. The family expected him to remit his wages, minus any expenses incurred while he was away on the job, to the household coffers. Male migrant laborers returned periodically to their villages and more often than not, retired there.

Peasant women were less likely to leave the village, but by the end of the nineteenth century as it became more difficult to earn income in the village, widows and unmarried older women, who were burdens on their families, sought their fortunes in the big cities. Those married women who wished to join their husbands had to obtain their spouses' permission to leave the countryside. If women attained that permission and the necessary passport, they normally left their children behind in the care of relatives, thus insuring the women would return home. Circumstances eased somewhat with the introduction of the Stolypin Reforms in 1907, which in transferring land ownership from the commune to households, allowed migrant laborers to abandon their village ties and beckon their wives and children to move to the city permanently.

In spite of the state's attempt to tie peasants to the land, the populations of St. Petersburg and Moscow more than doubled between 1860 and the outbreak of World War I, with St. Petersburg taking the lead. Most migrant laborers found jobs not in factories but rather in service industries, trade, artisanal pursuits, and construction. With the exception of domestic service, where employers provided room and board, migrants crowded together in small apartments, or in factory barracks, where privacy was nonexistent.

St. Petersburg offered special challenges to its inhabitants. It was not unusual for workers to live in moldy bug-infested cellars that were periodically inundated with a couple of feet of water. Although working-class neighborhoods existed within the city, some of the dank cellars were located in tonier apartment buildings where the wealthy occupied the upper floors. As a result, the differences between the living standards of the well-off and the poor were prominently on display. Lack of sanitation systems and contamination of the Neva River ensured that diseases such as typhoid fever and typhus were endemic to St. Petersburg. The fact that the city's booming steel mills, metalworking plants, and other factories constituted huge industrial complexes with over five hundred workers each contributed to workers' disaffection. This gigantism not only reduced workers to mere cogs in the machinery but also created the conditions for massive strikes.

Newly arrived migrants to the city had to learn how to navigate the streets, find shelter and work, and avoid the pickpockets and swindlers who could easily pick out "country bumpkins" because of their clothing and hairstyles. Like immigrants to New York and other major cities in the United States, peasants generally headed to the addresses of former neighbors and relatives who helped them settle in. Yet learning new ways proved to be a challenge. What sorts of difficulties did migrants to St. Petersburg confront? Why were they so dependent on the news they could glean from a penny newspaper such as Gazeta kopeika *(Kopeck Newspaper)? Why did strikes envelope large cities such as St. Petersburg?*

When sixteen-year-old Semen Ivanovich Kanatchikov moved to Moscow in 1895, the metropolis immediately made a "stunning impression" on him. In his autobiography, he later recalled how the brightly lit streets, abundant stores, multistoried houses, and "crowds of bustling people, rushing to un-known destinations for unknown reasons," made his new surroundings strik-ingly different from those of his native village. In Gusevo he had always lived among meadows, a sparkling brook, clean air, and familiar people. Now he felt like an "insignificant grain of sand" in a "hostile world." Along with the multitude of other peasants then migrating to Russia's urban areas, Kanatchikov had a lot to learn about his new home. Fortunately, resources were available to help ease migrants' transition to urban life. Historians are well aware, for example, of the practice of *zemliachestvo*, an informal net-work in which fellow villagers provided mutual aid to one another. *Zemli-achestvo* meant that, at least initially, peasant migrants often worked, ate, and lived with others who had also come from their home village. In Kanatchikov's case, a fellow villager had arranged a job for him before he ever arrived in the city.[1]

Migrants also learned about urban life from another source, though one less discussed in historical literature: the popular press. The same years that saw mass peasant migration to Russia's cities also witnessed the rise of the mass circulation newspaper. In St. Petersburg, Russia's capital, the popular daily *Gazeta kopeika* appealed specifically to lower-class urbanites. Though the newspaper's content was highly varied, the Daily Events column was report-edly its most popular section. Here *Gazeta kopeika* briefly chronicled note-worthy events in the life of the city: yesterday's suicides, accidents, thefts, as-saults, fires, and the merely unusual. In all likelihood, St. Petersburg's lower classes found Daily Events attractive for a few very practical reasons. First of all, although peasants who migrated were more likely to have developed ba-sic literacy than those who remained behind in Russia's villages, even many migrants lacked the ability to decipher complicated texts. For this semiliter-ate and newly literate population, then, the column's simple, formulaic lan-guage, which was easy to learn and understand, was an important considera-tion indeed. Second, entries in the column were so brief that readers might easily take in a section or two during spare moments they had in the course of their day—while waiting in line, traveling on the tram, eating lunch, and the like. Moreover, some readers may have occasionally discovered a specific connection with information presented in one of the column's entries. A bul-letin published on 15 January 1909, for example, relayed the following news: "At 1 a.m. on 14 January, an unmarried peasant girl, Marfa Dmitrieva, age 18, poisoned herself with morphine at the Paris Café." It is possible that a few readers found this information relevant because they were acquainted with Dmitrieva or (more likely) with the Paris Café. A reader or two might even have personally witnessed the event. But neither the entry's accessibility nor the occasional reader's direct knowledge of the people or circumstances

discussed is sufficient to explain the special attention that lower-class urbanites devoted to this section of the press. It is only when the account of
Dmitrieva's suicide is linked with many other, similar bulletins that a more
compelling explanation for turning to Daily Events emerges. Systematic examination of thousands of entries shows that the news contained in Daily
Events was useful to readers: it told them a good deal about how better to
cope with life in the city, or even how to opt out of it, as Dmitrieva sadly did.

But let us begin with the more obviously unwilling casualties of city life.
Among them, accident victims held the most prominent place.[2] In 1909,
nearly 20 percent of the entries in the Daily Events column concerned an accident of some kind; by 1915 that figure had mushroomed to 30 percent.
Daily Events readers learned of sudden explosions, unintentional shootings,
and unfortunate drownings in St. Petersburg's many canals. They read about
industrial workers who fell from great heights, suffered scalding from hot liq-
uids, or sustained bodily injury from falling debris. They encountered instances of poisoning from food and other sources, including the strange case
in which the servant Aleksandra Bashmakova mistakenly consumed roach
poison from a jar labeled "For Headaches."[3] Most of all, they learned that
stepping into the street was a dangerous proposition; St. Petersburg's newer
residents could easily fall victim to the disorienting forms of modern transportation that enlivened its busy streets. Even if an occasional automobile or
train had breezed through Kanatchikov's native village, the commotion that it
produced there would have been a startling interruption amid the quiet sounds
of meadow and brook; any villagers within the vicinity would naturally be
alerted to the vehicle while it was still far away. In a bustling, noisy metropolis like St. Petersburg, things were more complicated. In addition to the
crowds of people that Kanatchikov observed, private cars, taxis, buses, horse-
drawn carts and carriages, horse-drawn and electrical trams, and trains all
converged in urban centers. Evgenii Bauer's 1912 film *The Peasants' Lot*
vividly depicts the confusion that could beset individuals unaccustomed to
such a whirlwind of activity: as a peasant visiting the city desperately
searches for an address, trams pass within mere inches of her.

The peasant in Bauer's film safely reaches her destination, but Daily
Events shows that many lower-class pedestrians collided with automobiles,
trains, drays, and especially trams. Thanks to the rapid development of St. Petersburg's transportation system, the need to avoid collisions with trams was
somewhat of a novelty in the city itself, to say nothing of the disparity between modes of transportation in Russia's villages and in urban areas. As of
1870, trams in St. Petersburg had been limited to less than ten kilometers of
track, and these were horse-drawn trams. The city's very first electrical trams
went into service only in 1907. A mere three years later, in 1910, urban resi-

dents needed to be attuned to the presence of 525 electrical trams, 381 older horse-drawn trams, and 114 kilometers of track.[4] To cite but one of many mishaps, Daily Events reported on 7 August 1912 that Ivan Tomliakov, a forty-five-year-old worker, died as the result of an accident with a tram near Novodevich'ii monastery.

The column described most accident victims as "peasants," "workers," or members of particular laboring professions; middle- and upper-class individuals rarely appeared in this capacity. Similarly, Daily Events was most likely to report accidents that occurred in working-class districts of the city, as opposed to the city's administrative or more wealthy areas. While personal information about victims and their injuries is typical of accident reports, information about who was on the other side of the tram, automobile, or poison seldom is. Very rarely do accident reports appearing in Daily Events contain any suggestion that a driver, employer, or some other party might have been at fault for, or even a participant in, an accident. A common laborer in one of the city's working-class districts, Tomliakov was a typical accident victim in a typical accident place, at least insofar as Daily Events was concerned. Also characteristic is the sense that Tomliakov was callously destroyed by a nameless, faceless force. Despite the brevity of the accident report, readers learned quite a lot about Tomliakov, including his name, social position, age, and the time and place of his death. Readers also learned that this unfortunate man was "crushed to death," ending his life "under a tram." The incident's other "participant," a lifeless metal machine, presumably chugged away without damage. Lower-class urbanites who read Daily Events learned that they had to watch their own steps or literally be crushed by agents of modernity.

Accidents were not alone in making the street a dangerous place. As Daily Events makes clear, thieves, swindlers, and all kinds of ne'er-do-wells patrolled urban avenues for overly trusting, unwitting, or distracted targets. Consider, for example, the deceptive woman who encouraged two young girls on Panteleimonovskaia Street to view "the whole world" from a nearby church's bell tower. Though she kindly promised to watch the girls' valuable winter coats, the con artist was nowhere to be found when the youngsters returned from their adventure. In another, more typical case, a peasant named Smirnov was approached at Apraksin Market by two men who charged him with finding their lost wallet, which they said contained 750 rubles. To prove his innocence, Smirnov produced his own billfold, showing the strangers all the money he did have. Only later did Smirnov learn that, during their staged examination of Smirnov's wallet, the thieves had imperceptibly replaced his money with worthless pieces of paper.[5] He, not they, had been unlucky that day.

Since migrants to the cities were familiar with deception and theft in the life of Russia's villages, it might seem that they should have seen through such schemes. Urban thievery, however, had distinctive features. In the village, people were well acquainted with the character and property of almost everyone they encountered, and they could continue to live among the same people for years to come. In Russian villages, then, familiarity and social norms worked to discourage people from violating commonly accepted property rights. In contrast, in cities like St. Petersburg, residents continually experienced fleeting encounters with total strangers. A trusting soul could easily be hoodwinked by a seemingly honest individual and never see the thief again. The anonymity and deception characteristic of urban settings worked to the distinct disadvantage of inexperienced in-migrants. A thief's most common target was someone who did not recognize him. Furthermore, relatively few thieves were so bold as to arm themselves with revolvers or knives, nor did they really need to. Their most common weapons were lying, distraction, and the inattention of others. Migrants encountered so many new things in the city that it was difficult for them to distinguish probable from improbable encounters. For those new to urban life, it seemed entirely plausible that decent folks would lose wallets at the market or that strangers would kindly offer to guard bulky coats. Daily Events demonstrated to its readers that the wise urbanite needed to be ever vigilant for cons.

Of course, one could con as well as be conned, and Daily Events had something important to say about that as well. In brief: swindle they might—but swindlers *could* be arrested. Once they had adjusted to their urban lives, financially strapped newcomers to St. Petersburg might be tempted to become tricksters themselves, taking advantage of more recent arrivals, for example. Such was the case in October 1909, when a middle-aged man cheated one Shchetoleva, who had just arrived in the city, out of nine rubles, her passport, and her belongings. This incident was unusual, however, in that the perpetrator escaped punishment. Of all the situations regularly chronicled in Daily Events, reports on theft were most likely to include information about the perpetrator's arrest. Whether a thief had been arrested or remained at large was even more likely to be mentioned than the status of assailants and murderers. Thus, the column reported that the peasant A. Iakovlev was detained for stealing twenty-seven kopecks from a public church offering. More ominously for the city's affluent residents, struggling urbanites could be tempted by the ostentatious wealth of their employers. P. Spiridonova, for example, stole a sable boa and other goods valued at 2,500 rubles from the household that had retained her as a maid; Fedor Lednev similarly absconded with 900 rubles when his employer, a meat vendor, sent him to collect accounts. Daily Events points out, however, that both Spiridonova and Lednev suffered arrest.[6] The lesson for Daily Events readers was clear: thievery might be tempting, but it could also land one in jail.

Although theft and accident victims often suffered at the hands of seemingly anonymous entities, the bulletins in Daily Events did explore one type of urban victimization that frequently *was* personal. Between 10 and 18 percent of all incidents reported annually in the column were assaults and murders; in 22–38 percent of these cases, the injured party was attacked by someone specifically identified as an acquaintance, spouse, or family member. There was much that migrants could learn about urban life from the reports of physical assault. One important aspect was weaponry. Assailants overtaken by strong emotion made frequent use of whatever weapon they found nearby. On 8 February 1909 Daily Events reported that a certain Davikov, who would have used knives regularly in his work as a cobbler, stabbed a coworker six times during an argument. Readily available almost everywhere in early twentieth-century Russia, knives were cited in reports of assault and murder more than all other weapons combined. Angry individuals might also find a wide variety of other items—iron bars, wrenches, stones, bricks, rolling pins, acid, hot water, beer bottles, billiard balls—close at hand. Angry people did not need to look far to arm themselves.

Motive was another important dimension of the reports on assault and murder. Within this intimate world of aggression, assailants were typically angered by "an argument." Though there was nothing particularly "urban" about an argument and the column often failed to offer details, when it *did* elaborate Daily Events emphasized certain aspects of assaults. The center of dispute often was money. When the aforementioned cobbler Davikov stabbed his coworker, for example, he had been upset about his wages. Similarly, a disagreement over money prompted G. Lastochin to deliver deadly stab wounds to a coworker's breast and back.[7] In this connection, it is worth remembering that, for many of *Gazeta kopeika*'s lower-class readers, improving their family's standard of living had been the whole point of migrating to the city in the first place; moreover, migrants encountered the increased significance that money held in the city each and every day. Since the village economy was based more on subsistence agriculture and barter, people there could usually get by without much cash. It turned out that, in St. Petersburg, one needed it for everything, including food and shelter. If disputes about money were, in addition, an impetus for assault and murder, migrants learned that urban life harbored innumerable ways in which money, or the lack of it, could threaten their physical well-being.

So, too, could jealousy or other romantic difficulties. Many cases of assault illustrated how the city affected the intimate relationships of migrants. The jealous men and women featured in Daily Events attacked lovers and rivals; the vast majority were not married to the person they had assaulted. Thus, in one case from 1909, the jilted A. Liavdanskaia seriously burned Venedikt

Petrik's chest, face, and neck with sulphuric acid. In another, the cobbler K. Trokhachev stabbed O. Varfolomeeva, an acquaintance who would not pay attention to him when he pursued her.[8] Many male migrants had left their wives in the village, while St. Petersburg's smaller population of female migrants was predominantly unmarried. Even when both marriage partners lived in the city, they sometimes had to live apart in same-sex quarters provided by employers, because they could not afford common housing. These difficulties were compounded by the vastly increased number of potential partners and the relative anonymity available to urban residents. City life offered an abundance of new romantic choices, but readers of Daily Events were reminded that some opportunities could result in vicious jealousies.

A third group of assaults—those grounded in sexual predation—alerted migrants to another urban peculiarity: the special vulnerability of women in the city. Although the patriarchy of Russia's villages had oppressive aspects for women, it also sheltered them from aggression by men outside the household. In St. Petersburg, women were less likely to be shielded by a man who could intervene on their behalf. Typical was an incident reported on 6 November 1909, in which the cabby Makarov attempted to rape his unaccompanied passenger, Anna Frolova, near Semenovskii Square. And likewise a report from 18 January 1912 informed Daily Events readers that a group of "hooligans" had stabbed a young woman who had refused their "foul suggestions." If the rape victim had lived in a turn-of-the-century Russian village, it is unlikely that she would have required the services of an unfamiliar cabby at all; in the other young woman's case, the male head of her household would have been socially responsible for sheltering her and insuring that justice was properly meted out to such unruly hooligans. Daily Events demonstrated that peasant culture's tradition of male guardianship over women rang hollow in an urban setting. Female migrants to the city could not rely on male sanctuary. Such news may have reassured male migrants about the wisdom of leaving wives and daughters behind in the village. Migrant women, on the other hand, learned that they had to be especially careful and resourceful in looking out for their own welfare.

One hazard with which peasant migrants were more familiar was addressed by reportage on fire, consistently about 10 percent of all incidents appearing in Daily Events. Urban fires usually originated with a stove, faulty flue, or kerosene lamp, combined with inattentiveness or carelessness. But since none of these materials or behaviors was unknown in Russia's villages, descriptions of fire did not stress cause and prevention as much as the amount of damage that resulted from urban conflagrations. New urbanites needed to be reminded that fires could cause major destruction and injury, the more so in a congested, densely populated area. In 1912, specific estimates of monetary damages ranging from one thousand to one hundred thousand rubles were indicated for about half of all fires mentioned in Daily Events. Even the lower figure was an incredible sum for most of *Gazeta kopeika*'s readers: one thousand rubles would have been the equivalent of nearly three years' pay for an average worker in St. Petersburg. That fires produced damages into the tens of thousands must have seemed astonishing indeed, if not entirely inconceivable, to most migrants. Threats that urban fires posed to human life could also be immense. On 7 March 1912, for example, Daily Events reported that twenty-five panicked residents of one apartment building were wounded as they jumped from the structure's second floor to escape flames. An overturned lamp might well wreak havoc in a village, but a fire in the city put more people and more property immediately in harm's way. In urban St. Petersburg, migrants learned, everyone was more vulnerable to any misstep with fire.

Though most bulletins appearing in Daily Events fell into one of the categories already described, about 10 percent of the reports prior to World War I defied these classifications; that percentage increased to 22 percent after the onset of war. These miscellaneous snippets included reports of missing persons, abandoned children, counterfeiting, and illegal distilling. Readers learned, for example, about a zookeeper who lost his index finger to a lion, about rabid dogs and wolves that ran about the city frightening people, about instances of public nudity. They learned that some people wildly gesticulated in the street for no apparent reason, while others perpetrated "jokes" that the press and polite society deemed unamusing. These stories obviously appealed to prurient human curiosity. Even these incidents, though, told peasant migrants something they probably wanted to know. Migrants adjusting to the peculiarities of urban life could easily feel penniless, hungry, confused, adrift, or alone. They might well feel that attempting to live in the city was all too arduous. But perhaps many individuals who read Daily Events could also take some comfort in knowing that they were doing better than other, more unfortunate victims of modern urban life. Even if they were sometimes hungry or befuddled, most migrants had not embarrassed themselves with displays of insanity in the street, contracted rabies, or disappeared without a trace. They had not followed the example of Ivan Potapov, who attempted to earn a state-sponsored trip back to the village by throwing cobblestones through the window of a grocery.[9] They had not abandoned their children, surfaced as a lifeless body in a snowbank, or prankishly called on funeral bureaus to pick up nonexistent corpses. Nor had they, like Marfa Dmitrieva, abandoned life itself through an overdose of morphine.

We return now to that young woman's fateful decision, for many, many other individuals similarly chose to leave the city through suicide. Indeed, prior to the onset of World War I, when involuntary death was to become an all too pervasive feature of Russian political culture, *Gazeta kopeika* was brimming with comparable reports: over 25 percent of Daily Events' contents concerned successful or attempted suicide, making it the segment's dominant news. In 1909, the column reported an average of twenty-six suicides each month; by 1912 the average monthly rate had jumped to thirty-seven. For individuals who chose to end their lives, selecting their manner of death was an unavoidable imperative. When examined along with hundreds of other suicide reports, Dmitrieva's solution emerges as a typical exit strategy, especially for female suicides. While men were much more likely than women to end their life at the point of a dagger, barrel of a gun, or end of a rope, both male and female suicides were most likely to opt for some form of poison. Where Dmitrieva *was* unusual was in her choice of toxin. Drugs like morphine, cocaine, and opium, which were expensive and difficult to obtain, were rarely mentioned in Daily Events reports. The poison of choice was instead an ordinary household item—essence of vinegar. The acidic burning of the digestive tract produced by this concentrated form of vinegar could not have made for a pleasant death.

The advantage of vinegar essence was that it was an inexpensive, readily available alternative. The choice of lethal agent thus helps to illuminate an important motivation for suicide, which was often left unclear in *Gazeta kopeika*. Despite what must have been many readers' natural curiosity, Daily Events offered an explanation for suicide in only one of every two cases, and even then it might merely stipulate that an individual's reasons were "unknown." The death of Dmitrieva was simply one of many instances shrouded in such mystery. Her motivation, perhaps, simply could not be determined. When a fuller explanation for a suicide was forthcoming, it could encompass anything from mental illness, to romantic disappointment, to family difficulties. But of all the suicidal motivations mentioned by Daily Events, those that figured most prominently were all linked to poverty: "need," unemployment, hunger, and "a lack of means to live." Another group of individuals—those said to be "dissatisfied with life" or "sick of life"—is also likely to have included suicides who suffered from financial difficulties, though it is impossible to say for certain how many. Dmitrieva's own ability to make ends meet in an urban setting remains unclear. But if she was able to bypass the common method of acidic poisoning by vinegar essence and to obtain a relatively comfortable sedative like morphine, she was among the "luckier" suicides.

Suicide reports in Daily Events thus carried several lessons for *Gazeta kopeika*'s readers. Financial incentives were a key factor in peasant migration to the city: some had hoped for a better life there; others hoped to return to their villages with increased wealth and status. But Daily Events showed that there was no guarantee of economic success. Even if *zemliachestvo* buffered the vulnerability of many migrants, many lower-class urbanites found themselves financially awash with few resources to draw upon. Some individuals who took their lives had reportedly made unsuccessful attempts to borrow money from blood relatives before ending their lives; a few people dramatically ended their lives together with romantic or spiritual partners. But the dominant picture that emerges from Daily Events is one of destitute urbanites dying alone, albeit often in view of others. Perhaps unintentionally, in its failure to offer any other, useful suggestion to financially troubled readers, Daily Events presented suicide as a logical way to avoid a life of poverty. People were apparently able to make disturbing use of that information, despite the spareness of suicide reports. Indeed, during *Gazeta kopeika*'s early years, the Daily Events column seems to have unwittingly taught its readers about the means available to end life. In 1909, vinegar essence was specifically named in 39 percent of the suicidal poisonings described. But by 1915, interestingly, the column failed to mention vinegar essence even once. The same trend applies to other poisons as well. Whereas the column reported deaths by carbolic acid, hydrochloric acid, arsenic, cyanide, creosote, ammonia, and more in 1909, none of these toxins was specifically mentioned by 1915. By then, readers learned only that suicides had died from "a poison." When it came to suicide, the succinctly written column nonetheless appears to have told readers more than its editors ultimately thought they should know.

As a commercial paper dependent on its customers for success, St. Petersburg's *Gazeta kopeika* was obliged to publish material that was of interest to a lower-class readership. While it would be easy for historians to attribute the popularity of Daily Events to nothing more than idle human curiosity, the column's bulletins followed a certain logic, especially for urban Russia's large population of peasant in-migrants. The patterns that emerge from the thousands of bulletins published in Daily Events show that even if *zemliachestvo* eased many migrants' transition to urban life, the practice failed to shield a great many others from poverty and other hazards of turn-of-the-century cities. Directing its attention to facets of urbanity highly relevant to the new life in-migrants had chosen, it ensured that fellow villagers were not the sole source of knowledge available to St. Petersburg's new residents. The practical value of this knowledge varied, to be sure. New arrivals to the city could use Daily Events to learn how to escape the lonely victimization of urban life by committing suicide. But they could also learn to remain ever vigilant for the occasional rabid dog, keep flammables under control, be wary of monetary and romantic disputes, question the integrity of innocent-looking swindlers, and always look both ways before stepping into the street. If they managed to do all that, scores of misfortunes chronicled in

Daily Events reassured them that, whatever other problems they might have, they were not doing so bad.

NOTES

I want to thank Ann LeBar, Loyal Cowles, and Alison Smith for their helpful comments. Grants from the Northwest Institute for Advanced Study supported the research and writing of this article.

1. Reginald E. Zelnik, trans. and ed., *A Radical Worker in Tsarist Russia: The Autobiography of Semen Ivanovich Kanatchikov* (Stanford, CA: Stanford University Press, 1986), 6–8.
2. The characterizations of Daily Events (Proisshestviia) presented in this chapter are drawn from a database compiled from the 1909, 1912, and 1915 editions of *Gazeta kopeika*.
3. *Gazeta kopeika*, 23 September 1912.
4. James H. Bater, *St. Petersburg: Industrialization and Change* (Montreal: McGill-Queen's University Press, 1976): 270–73.
5. *Gazeta kopeika*, 19 October and 5 March 1909, respectively.
6. *Gazeta kopeika*, 22 October, 12 December, 15 January, and 17 July 1909.
7. *Gazeta kopeika*, 18 January 1909.
8. *Gazeta kopeika*, 29 August and 29 September 1909.
9. *Gazeta kopeika*, 2 November 1909.

SUGGESTED READINGS

Bater, James H. *St. Petersburg: Industrialization and Change*. Montreal: McGill-Queen's University Press, 1976.

Bradley, Joseph. *Muzhik and Muscovite: Urbanization in Late Imperial Russia*. Berkeley: University of California Press, 1985.

Brooks, Jeffrey. *When Russia Learned to Read: Literacy and Popular Literature, 1861–1917*. Princeton, NJ: Princeton University Press, 1985.

Burds, Jeffrey. *Peasant Dreams & Market Politics: Labor Migration and the Russian Village, 1861–1905*. Pittsburgh: University of Pittsburgh Press, 1998.

Engel, Barbara Alpern. *Between the Fields and the City: Women, Work, and Family in Russia, 1861–1914*. Cambridge: Cambridge University Press, 1996.

Frank, Stephen P., and Mark D. Steinberg, eds. *Cultures in Flux: Lower-Class Values, Practices, and Resistance in Late Imperial Russia*. Princeton, NJ: Princeton University Press, 1994.

Johnson, Robert Eugene. *Peasant and Proletarian: The Working Class of Moscow in the Late Nineteenth Century*. New Brunswick, NJ: Rutgers University Press, 1979.

McReynolds, Louise. *The News under Russia's Old Regime: The Development of a Mass-Circulation Press*. Princeton, NJ: Princeton University Press, 1991.

Paperno, Irina. *Suicide as a Cultural Institution in Dostoevsky's Russia*. Ithaca, NY: Cornell University Press, 1997.

Ransel, David L., trans. and ed. *Village Life in Late Tsarist Russia: An Ethnography by Olga Semyonova Tian-Shanskaia*. Bloomington: Indiana University Press, 1993.

Worobec, Christine D. *Peasant Russia: Family and Community in the Post-Emancipation Period*. Princeton, NJ: Princeton University Press, 1991.

Zelnik, Reginald E., trans. and ed. *A Radical Worker in Tsarist Russia: The Autobiography of Semen Ivanovich Kanatchikov*. Stanford, CA: Stanford University Press, 1986.

Chapter Nine

Freedom and Its Limitations

A Peasant Wife Seeks to Escape Her Abusive Husband

Barbara Alpern Engel

Until the February Revolution of 1917 marriage in Imperial Russia remained under the jurisdiction of religious authorities. For Orthodox believers, the ec-clesiastical courts of the Russian Orthodox Church adjudicated divorce peti-tions. Like its Catholic counterpart in Western Europe, the Russian Orthodox Church viewed marriage to be a sacrament and therefore a religious union that could be sundered only in exceptional circumstances. Theoretically, these circumstances included adultery, bigamy, disappearance of a spouse for over five years, exile to Siberia on a charge of felony, sexual incapacity that pre-dated the marriage, premarital insanity, and some lesser grounds. In practice, however, the nineteenth-century Orthodox Church granted divorce only in cases of bigamy and Siberian exile of a spouse. Unlike the Western Catholic Church, it did not facilitate annulment and separation. Petitions from the lower classes, including peasants, became increasingly entangled in a web of ecclesiastical red tape. Contested divorces languished for years without res-olution. Nonetheless divorce petitions to ecclesiastical authorities grew dra-matically in the last decades of the imperial regime, especially as increasing migratory labor to towns and cities separated families and placed a strain on peasant marriages. The church's inability to deal adequately with the demand for divorce helped undermine that institution's authority.

Outside of deserting a spouse and cohabiting with a partner outside of marriage, subjects of the tsar did have recourse to another body for the ad-judication of marital separations, and that was the tsar's own Chancellery for Receipt of Petitions. In the autocratic system (as had been true of European absolutist systems), it was not unusual for the ruler to sidestep already exist-ing, but inefficient, bureaucratic structures that provided necessary employ-ment for noblemen by opening new, more-efficient offices. A creation of the

1880s, the chancellery acted as a supralegal secretive and benevolent institution. It represented the monarch's personal justice as it sought to mitigate some of the harsher aspects of civil and ecclesiastical law, including the legal provision prohibiting marital separation.

Thousands of discontented women, like Evdokiia Ivanovna Kulikova, the subject of Barbara Alpern Engel's chapter, took advantage of the chancellery's existence by petitioning the tsar for legal separation from their spouses and a residency permit to live apart from them. Between 1890 and 1902 approximately 20 percent of these petitioners were successful in achieving their freedom, although some of them, like Kulikova, had to pay a heavy price for that freedom.

As you read Kulikova's story, consider the following questions: What was the nature of patriarchal authority in the peasant household? Why might villagers have sided with the husband and middle-class lawyers with Kulikova? Why was there such a dizzying array of narratives about Kulikova and her spouse's individual characters and relationship? Can we ever know the truth about Kulikova's relationship with her husband? Why was Kulikova's infidelity to her husband an issue of concern when he had clearly abandoned her, and she was earning an independent income? How was Kulikova transformed and empowered by her urban experience? Were the chancellery officials acting in a paternalistic and arbitrary fashion? Finally, how did the chancellery's existence contribute to a growing disdain for the autocracy's authority?

> I come from a peasant family with a place in the village of Mozhaevo, Kisemskii district, Ves'egonsk township, Tver, where my family spends the summer; winters, they live in the town of Krasnoi Kholm. I had not yet reached the age of sixteen [the legal age of marriage] or become a woman when my parents . . . , having overcome my resistance, married me off to the nineteen-year-old peasant Dmitrii Kulikov . . . who had already become corrupted.[1]

Thus began the petition, five type-written pages in length, that Evdokiia Ivanovna Kulikova addressed to Tsar Nicholas II on 11 June 1897. Claiming to have endured virtually every abuse that a peasant household could inflict upon a woman, Kulikova requested the right to separate formally from her husband. Her marriage had been loveless from the first, she wrote. His parents had forced Dmitrii, too, into marriage, hoping he would abandon his "dissolute, debauched and drunken way of life." Instead, he persisted and spent all his time with another woman or drinking and carousing. All Evdokiia's efforts to be a good wife notwithstanding, Dmitrii "tyrannized" and mistreated her, regarding her merely as an obstacle in the path of his pleasure. He had even tried to murder her, she claimed, by abandoning her alone in the depths of a forest. Evdokiia came to hate him. Once she got so angry that—God forgive her—she had gone after Dmitrii with an axe and nearly murdered him. But life became even harder following his recruitment into the army. Dmitrii's absence left Evdokiia without protection in her widowed father-in-law's household. The father-in-law, already conducting an affair with another daughter-in-law, had begun to show sexual interest in Evdokiia as well. So, "fearful and indignant at such debauchery," she fled. Having worked for a while as a chambermaid, she currently earned her living as a seamstress in the city of St. Petersburg.

Her husband's reappearance in her life had prompted Kulikova to petition the tsar. Until Dmitrii's term of service ended the previous August, she had heard nothing from him. But now back home in the village, Dmitrii demanded that she join him and threatened to force her return under police escort if she refused. Desperate to avoid her former misery and fearful that this time she might really murder her husband, Kulikova requested the internal passport that would enable her to live apart from him.

Kulikova's request was by no means unusual. Between 1884 and 1914, tens of thousands of married women addressed petitions to the tsar seeking relief from Russia's patriarchal family laws. Governed by the church, which permitted divorce only under exceptional circumstances, Russian family law subjected a wife almost completely to her husband and strictly forbade the separation of spouses. Under the law, a wife required her husband's permission before she could take a job, enroll in school, or acquire the internal passport she needed to reside more than thirty miles from her husband's place of residence. Kulikova's petition was forwarded to the Imperial Chancellery for Receipt of Petitions, which served as a kind of final court of appeals for unhappy wives. Acting in the name of the tsar, the chancellery held the power to supercede the law forbidding spousal separation and to grant a woman a passport of her own.

Until the early twentieth century, the vast majority of women petitioners (about 80 percent) belonged to the peasant estate, as did the vast majority of Russia's population. The preponderance of peasant wives, however, was mainly a result of the tension between the economic and cultural changes that swept Russia in the final decades of the nineteenth century and the conservative institutions of peasant life. Encouraged by the government's policy of industrialization and the growing importance of cash in the countryside, tens of thousands of peasants left their homes to seek work elsewhere. Economic change brought new opportunities for social mobility, while a burgeoning consumer culture began to transform the tastes of Russia's rural as well as urban population. Nevertheless, peasant choices continued to be limited, especially if the peasant was a married woman. Until 1906, the law required a peasant who wished to live and work elsewhere to obtain permission from both village and household authorities, which if she were a married woman, meant her husband. If the husband severely mistreated and neglected his wife, village authorities could let her go without his approval, thanks to a Senate decision of 1888. However, peasant authorities exercised this option only in exceptional cases. Wife beating was commonplace, if not ubiquitous, in peasant villages. "The more you beat your wife, the tastier the cabbage soup," opined one peasant saying. A wife's desire to escape an abusive husband often elicited little sympathy from fellow villagers. Her desire to live elsewhere, especially in a city, aroused still less sympathy. Peasants placed the economic well-being of family and community above the well-being of the individual and tended to distrust the individualism and to fear the moral corruption that they associated with urban life. Unless a husband had ruined his household economy, peasant authorities were disinclined to separate a married couple by allowing his wife to leave the village.

More sympathetic to the plight of an abused wife, the chancellery officials who considered Kulikova's petition nevertheless had similar concerns. To convince the officials to grant her request for separation, a wife had to demonstrate not only that her husband had severely abused or neglected her for no reason, but also that she was a virtuous woman. By the time that Kulikova petitioned, the chancellery had developed a set of guidelines for decision making in such cases. Among the husbandly failings that alone or, preferably, in combination might earn a wife her freedom were coarse, cruel, disreputable, or insulting behavior; drunkenness; failure to support the family; insanity; sexual incapacity; and adultery. Adultery and sexual incapacity also figured among the grounds for divorce, but because the church applied far more stringent rules of evidence, a woman stood a far better chance of obtaining a separation. At the same time, chancellery officials shared the widespread concern about the sexual conduct of women no longer under the tutelage of husband or father. Thus, if they learned that a wife had conducted herself immodestly or licentiously during her marriage or after parting from her husband, her likelihood of obtaining a separation became significantly reduced.

Neither these guidelines nor even the fact that the chancellery entertained petitions from abused wives was ever publicized by the chancellery itself. Such secrecy served to conceal the fact that by granting separation to seriously abused wives, the chancellery actually violated imperial law forbidding marital separation; secrecy also protected officials from being inundated by separation petitions. To preserve this secrecy, officials based all their decisions exclusively on written evidence, thus leaving a rich record for the historian. Instead of confronting one another in court, both husband and wife testified to an investigating officer, who was supposed to record oral testimony word for word; witnesses were similarly questioned. Officials then considered this evidence behind closed doors, explicitly barring lawyers from participation in the process. If, having considered the results of the preliminary investigation, officials found themselves unable to resolve a case, they could request that the police investigate further "the habits and way of life" of both spouses. These subsequent investigations usually involved secret police surveillance of one or both parties.

Neither the substance of Kulikova's complaints nor the procedures that the chancellery followed differed significantly from those I have found in the eighty-five other cases involving peasant couples that I have read so far. One of the things that distinguishes the Kulikova case from the rest is that lawyers became involved—deeply and emotionally involved—at every stage of Kulikova's appeal, despite chancellery regulations mandating their exclusion. Her case was precisely the sort to elicit jurists' sympathy. From the mid-nineteenth century onward, liberal jurists had been actively engaged in efforts to reform the very marital laws that made Kulikova's life so difficult. Seeking to remove family law from the clerical domain, to ease the laws governing divorce, and to facilitate legal separation, progressive jurists pursued a more ambitious goal: to enhance the rights of the individual and to limit the exercise of arbitrary authority. And to underscore the necessity of marital reform, jurists published grisly accounts of the victimization of peasant women at the hands of ignorant and brutal husbands. Bearing titles such as "Women's Moans,"[2] these accounts described in painful detail the consequences for women of the lack of limits to men's domestic authority. The jurists who became involved in Kulikova's case shared the propensity to view peasant women as victims. By helping her to present her story, they also tried to ensure that chancellery officials would view her that way, too.

That others might tell Kulikova's story differently became evident almost as soon as the investigation began. The first to testify were the peasants of her husband's village of Aleksino, Tver. In their version of the story, Dmitrii became the innocent party and Evdokiia, the villain. Displaying the united front that peasants often presented to outsiders, the villagers spoke unanimously in favor of Dmitrii in response to the investigator's questions. Pavel Plyshakov, the village elder, testified that he knew nothing bad about Dmitrii; Dmitrii drank no more than other peasants did. Similarly, the village guard maintained that there was never any talk about Dmitrii mistreating his wife. According to him, Dmitrii lived a "sober lifestyle" and was just "an ordinary guy," who behaved no differently from other peasants, a testimony that other villagers repeated virtually word for word. Even Kulikova's best friend, Anna Volkova, on whom she had counted for support, testified that the couple had gotten along well while they lived in the village. Most peasant witnesses blamed Evdokiia instead of Dmitrii for the breakdown of the marriage. While he really was uncertain why the couple separated, the village guard supposed that her "light [i.e., immoral or unseemly] conduct" was responsible. The village elder claimed that Evdokiia had "abandoned" her husband when he was drafted into the army and then refused to return to the village.

To make matters worse, since moving to St. Petersburg, Kulikova had changed in ways that aroused villagers' suspicions. In provinces with high levels of peasant out-migration, such as Kulikova's native Tver, peasants, the young in particular, commonly donned urban-style clothing and footwear for special occasions, while visiting migrants liked to flaunt their new possessions. However, judging by villagers' response to Kulikova's self-presentation, there were limits to how fashionable a peasant might become before ceasing to be a peasant. To the village elder, Kulikova had on her last visit to the village appeared to be just like a wealthy woman, "a lady." Sporting a gold watch and "French clothing," she had become, in his opinion, "unfit" for village life. He doubted that she earned her living "by honest labor." Kulikova's transformation impressed the township elder, too. Looking like a "wealthy person," she had ceased entirely to be a peasant. A third articulated explicitly the sexual suspicions that provided the subtext of others' statements: Kulikova was assuredly "a kept woman." How else could she afford to live in comfort in St. Petersburg in her own apartment and dress in the "latest fashion"? Besides, he claimed, she had conceived a child while her husband served in the army.

Even Kulikova's parents contradicted portions of her initial narrative, refusing to endorse her account of victimization at their hands. The mother testified that her daughter had married at age seventeen or eighteen, not at fifteen as the girl claimed; moreover, Evdokiia herself desired the marriage. While acknowledging that he and his wife did "advise" their daughter to marry Dmitrii because his family "lived better" than theirs did, her father also denied applying any pressure. And while the parents otherwise substantiated Evdokiia's story of marital abuse and supported her request for separation, their version of her story also differed in other key respects. Thus, they agreed that she had begun to complain of Dmitrii's ill-treatment almost immediately after the wedding and claimed that they themselves had seen him strike her. However, they explained their daughter's departure from her in-laws' household in rather different terms than had Evdokiia herself: rather than abuse, sexual harassment, and moral revulsion, it was the fact that his family denied her support while her husband served in the army that forced Evdokiia to leave their household.

At this point, Kulikova, having learned that villagers had contradicted her story, began to fear for the outcome of her case. So in a second letter to the chancellery, typewritten like the first, she sought to discredit their account. Her father-in-law had forced his fellow villagers to testify in his family's favor by threatening to cripple or kill them and then destroy their property if they upheld her story, Kulikova's letter alleged. Moreover, her husband complained about her incessantly, and since he knew everyone, he had succeeded in turning people against her. In consequence, no one was prepared to speak in her favor. "Even my old father is afraid to step out on the street," Kulikova claimed, because her husband had threatened to murder him and village opinion was so set against him. Identifying twelve more witnesses who would verify her story, she asked that they be questioned.

Meanwhile, the investigation continued to yield alternative versions of Kulikova's story. Before moving to St. Petersburg, Kulikova had worked as a cook in the town of Krasnoi Kholm, Tver, where her parents spent the winter. Her former employer, Olga Suslova, had nothing but good things to say about Kulikova's character: honest, hardworking, and modestly behaved, Kulikova never left the apartment and received no visitors. Yet despite the fact that she clearly wished Kulikova only well, Suslova cast serious doubt on her former servant's account of being forced into a loveless marriage. She married for love, Kulikova had confided to Suslova, and she eagerly anticipated her husband's return from military service.

Still more damaging to Kulikova's case was the testimony of the next set of witnesses, the two yardmen (*dvorniki*) who served in the building in St. Petersburg where Kulikova worked as a chambermaid after leaving Krasnoi Kholm. Every urban apartment house had at least one yardman, usually a peasant migrant, whose responsibilities included keeping an eye on the activities of the building's residents and reporting anything suspicious to the police. According to the senior yardman, Kulikova lived "an immoral life" when she resided in his building: she engaged in "indecent conduct" with the junior yardman while simultaneously conducting an affair with a carter. The carter confirmed this account: he was sexually involved with Kulikova for about two months, but then ended the relationship when he learned that she was seeing other men. The junior yardman confirmed the story, too. Acknowledging that he had "courted" Kulikova, the junior yardman maintained that he stopped seeing her when he realized that she was going out with other men.

For servants such as Kulikova to engage in extramarital sexual relations was hardly unusual, although to enjoy multiple partners, as the yardmen claimed she had, was no doubt less common. During the 1890s, over eight thousand women, most of them domestic servants, bore out-of-wedlock babies in St. Petersburg every year. Kulikova, too, became pregnant, as she acknowledged in subsequent testimony. Unable to deny the fact of her "illicit" sexual behavior, for which a baby served as irrefutable evidence, she nevertheless explained her pregnancy in terms that cast her in a more favorable light than had the yard-men's story. She had had only one lover, Kulikova claimed, a man of a higher social status than hers: he was a student whom she had met on the street and whose name she refused to divulge.

Whatever the truth (and chancellery officials had their doubts about the student), Kulikova's pregnancy appears to have represented a turning point in her life. Instead of handing the baby over to a foundling home and to almost certain death, as did so many servant mothers of illegitimate children, Kulikova chose to keep her infant and support the two of them. Even more atyp-ically, Kulikova obtained the vocational training that enabled her to accom-plish this. Somehow—she herself claimed that her student-lover encouraged and supported her—she managed not only to maintain herself and her infant for a while without holding a job but also to enroll in Xavier Glodzinski's tai-loring courses, where she mastered the craft of sewing women's clothing and men's and women's underclothes. According to the elegant diploma pre-served in her file, Kulikova became a first-rate student of fashion, complet-ing both "the theoretical and practical course with great success."

Somewhere along the line, Kulikova evidently learned to refashion herself as well. The child of an impoverished peasant household who had spent her first twenty years in the village, she had acquired by the time she came into contact with three St. Petersburg jurists, the look of "a lady" and something of the demeanor of one, too. This is clear from the testimony of one Lev L'vovich Breitfus, a judge in the St. Petersburg Circuit Court, to which Ku-likova turned for help after village authorities revoked her passport at her hus-band's request. Explaining to her that the court could not assist her to obtain another passport, Breitfus recommended that she petition the chancellery in-stead. But he also felt sufficiently touched by Kulikova's plight to offer per-sonal assistance, too. "Seeing her embarrassment and despair, and recogniz-ing from her petition that I was dealing with an inexperienced and genuinely unhappy woman," as he put it, he suggested that she consult with a friend of his, Vladimir Evgenievich Golovin, a well-known St. Petersburg divorce lawyer. Breitfus also encouraged her to turn to him, Breitfus, should she re-quire help in the future. Then he lost track of her until she turned up one day to ask for help finding work. Recognizing her need and displaying a remark-able level of trust toward a woman who was, after all, almost a perfect stranger, Breitfus invited her to live in his family's empty apartment while they were away at their dacha (summer house). After their return, the family hired Kulikova as a seamstress. Sewing "with skill and taste," she produced all the clothing that Mrs. Breitfus wore.

Kulikova won the support as well as the trust of Breitfus, his family, and several friends. Golovin, the divorce lawyer, having agreed to assist her, helped her to craft (and no doubt asked a clerk to type) both her initial petition and the subsequent letter to the chancellery. In addition, Breitfus brought Kulikova into contact with a third jurist, Anatolii Alekseevich Khodnev, a judge in the St. Petersburg Court of Appeals, for whose family she worked as a seamstress, too. Khodnev also became involved in assisting Kulikova to obtain a separation. Breitfus and Khodnev both wrote letters to the investigating police, stressing Kulikova's gentility, her modesty, her industriousness, and the misery and nervous exhaustion to which her husband's demand for cohabitation had reduced her. In his letter Breitfus recounted how his entire family had been won over by Kulikova's "gentle demeanor" and come to empathize deeply with her grief. Casting Kulikova in as favorable a light as possible, Breitfus sought to counteract the potentially damaging consequences of her earlier, "disreputable" behavior. He was "profoundly and sincerely" convinced, he wrote, that Evdokiia Ivanovna fully merited his kindness. A "decent woman in all respects," she earned her daily bread with her own honest labor. Like the Breitfus family, Khodnev, too, felt "deep sympathy" for Evdokiia Ivanovna on account of her "difficult family position," and he, too, attested to her excellent character and impeccable conduct: Evdokiia Ivanovna is "industrious to the highest degree, honest and indisputably moral."

It was customary for employers to compose letters of reference testifying to the character and trustworthiness of their employees and, more rarely, even to support them in troubled times. However, the jurists' involvement with Kulikova was of an entirely different order. They not only acted as her patrons, financially as well as legally, but also appear to have regarded her almost (but not quite entirely) as one of their own: even in their private correspondence, they never referred to her otherwise than by name and patronymic (Evdokiia Ivanovna), that is, in a formal and respectful fashion, rather than by first name, or diminutive, which is how employers customarily addressed their lower-class employees. Moreover, on Kulikova's behalf, they attempted to draw upon the social connections that like a web linked members of the educated, professional elite in the city of St. Petersburg. On 16 April 1898, Khodnev sent a personal note to Baron Aleksandr A. Budberg, then assistant to the director of the chancellery. The Kulikova case had already languished in "thy Chancellery" for some time, Khodnev wrote, employing the familiar form of address. The investigation report had been in the chancellery's possession since 22 March, Khodnev reminded Budberg. Why the delay? Apologizing in advance for the bother, for the sake of their "old friendship" Khodnev asked Budberg to do everything that his "kindly heart dictates" on Kulikova's behalf. Khodnev's letter prompted Budberg to turn his attention to the case—"I request that you send me the file" is written across the top in Budberg's hand.

However, the outcome was not resolution, but further investigation. The chancellery addressed a letter to the governor of Tver province, describing the conflicting evidence that had been collected thus far. On the one hand, village witnesses all concurred that Dmitrii was not responsible for the breakdown of his marriage. On the other, the local land captain, a noble official with jurisdiction over peasant institutions, had submitted a negative report about Dmitrii, claiming that he spent his wages on alcohol and was incapable of supporting a wife. "From Kulikov's own words," the land captain concluded, "I understood that he wants nothing more than to extort money from his wife." The chancellery wanted to know which version was true. The governor's response of 12 June upheld Dmitrii's story, not his wife's. Dmitrii belonged to a well-to-do peasant household that possessed two huts and a storeroom, two barns, a horse, three cows, five sheep, and ten chickens. Such a household was perfectly capable of supporting a wife "in the peasant fashion," asserted the governor. Dmitrii currently worked as a cabbie, sending his wages home to his father. He very much wanted to live with his wife again and should be permitted to do so, recommended the governor's report.

Unaware of this course of events and growing increasingly uneasy about the outcome of her case, Kulikova sought a meeting with Baron Budberg. Afterward, she visited Breitfus and Khodnev at their dachas, recounting to them what had transpired. These visits elicited another round of correspondence, in which Breitfus wrote Khodnev, and Khodnev, enclosing Breitfus's letter, addressed another note to Budberg, reminding him of his "promise" to resolve the Kulikov case before he, Khodnev, returned from his summer leave. "Don't refuse, my dear, to do everything that your kindly heart tells you," he urged once again. Breitfus, too, was becoming alarmed, as indicated by the following account of Kulikova's travails, excerpted from his letter to Khodnev:

> According to Evdokiia Ivanovna's account, Baron Budberg was rather surprised to see her among the petitioners and . . . asked: "Is your business really unresolved?" Receiving from her a negative response, he inquired, "Do the police bother you?" Receiving another negative response, he remarked, "So much the better." From these words, I conclude that Baron Budberg has completely forgotten about our protégé Evdokiia Ivanovna or that the case has been resolved in an unfavorable manner, but that she has not yet been told. Of course I said not a word to her about my fears. If you, good Anatolii Alekseevich, find it possible to take the side of this unhappy woman, then don't abandon her now, when as the lawyers say, the "danger lies in the delay." Perhaps we can still save her.

Save her from what, exactly? From her brutal, drunken peasant husband, of course, but also from the demeaning procedures to which the chancellery routinely subjected its supplicants in separation cases. The previous spring, Breitfus had spoken to a minor chancellery official, who informed him that even when the chancellery resolved a case in the petitioner's favor, it usually approved only a temporary, one-year passport at first, subjecting the petitioner to a new investigation when she sought to renew it. This process would be repeated for four years; only if all reports were positive would the chancellery approve a final, permanent passport, freeing the woman once and for all from her husband's authority. Breitfus found such a prospect horrific even to contemplate. "You cannot imagine, dear Anatolii Alekseevich, what that means," he wrote. "During that entire time, Evdokiia Ivanovna must literally pay court to the yardmen of the building she lives in, as well as a pack of agents from the criminal investigating department of the police," a process she had already endured for over a year. "If you want to perform a truly Christian act," he pleaded, "then free her from that horrible yoke and obtain for her the right to a separate passport without further restrictions. Evdokiia Ivanovna is without doubt a decent and honorable woman and that kind of surveillance cannot demonstrate the circumstances of this case."

When it came, the resolution of the Kulikova case satisfied her protectors only in part. On 20 September 1898, fifteen months after receiving Kulikova's initial petition, the chancellery arrived at a decision. New evidence had tipped the scales in mid-August. A police report revealed that Dmitrii Kulikov had quit his job as a cabbie and vanished without a trace, while the depositions of witnesses named in Kulikova's second letter verified key details of her story: a land captain had once found Dmitrii, having tumbled from his sled, lying in the snow in a drunken stupor; the peasant who discovered Evdokiia confirmed that she had been abandoned deep in the woods; and so on. A lengthy summary of the evidence, intended for the eyes of the tsar alone, explained why the chancellery had found in Kulikova's favor despite her sexual transgression. "Taking into consideration that Kulikov has insufficient means to support a wife, that he refuses to supply her with a passport in order to extort money from her, that he abuses alcohol and himself forced the petitioner to live separately from him, and that Kulikova, having permitted herself earlier to betray her vows is now virtuous," the chancellery approved a one-year passport over her husband's objections and recommended that the couple "come to some agreement during that year." So, while Kulikova received her separation, she was not spared the need to appeal for its renewal over four more years.

There is nothing in her file to indicate what happened between September 1898, when Kulikova received her one-year passport, and February 1900, when the case resumed, but it seems likely that when her document ran out, she petitioned again and then, faced with the prospect of another investigation and renewed police surveillance, resolved upon a more decisive course

of action. In any event, on 9 February 1900, the chancellery received a letter
from husband and wife, outlining the agreement they had reached on their
own. According to its terms, Dmitrii agreed to grant Evdokiia her freedom,
renouncing all his rights over her; for her part, Evdokiia renounced all future
claims on him and promised to pay him the sum of one thousand rubles in two
installments, the first immediately after the agreement was confirmed and the
remainder within three months. Two weeks later, the husband submitted a letter to the chancellery in which he "solemnly and finally affirmed [his] renun-
ciation of Evdokiia Ivanovna and any children she might bear." The chancellery asked the Tver governor to issue Kulikova a passport, and there the
case closed. Thus, in the end, to receive the unrestricted freedom she sought,
Kulikova (or more likely her protectors) had to purchase it, and for the substantial sum of one thousand rubles, over three times Kulikova's yearly income, which amounted to twenty-five to thirty rubles a month according to
police reports.

What does Evdokiia Kulikova's experience tell us about the options available
to a migrant peasant woman in turn-of-the-century Russia? On the one hand,
her story provides a vivid illustration of the ways that urbanization, the expanding market economy, and burgeoning consumer culture of the late nineteenth century could expand the menu of choices available even to a peasant
woman. They encouraged a new individualism, as evidenced, for example, in
Kulikova's decision to acquire the skills of a seamstress and to obtain a separation from her husband, come what may. And as her transformation into a
"lady" demonstrates, they provided unprecedented opportunities to refashion
one's self, thus helping to blur the social boundaries that separated elites from
masses or, in this case, Kulikova from her protectors. However, Kulikova's
experience also reminds us of the structural factors that could limit individual
autonomy—in this case, the autonomy of a married peasant woman. Having
transformed herself into a lady, in the eyes of city folk and villagers alike,
Evdokiia Kulikova nevertheless remained a peasant's wife in the eyes of the
law. Her legal status left her subject to her husband's will, to marital laws that
forbade the separation of spouses, and to passport laws that restricted her mobility and granted villagers the power to decide where she should live. To escape these restrictions, she had to present herself not only as a victimized wife
but also as a virtuous woman who had mended her ways after a brief lapse,
which her jurist-protectors helped her to do. Still, for almost a year, Kulikova's everyday activities had been subject to the scrutiny of yardmen and
police agents, and she managed to avoid another round of surveillance only
because she produced the money to purchase her freedom. But restrictive
laws and arbitrary administrative practices continued to limit the autonomy of

others. They were experienced as particularly burdensome by professionals, which is one reason why the jurists empathized so fully with Kulikova in the first place and reacted so negatively to the prospect of further surveillance. Even as we note the transformations wrought by urbanization, the market economy, and the new consumer culture, we would do well to remember the limitations, too. Otherwise, how do we explain the revolutionary upheavals of 1905 or, perhaps, even of 1917?

NOTES

Research for this chapter was supported in part by grants from the Council of Research and Creative Work at the University of Colorado at Boulder and the International Research and Exchanges Board (IREX), with funds provided by the National Endowment for the Humanities, the U.S. Department of State, and the U.S. Information Agency.

1. The records of the case described in this chapter are located in the Russian State Historical Archive (RGIA), *fond* 1412, *opis* 221, *ed. kh.* 204 (Kulikova). Unless noted otherwise, all quotations are taken from these records.
2. Iakob Ludmer, "Bab'i stony," pts. 1–2, *Iuridicheskii vestnik*, nos. 11–12 (1884): 446–67, 658–79.

SUGGESTED READINGS

Engel, Barbara Alpern. *Between the Fields and the City: Women, Work and Family in Russia, 1861–1914*. Cambridge: Cambridge University Press, 1994.
———. "In the Name of the Tsar: Competing Legalities and Marital Conflict in Late Imperial Russia," *Journal of Modern History* 77, no. 1 (March 2005): 70–96.
———. "Marriage and Masculinity in Late-Imperial Russia: The 'Hard Cases.'" Pp. 113–30 in *Russian Masculinities in History and Culture*, edited by Barbara Evans Clements, Rebecca Friedman, and Dan Healey. Houndmills, England: Palgrave, 2002.
———. "Russian Peasant Views of City Life, 1861–1914," *Slavic Review* 52 (Fall 1993): 444–59.
Engelstein, Laura. *The Keys to Happiness: Sex and the Search for Modernity in Fin-de-Siècle Russia*. Ithaca, NY: Cornell University Press, 1992.
McReynolds, Louise. "'The Incomparable' Vial'tseva and the Culture of Personality." Pp. 273–94 in *Russia. Women. Culture*, edited by Helena Goscilo and Beth Holmgren. Bloomington: Indiana University Press, 1996.
Ruane, Christine. "Clothes Make the Comrade: A History of the Russian Fashion Industry," *Russian History/Histoire Russe*, 23 (Spring/Summer/Fall/Winter 1996): 311–43.
Wagner, William. *Marriage, Property and Law in Late Imperial Russia*. Oxford: Clarendon Press, 1994.

Chapter Ten

"She Done Him In"

Marital Breakdown in a Jewish Family

ChaeRan Y. Freeze

The Russian Empire acquired a significant Jewish population as a result of Catherine II's partitions of Poland at the end of the eighteenth century. By her decree of 1791, Jews were confined to live in an area called the Pale of Settlement, which included the Belarusian, Latvian, Lithuanian, Polish, and Ukrainian provinces. In the 1880s the Russian government allowed over three hundred thousand Jews to live elsewhere in the empire. Generally, these were individuals officials regarded as being beneficial to the realm, including successful merchants, some artisans, and graduates of institutions of higher education. According to the 1897 census, there were 5.1 million Jews in the empire's total population of almost 129 million. Encouraged to assimilate into the dominant Russian culture, Jews nevertheless experienced discrimination and from the 1870s onward often became victims of anti-Semitic pogroms— acts of violence against Jewish persons, homes, and businesses.

Although the state granted each religious confession authority over the intimate matters of marriage and divorce, the modernizing autocracy began to question the traditional practices of rabbis and rabbinical courts in these matters. Indeed it encouraged individuals, especially women, to appeal to secular courts for justice and redress. Unlike the sessions of the Imperial Chancellery for Receipt of Petitions, those of the civil courts were open to the public and their outcomes were consequently part of public discourse. But as in the testimonies of plaintiffs, defendants, and witnesses before the chancellery, these depositions before the civil courts were complicated by community needs, gender norms, self-interest, and rising expectations of justice.

In what ways does the story of Masia Zalkind compare with that of Evdokiia Ivanovna Kulikova in the previous chapter? Did the Jewish shtetl evince a different type of patriarchal culture than the one that existed in the

Russian peasant village? Will we ever know the true story of Masia Zalkind's married life and whether or not she killed her husband? What types of changes were taking place in Jewish family life in the Western provinces at the turn of the twentieth century and why?

On 19 November 1911, after Abram Zalkind spent the morning studying Torah in the local synagogue, he returned home for a lunch that consisted of some "not-so-fresh minced liver" and a small glass of vodka. He had barely finished eating when he was suddenly stricken with severe abdominal pain and nausea. The family summoned a doctor, but the latter found nothing seriously wrong and merely prescribed a "fizzy powder drink" to relieve the pain. A couple hours later, his wife, Masia, summoned a second physician, who recommended different medication to alleviate the husband's vomiting and diarrhea. By early evening, Abram's condition had deteriorated, his heartbeat faint and his pulse weak; a few hours later he was dead. Such, at least, was the wife's account. Jewish residents of Smorgon (a small town in Lithuania with 10,200 residents, two synagogues, and fourteen Jewish prayer houses), however, suspected foul play and sent a denunciation to the state court, accusing Masia Zalkind of lacing her husband's food with arsenic to end their miserable marriage.[1]

Spousal murder, though a relatively rare form of homicide, captured the public's imagination and triggered a close scrutiny of the couple's relationship for signs of animosity, infidelity, and avarice. Most spousal homicides in Imperial Russia were in response to physical and mental abuse. According to one commentator for the Russian press, such crimes "result from the barbaric relations between husband and wife that are considered normal among the lower strata of the population."[2] But was the Zalkind case really a desperate case of mariticide or simply food poisoning? Whatever the truth of accusations that Masia Zalkind had murdered her husband, the court trial revealed much about Jewish expectations of marriage, prevailing attitudes toward domestic strife, and the politics of divorce in a close-knit Jewish town in Lithuania, where everybody knew everybody's business and family secrets were difficult to conceal.

Indeed, family matters *were* community business: the Jewish community (specifically through the rabbi) controlled the making and unmaking of marriage. This was the special privilege of the Jews: down to its final overthrow in 1917, the ancien régime in Russia made marriage and divorce the responsibility of each religious confession. In contrast to most European countries, which gradually brought marriage under the control of the secular state, the Russian government gave each confession the power to regulate this important institution. In some measure, this "unmodern" feature—the state's failure to secularize and establish its own control—reflected the exigencies of a multiconfessional, multinational empire. Faced with the myriad traditions, customs, and religious rites of different Christian and non-Christian groups, the ancien régime elected to let each faith handle such matters: "Each tribe and nation, including the heathens, is permitted to enter into marriage by the regulations of their laws and accepted customs, without the participation of a civil authority or Christian spiritual leader."[3] As a result, in the case of Jews, rabbinic law governed family life.

That law was extremely liberal on the matter of divorce. Whereas the dominant Russian Orthodox Church treated marriage as an almost indissoluble sacrament, Jewish law viewed the institution as a voluntary union that entailed mutual responsibilities and benefits—the violation of which constituted grounds for dissolving a union. Hence, Jewish law recognized a broad and liberal set of grounds for divorce—from adultery to childlessness, from insults to in-laws to laxity in religious observance. Couples could even divorce by mutual consent without attributing fault to either party. Jewish metrical books from Moscow, for example, routinely cited "mutual hatred" as the grounds for marital dissolution.

Jewish divorce laws were also unabashedly patriarchal, according extraordinary privilege to males: the husband had the sole prerogative to divorce his wife and, under special circumstances, could even do so against her will. In the presence of ten male witnesses, he would place the bill of divorcement in his wife's hand and recite the following words: "Behold, this is your *get*; you are divorced by it from me and you are [hereby] permitted to marry any man." In theory, a woman also could initiate a divorce for a variety of reasons (e.g., intolerable odors from the husband's mouth or nose, leprosy, failure to materially support his wife, refusal to perform his conjugal duties, impotence, and conversion to another faith). There was one major catch, however: she could only obtain such a divorce with her husband's consent.[4] According to Masia's neighbors, precisely this reason—her husband's refusal to grant the bill of divorcement—drove her to commit murder. It was not that Abram still loved her; like a growing number of Jewish husbands in late Imperial Russia, he saw divorce as tantamount to financial ruin. As the couple fought and bickered, the mutual estrangement only intensified. That bitter conflict and Masia's position led friends and relatives to suspect that she had indeed resorted to poison.

Indeed, the most common of marital distress—finances—only helped to intensify the community's hostility toward Masia. Abram's brother, for example, testified that Masia had deliberately defrauded her own husband and extorted a large sum of money. She allegedly had demanded an arrangement guaranteeing her financial support in the event of his death (on the grounds of his fragile health). Abram unwittingly signed the contract (without even reading it), agreeing to pay 1,500 rubles at any time of his wife's choosing. She did not tarry in exploiting his trust: she filed and subsequently won a suit in the Vil'na regional court that mandated immediate payment. Since her husband lacked the capital to satisfy the court injunction, Masia put a lien on their own house. "No matter how much money my brother provided for her expenses," his kinsman bitterly complained, "she always said it was not enough and demanded more money from him."

It was not simply avarice and deceit that outraged her fellow Jews in Smorgon: Masia had gone outside the community and solicited the intercession of a Russian state court against her spouse. Jewish society deeply resented the intrusion of gentile authorities into communal affairs and especially in private family matters, let alone at the initiative of a female litigant. For centuries, Jews had maintained autonomous courts and strictly forbade coreligionists to appeal to "outside" authorities. Indeed, the community had traditionally treated offenders with the utmost severity: "[The elders of the community] shall inscribe his [the offender's] name in the record-book, so that when the time comes, his son shall not be circumcised, nor marriages performed for his children, as well as other matters concerning him as a Jew."[5] Such ethnic boundaries of defense persisted in the Russian Empire. As late as 1881, tsarist officials complained about the tenacity of these unofficial Jewish courts, but conceded that they often alleviated the congestion in state courts by resolving religious and minor civil cases.

Masia Zalkind was, in fact, not the only woman to take advantage of the state courts. Indeed, after the judicial reform of 1864, the new system of courts not only offered quick, inexpensive justice but promised equal treatment for men and women. Little wonder that the courts unleashed a tidal wave of litigation, not only among Russians, but also among Jews. The surging caseload of the judicial system provoked a rising chorus of concern about this destructive "litigiousness," not so much because of the excess burden as because of the fear it was dissolving the social fabric. A government report in 1881, for example, sharply criticized the ubiquitous presence of Jewish lawyers in "every town and village," who promised to help draft petitions and legal instruments. Even the grassroots ecclesiastical supervisors of the Russian Orthodox Church in Lithuania complained that the "profusion of frivolous litigation" exacerbated social tensions and led to corruption in the courts.[6]

Despite such criticism, the Zalkind case shows why Masia—like many other women—felt that only the state court held out any prospect of justice. So long as she stayed within the community, the wife apparently believed that there was little reason to expect fair treatment. In fact, the tale of Masia's monetary extortion was far from accurate. As court records show, her brother-in-law had deliberately omitted a crucial detail: the house had originally belonged to Masia (a bequest from her deceased father that she had put in her husband's name to preclude any claim by her sister). Problems ensued, however, when he subsequently refused to transfer the property back to her name. Determined to reclaim her property, the wife took the matter into her own hands. But in doing so, she broke a strong taboo: rather than negotiate with her husband and relatives, she turned to the tsarist state. Masia also bypassed the rabbinical court, no doubt fearing that it would side with her spouse—a well-respected and prominent member of the religious community. Her apprehensions were not unfounded; the majority of hostile witnesses at her murder trial were men who had studied Torah with her husband in the local synagogue. As Jewish women like Masia Zalkind elected to resolve their domestic (especially monetary) conflicts in state courts, both husbands and religious authorities saw such litigation as a challenge to patriarchy and Jewish communal autonomy. Although Masia won the civil litigation, she made herself a virtual pariah in her hometown; this cloud of ill will would play a major role in the murder trial at the criminal court.

Significantly, much of the testimony about Masia's character was deeply gendered: to undercut her credibility, witnesses were at pains to prove that Masia was a bad wife and mother—hence, someone so abnormal that she could indeed have perpetrated so dastardly an act. The male witnesses, in particular, emphasized Masia's "unusually ill-tempered shrewish character" and also claimed that her lack of maternal concern for her children was the real cause of the marital strife. Thus one neighbor testified that "[she] did not love her older children—a son and daughter—and eventually forced her husband to send them away from the house." Another witness claimed that she neglected her family: "Masia Zalkind often abandoned her husband and children for prolonged periods to travel to Vil'na." He also volunteered the rumor that she had a lover. The witnesses, by contrast, praised Abram as a good father who "strongly loved his children." The local rabbi also confirmed that the husband had complained about his wife's "difficult disposition and her cold and unmaternal relationship to the family."

It was specifically these kinds of gendered denunciations that were characteristic of Jewish divorce cases: given the conservative family-centered ideology and politics of the tsarist state, such testimony was critical in undermining the good character and credibility of female litigants. That is why witnesses often sought to denigrate a woman by exposing her "poor mothering," thereby invoking popular assumptions about the female's "innate" capacity for nurturing and self-sacrifice. In one poignant case, where a woman sought to study in Odessa so as to ensure her economic independence, her husband initially agreed but later reneged and demanded that they reestablish traditional gender roles. Interestingly, in this case, it was the male who resorted to the state, asking that the wife be forced to return on the grounds that his "small children suffer worse than orphans being left without the tenderness and care of their natural mother." His wife rejected the traditional definition of gender roles, especially "with respect to the meaning of the family, the role of the mother, and concern about the upbringing of the children." She explained that she sought to study dentistry not only to satisfy "my thirst for knowledge" but also so that "I can support myself and the children in the event of a divorce."[7] Such views, slowly but inexorably gaining ground in late Imperial Russia, posed a direct challenge to traditional patriarchy. Despite the many cultural differences, Jewish society also expected women to prefer the traditional maternal role, which in their view was linked to the female's reproductive capacity. Failure to exhibit a "maternal" nature provoked harsh censure. As the witnesses at the Zalkind trial argued, if Masia lacked the maternal "instinct" to care for her biological children, how could she have been anything but an unfeeling, evil, and coldhearted wife?

Masia's trial brought to light some new interesting elements that reflected the changes overtaking the culture and values of a traditional Jewish shtetl. Perhaps the most striking testimonies came from witnesses who attributed the marital breakdown to an absence of love. As one close neighbor declared, "In my opinion, Masia Leia did not love her husband at all." The lack of love was reciprocal; as a friend of the husband testified, "Abram Zalkind always said that he never loved his wife and thus it was impossible to live together with her." While such testimony served to enhance the prosecution's case for motive, its very invocation reflected a tacit recognition of romantic love. Not surprisingly, whether disingenuous or not, Masia contested such assertions and sought to affirm the authenticity of her marriage, claiming that "on the contrary, I loved him very much; he was my all." Indeed, Masia even invoked a patriarchal trope to enhance her credibility as a loving wife: "When I became a orphan, he was not only a husband, but a father to me." Her "estranged" son confirmed her statement, testifying that despite their constant fighting, "I have no doubt that my mother loved the deceased."

Whatever the truth of these conflicting assertions, the depositions reveal that Jewish society—where arranged marriages were still common—now expected some degree of affection ("love") in marriage. To be sure, the concept of "love" was not entirely new: records from Vil'na from the late 1830s show that 20 percent of the divorces were on the grounds that "they do not love each other." In the following decades the "modern idea" of the companionate marriage, based on mutual respect, emotional compatibility, and affection, gradually gained such a strong foothold that witnesses at Masia's trial involuntarily invoked this new norm.

A host of broader developments helped to foster and disseminate the new ideal of marriage. One was the influence of the Jewish enlightenment movement, which sought to modernize Jewish society through a fundamental reform of its values, institutions, and customs. It sharply criticized arranged marriages as commercial transactions devoid of sympathy for personal feelings. The proponents of enlightenment demanded that children be granted complete freedom of choice in marriage, instead of being led to the wedding canopy "like sheep to the slaughter." A second related factor was the rise in secular education and the broad circulation of romance novels particularly among Jewish women, who voraciously consumed Yiddish chapbooks and European literature by Johann Goethe, Friedrich von Schiller, and Alexander Dumas. This new culture valorizing love raised new expectations of emotional and intellectual compatibility in marriage. A third factor was demographic, signified by a sharp rise in the age of first marriage; whereas Jews had previously married in their early teens, by the early twentieth century, over 50 percent of Jewish brides entering marriage for the first time were aged twenty-one to twenty-five and grooms twenty-six to thirty. This meant that prospective spouses were more economically independent, psychologically mature, better educated, and often insisted on choosing their own spouses.

The result of this new ideal of marriage was a strong sense of "self" and a new desire for respect and consideration, especially among women. Ester Saet, the wife of a jeweler in Kronshtadt, called her marriage of twenty-two years "the most miserable union" and explained why: "In recent years, his attitude toward me has been hostile and contemptuous and for four years we have lived together like complete strangers, not like man and wife."[8] Another Jewish woman in Rostov was adamant that only passionate romance could satisfy her expectations of marriage and that an arranged match was intolerable: "I categorically told my mother that I will not live with my husband because I do not love him and that I could not possibly love him after our three-day acquaintance." Her mother's retort—"Get used to him and you will come to love him"—sought to reassert parental authority over matchmaking and to resist the new conception of a conjugal union based on affection.[9] But such parental authority was on the wane. Even the traditional residents of Smorgon were influenced by the new idea of a love-based marriage: they regarded the lack of mutual affection between the Zalkinds (not to mention the public scandals, alleged infidelity, and lawsuits) as a clear symptom of a failed union.

In contrast to the cascade of testimony from the husband's friends and relatives, Masia's voice is remarkably silent in the court record. In fact, her only appearance in the trial record is a brief interview with the medical examiner and a couple letters to her family from prison. According to Masia, the marriage had broken down for two main reasons—significantly, reasons that all the witnesses (save her uncle and the town rabbi) had chosen to omit or ignore. One was the intolerable meddling of her husband's kin and friends into their private affairs. In Masia's own words, their relationship had been fine "until her husband came under the influence of [his] friends and brother." In a letter from prison, she castigated these individuals as "evil people, who deceived me" and had brought about her "ruin." Her grievance certainly had the ring of truth; Jewish memoirs attest that the invasive meddling of in-laws, siblings, relatives, and close friends was a significant source of marital strife. Parents and older siblings deemed it their right to intercede if their own interests were at stake. Such was the case of the Hebrew writer Avraham Mapu, who constantly meddled in his younger brother Matityahu's financial affairs. Thus in a letter dated 15 March 1858, Mapu admonished him to prevent his wife's careless dissipation of their assets: "Do not give in to the wishes of your wife, who desires to journey to Italy or to the sea of Tiberius [Crimean Sea]." He warned, "Take pity, brother. Take pity on your soul and put the money on guard in a place where it will not fall into her hands."[10] Such interference caused Matityahu's mother-in-law to blame Mapu for destroying her daughter's reputation and marriage. Whatever the truth of Masia's complaints, they touched a raw nerve in family relations and had the ring of authenticity.

The second reason for the Zalkind's marital breakdown was domestic abuse. Interestingly, even Masia was reluctant to air this matter in public. Her brother-in-law conceded some "violence" in the household, but blamed it on both spouses: "Their arguments sometimes even turned into brawls." The local rabbi, however, was more forthcoming in his testimony and cited the wife's recurrent complaints that Abram Zalkind "subjected her to hunger, that he was a heartless individual who often beat her and restricted her freedom." Masia Zalkind's own reticence in court is surprising, since such domestic abuse was certain to elicit the sympathetic support of the state court. Although she may have been seeking to avoid giving motive to her alleged crime, it is more likely that she simply viewed her husband's behavior as "un-Jewish" and "shameful." Her silence was, in fact, not unusual: the social stigma was so great that, in another case, a Jewish woman from Kovno confessed: "I experienced such shame that I would have preferred to die." Even Dora Faivelivich, from cosmopolitan St. Petersburg, admitted the same feelings: "I was not able [to tell] anyone of these complaints and to shame my close ones, so

I alone carried this heavy cross [a strange metaphor for a Jewish woman to use]." An additional motive for silence was the presence of children. Faive-livich declared that "I tolerated everything as long as my strength would allow . . . until I could no longer endure the beatings" for her children's sake. Another woman told the local rabbi that her husband treated her "in an extremely evil, crude, and barbarous manner" but she stayed "as a mother who would sacrifice her life gladly for her children."[11] Although it is difficult to judge the severity of abuse in the Zalkind case, it evidently played a role in the breakdown of the marriage.

Whatever the exact mixture of factors that triggered conflict in the Zalkind household, the fact of marital breakdown was hardly a cause of surprise among Jews in late Imperial Russia. Far from viewing marriage as an ideal institution, Jewish social critics like Avraham Mapu wrote that "only one in a thousand will derive joy from family life and even that will be a façade."[12] Similarly, in 1909, the Yiddish newspaper the *Matchmaker* directly confronted the burning question of the day: "Why are there so many families that lead unhappy lives?"[13] Indeed, contemporaries and statistics suggest that the "family crisis" was particularly acute among Jews in the Russian Empire. Thus, the 1897 census showed that .33 percent of the Jewish population was divorced, compared to just .07 percent of the total population. Indeed, the rate among ethnic Russians, Ukrainians, and Belarusians (most of whom belonged to the Russian Orthodox Church) was about half the national average. In other words, the Jewish divorce rate was almost five times that of the national average and about ten times that of the average of Slavs in the Russian Orthodox Church.[14]

Significantly, the Jewish divorce rate actually declined in the late nineteenth century. To be sure, marital discord did not necessarily drop and, under the pressures of modernization, may even have increased. Nevertheless, couples became increasingly reluctant to obtain a formal Jewish divorce. One factor was the financial and legal impediments that made a formal divorce difficult and undesirable. A key element—evident in the Zalkind case—was financial: Abram simply could not afford to divorce. Jewish law required two payments upon the dissolution of a marriage: the *ketubah* (a sum that the husband agreed to pay the wife upon the dissolution of the marriage) and full restitution of the wife's dowry. While the financial dilemmas were hardly new, the specter of litigation in state courts, which had real coercive power, represented a new phenomenon. Fear of such judicial power inspired the categorical language of Jewish divorce agreements: "We have no present or future claims against each other." A second consideration, especially important for women, was the impact of divorce on their legal status and rights of residency. This issue was especially critical for Jews given the fact that they were restricted to the Pale of Settlement (a bloc of western and Polish provinces). Only those in exceptional categories—including first-guild merchants, ex-soldiers, skilled artisans, and university students—obtained permission to reside in the internal Russian provinces. Since the woman's status derived from her husband's, divorce cast doubt on her ability to reside outside the Pale of Settlement. Many Jewish women, therefore, preferred separation to divorce in order to avoid the nightmares of dealing with the tsarist bureaucracy to obtain new passports and residence permits.

The drop in the divorce rate also resulted from the fact that increasingly rabbis were unable to force recalcitrant husbands to grant their wives a divorce. In part, this was due to restrictions in imperial law, which now forbade the use of traditional methods of coercion (such as flogging and communal ostracism). But the problem of enforcement also stemmed from the growing refusal of males (especially in more cosmopolitan areas) to heed rabbinical injunctions. Whatever the motive, couples like the Zalkinds, whose marriages had failed, remained officially married, a situation that generated escalating tensions that, as Masia's neighbors suspected, led her to poison her husband.

On 17 September 1911 jurors (none was Jewish) handed down the verdict that decided Masia Leia Zalkind's fate. It paid no heed to her half-hearted attempt to mitigate her plight by invoking a "mental" defense with the claim that "she did not feel that her mental facilities were in order." Such ideas were then in vogue, with the notion of "female hysteria" purportedly based on the special reproductive physiology of women. But the court rejected this argument; the state doctor, who found no family history of mental illness or irregularities in the patient's menstrual cycles, pregnancies, and births, declared her psychologically fit to stand on trial. What proved critical in the jurors' minds was the official autopsy report, which found a "rather significant amount of arsenic" in the husband's stomach. What Michel Foucault has called the "power of knowledge" (and what foreshadows modern DNA evidence) had already come to dominate court procedures in late Imperial Russia. Without direct proof (Masia's eleven-year-old son, indeed, testified that the entire family had eaten the same chopped liver and herring from one plate), the jury concluded that given the testimony about marital discord, the defendant was clearly guilty of murdering her spouse. It sentenced her to the deprivation of all her rights and hard labor. Perhaps as a tacit acknowledgment of female "hysteria," the jury ruled that the crime was not premeditated and therefore reduced her sentence from fifteen to ten years of hard labor.

As in many court cases, especially in postreform Russia, it is difficult to assess the justice of such a verdict. Given the inconclusive forensic evidence (which did not prove that Masia was directly responsible), the jury had to rely mainly on its own assumptions and perceptions. The testimony of neighbors and relatives was also critical; it established motive and invoked images that made the alleged murder entirely credible to the jury. It is clear that Masia had few friends and supporters, not least because she violated community taboos (against appeals to the tsarist state) and its prescribed norms for female maternal behavior. Her neighbors in Smorgon and the jury in Vil'na found it easy to believe that Masia Zalkind had indeed "done him in."

NOTES

1. The Masia Zalkind court case is preserved in the Historical State Archive of Lithuania (LVIA), f. 448, op. 7, d. 479. Unless noted otherwise, all quotations are taken from this case.

2. "Smert ot strakha pred nagaikoi," *Kazanskii telegaf,* 2712 (1901): 2, as cited in Stephen Frank, *Crime, Cultural Conflict, and Justice in Rural Russia, 1856–1914* (Berkeley: University of California Press, 1999), 170.

3. *Polnoe sobranie zakonov Rossiiskoi imperii,* 1st series, 45 vols. (St. Petersburg: Tip. II otdeleniia sobstvennoi ego imperatorskago velichestva kantseliarii, 1830), 10:90.

4. Rachel Biale, *Women in Jewish Law: The Essential Texts, Their History, and Their Relevance for Today* (New York: Schocken Books, 1995), 70–101.

5. Shmuel A. Cygielman, *Jewish Autonomy in Poland and Lithuania until 1648* (Jerusalem: [s.n.], 1997), 93.

6. Russian State Historical Archive (RGIA), f. 821, op. 9, d. 137, l. 50. Gregory Freeze, "Russian Orthodoxy on the Periphery: Decoding the *Raporty Blagochinnykh* in Lithuania Diocese," p. 127 in *Problemy vsemirnoi istorii: Sbornik statei v chest' Aleksandra Aleksandrovicha Fursenko,* ed. B. V. Anan'ich et al. (St. Petersburg: D. Bulanin, 2000).

7. RGIA, f. 1412, op. 215, d. 104, ll. 5–5 ob.

8. RGIA, f. 1412, op. 228, d. 23, l. 56.

9. RGIA, f. 1412, op. 213, d. 1, l. 1.

10. Ben Zion Dinur, ed., *Mikhtavei Avraham Mapu* (Jerusalem: Mosad Byalik, 1970), 29.

11. RGIA, f. 1412, op. 231, d. 1, l. 1 (case of Dora Faivelivich); f. 821, op. 9, d. 16, l. 16–16 ob. (case of Sara Shternfeld).

12. Dinur, *Miktavei,* 133.

13. "Gliklikher familien leben," *Der shadkhon* 1 (1909): 3.

14. Andreas Kappeler, Henning Bauer, and Brigitte Roth, *Die Nationalitäten des russischen Reiches in der Volkszählung von 1897,* vol. 2 (Stuttgart, Germany: F. Steiner, 1991), 137–40.

SUGGESTED READINGS

Biale, David. "Eros and Enlightenment: Love against Marriage in the East European Jewish Enlightenment." *Polin* 1 (1986): 59–67.

Feiner, Shmuel. "Haisha hayehudiyah hamodernit: mikre-mivhan beyahasei ha-haskalah vehamodernah." *Zion* 58 (1993): 453–99. Examines the problem of the "modern Jewish woman" as a test case in the relationship between the Jewish enlightenment and modernity.

Freeze, ChaeRan Y. *Jewish Marriage and Divorce in Imperial Russia.* Hanover, NH: Brandeis University Press, published by University Press of New England, 2002.

———. "The Litigious Gerusha: Jewish Women and Divorce in Imperial Russia." *Nationalities Papers* 25, no. 1 (1997): 89–101.

Hyman, Paula. *Gender and Assimilation in Modern Jewish History. The Roles and Representations of Women.* Seattle: University of Washington Press, 1995. See chapter 3, "Seductive Secularization." Analyzes the process of acculturation among Jewish women in tsarist Russia and Poland in the nineteenth and early twentieth centuries.

Parush, Iris. "The Politics of Literacy: Women and Foreign Languages in Jewish Society of Nineteenth-Century Eastern Europe." *Modern Judaism* 15 (1995): 188–90. Discusses the impact of secular literature on Jewish women's acculturation and secularization.

Stampfer, Shaul. "Hamashmaut hahevratit shel nisuei boser bemizrah Eiropa." Pp. 65-77 in *Studies on Polish Jewry: Paul Glikson Memorial Volume*, edited by Ezra Mendelsohn and Chone Shmeruk. Jerusalem: Zalman Shazar Center, 1987. Examines the myth of child marriages in East European Jewish society.

Wengeroff, Pauline. *Rememberings. The World of a Russian-Jewish Woman in the Nineteenth Century.* Translated by Henny Wenkart and edited by Bernard Dov Cooperman. Potomac: University Press of Maryland, 2000.

Zborowski, Mark, and Elizabeth Herzog. *Life Is with People: The Culture of the Shtetl.* New York: Schocken Books, 1962.

Chapter Eleven

Serving the Household, Asserting the Self

Urban Domestic Servant Activism, 1900–1917

Rebecca Spagnolo

Rapid industrialization and urbanization in late Imperial Russia, as elsewhere in the industrializing world, brought in their wake not only poor working and living conditions but also a growing sense of dignity and self-respect among the laborers who chafed at the degradations they had to face on a daily basis. Strikes became commonplace in the last decades of the Romanov dynasty as workers organized illegally (before 1905 and after 1907) to protest such issues as meager wages; long hours; lack of job security, insurance, and safety measures; and the hiring of scab labor.

The Russian working class, however, was heterogeneous, marked by differing skill levels, occupations, and gender. Factory workers and domestic servants had steadier employment and better pay than workers in various nondomestic service industries and artisanal trades. Among factory workers, a hierarchy of workers developed that favored skilled workers over semiskilled and unskilled laborers as laborers at higher levels sought to protect their higher wages and advance their positions against others. Unfortunately, women generally fell into the categories of semiskilled and unskilled workers, but even in those groups they were considered by their male counterparts to be second-rate and threats to men's livelihoods because women's wages were considerably lower (between a half and two-thirds) than men's wages for the same type of work. Furthermore, employers were inclined to hire more women due to their reluctance to jeopardize their family's needs by participating in strikes. A masculine work culture pervaded the factory floor: Men subjected women workers to coarse and abusive language as well as physical harassment. Men controlled the mutual aid organizations and other associations of workers even in industries (such as textile and food production) where women predominated, leaving women less likely to have representation.

Women, nonetheless, did participate in the growing strike movement, espe-
cially as economic conditions deteriorated in the early twentieth century and
rising expectations for change culminated in revolution in 1905 after a peace-
ful demonstration of workers and their families was fired upon by government
troops at the Winter Palace.

   As Rebecca Spagnolo points out in this chapter, it has long been thought
that domestic servants, who were overwhelmingly female, were less likely to
organize themselves than female factory workers because of their isolation
from one another and lack of leisure time. Historians have also presumed that
domestic servants enjoyed better working conditions than their factory coun-
terparts. They have assumed that housework even before the invention of mod-
ern conveniences was not particularly onerous and that domestics were likely
to ape their middle- and upper-class employers in speech and have higher as-
pirations. Unlike major factories that employed anywhere from a hundred to
several thousand laborers, typical middling urban families that lived in apart-
ment blocks and had disposable income hired a single servant. Only the
wealthiest of households could meet the expectations of Elena Molokhovets,
Russia's equivalent of Mrs. Beeton, that fashionable households be run by an
army of servants. Although factory work involved long hours and backbreak-
ing work, industrial laborers did not have to work eighteen hours a day, seven
days a week or be on call the other hours, whereas servants did. Strikes had
resulted in an 1897 factory law restricting the working day to eleven and a half
hours. It is therefore not surprising that domestic servants asked for a shorter
working day to gain equity with factory workers and, in 1905, adopted the fac-
tory laborers' demand for an eight-hour day.

   What other grievances did domestics have and how might those grievances
have made them more vulnerable and insecure in their positions than factory
workers? To what degree were domestics dependent upon charity? To what
degree could they take action themselves? Why did domestics, like other
workers, insist on demanding respect from their employers when they had
other issues to complain about? Why might domestics have had greater suc-
cess in organizing themselves than historians previously thought?

   A servant should serve. She should serve in the morning, she should serve
   during the day, during the evening, after midnight, she should serve on
   weekdays and on holidays.[1]

By the end of the nineteenth century the character and composition of Russian urban society was changing dramatically. Thousands upon thousands of
peasant migrants were flocking to urban centers, particularly to St. Petersburg
and Moscow, in search of jobs and new opportunities. For example, whereas

in 1850 the population of St. Petersburg and its suburbs numbered approximately five hundred thousand, by 1914 their populations had more than quadrupled to almost 2.2 million. Not all of these recent arrivals were destined for employment in factories and workshops, as many entered the growing retail, construction, communications, and transportation sectors of the economy. The most populous employment sector, and therefore the main prospect for many of these internal migrants, was service, with its largest subgroup—domestic service.[2] By 1887 the number of domestic servants had increased to over 1.3 million throughout Russia.

Not only had domestic service continued to grow in size during the late nineteenth century, but it had also been feminized. By the early twentieth century only a small, though not insignificant, percentage of males remained in service. In 1882 less than 70 percent of Moscow domestic servants were women, but by 1912 their percentage had increased to 93. A similar change took place in St. Petersburg where the composition of service went from 50 percent female in 1864 to 91 percent in 1900. As a result, service remained the single largest occupation for employed women in urban centers such as St. Petersburg, Moscow, Odessa, Khar'kov, and Kiev. By 1900 their ranks in St. Petersburg and Moscow had swollen to 128,045 and 78,728 women, respectively. Even as late as 1912, twice as many women were engaged in service as worked in factories.

In spite of the fact that service comprised, after agriculture, the second most populous occupational category in Russia, domestics have been conspicuously absent from history books. There are at least three reasons for this regrettable neglect, one evidential and the others interpretative. First, servants were not in a position to leave behind a complete or readily accessible documentary legacy. Handicapped by a literacy rate lower than that of skilled female factory workers and with only a marginally higher rate than female textile workers, domestics left little in the way of personal letters or memoirs.[3] The problem of documentary sources has been further complicated by the fact that domestic servants did not work in larger institutions such as workshops, mills, or factories that usually generated ample records. Most Russian domestic servants, like the proverbial English "maid-of-all-work," labored alone in thousands of households scattered throughout Russia's cities and towns.

Second, domestics have suffered from historians' traditional gender-based disregard of an occupation with a disproportionate representation of women. In instances where scholars have acknowledged their presence, their role has traditionally been eclipsed, if not demeaned, by a definition of work and workers that has privileged the achievements of factory workers over all other laborers. Consequently, historians have relegated the experiences of the domestic to the odd page and passing footnote. Some exceptions have appeared in the works of Barbara Alpern Engel, Rose Glickman, Catriona Kelly, and Angela Rustemeyer. However, even these scholars focus largely on the socioeconomic vulnerability of the individual domestic servant rather than on the contribution of service to the formation of an organized female workforce in Russia's modern urban society.

With a view to restoring the domestic servant to her rightful place as an integral player in the organization of Russia's women workers in the first two decades of the twentieth century, this chapter explores the initial steps undertaken by and for the domestic servant that aimed at enhancing her quality of life and her ability to adapt to a changing urban environment. The experiences of domestics, culled from archival sources including servants' letters and newspaper articles about domestic service, demonstrate that these women confronted seemingly insurmountable obstacles to secure their goals and that many of their achievements were often "more honor'd in the breach than the observance." However, the extent to which domestics were able to assert themselves as organized members of a rapidly growing urban workforce, while simultaneously serving their employers in isolation, was unparalleled in the modern world in the early twentieth century.[4]

The life of domestic servants at the turn of the twentieth century was bleak. Domestics faced difficulties in asserting themselves as individuals and satisfying the onerous demands of the households they served. Employers forced them to provide almost uninterrupted repetitive labor for the household's benefit. In this and other respects domestic servants were akin to workers in the early days of the Industrial Revolution. They had to be the first to arise, usually no later than 6:00 a.m., and the last to retire, often past midnight. In fact, a standard joke had it that the life of a domestic in the employ of a member of the intelligentsia was more pitiable than any other, as the intelligentsia were constitutionally unable to retire before midnight! Regardless of their social standing, family members when they arose in the morning expected the servant to have the samovar and breakfast already prepared. During the day, the domestic had responsibility for all the cleaning, the laundry, the shopping, and the minding of small children. By evening her employers counted on her to feed and put the children to bed, have dinner prepared, and provide a never-ending supply of tea for adult family members and their occasional guests. A servant was allowed rest periods of an hour or two, or even more in what could be an eighteen-hour day, but because these breaks were usually of varying lengths and idiosyncratic to the family's needs, they were rarely predictable or fully enjoyable. Even time off on Sundays turned out to be an irregular luxury, and holidays were virtually unheard of.

In addition to being overworked, a domestic could be subjected to her employers' whims and caprices and sometimes abuse. For example, in one letter a young servant girl noted that she was forbidden to leave the house for more than two hours per month, and then only to go to church. Her living quarters, she bemoaned, consisted of a dark corner of the apartment that she shared with the garbage. Another young woman described how her "soul was poisoned with the vulgarity" of the various male members of her household. Not only had these sons of "pious mothers" infected her with their diseases, she decried, but they had also subsequently thrown her out onto the street where she was fit for little more than the career of a prostitute.[5] Like the industrial laborer, a domestic had to face instances of sexual harassment and assault in the workplace; however, unlike other female laborers, a servant had to do so with the added pressures of physical and psychological isolation. It was not uncommon for a servant to fall prey to the unwanted advances of an employer, a fellow servant, or a tradesperson.

On the eve of the twentieth century a servant's wages were equally unrewarding. She received little compensation for the hard work and indignities she endured—a handful of rubles each month—and even then only if she was among the fortunate. There was no formal compulsion for the employer to pay a servant anything, let alone abide by a wage scale or definition of what constituted suitable room and board. There were numerous cases of ungrateful employers denying their servants adequate working and living conditions and refusing to pay them for months at a time. While the prerevolutionary period witnessed the introduction of legislation designed to improve the living conditions of other working-class groups, especially female factory workers, it ignored the domestic servant. As always, she found herself at the mercy of the customary law of individual families.[6]

The absence of legislation to protect domestic servants, however, did not leave them completely defenseless. In the late nineteenth century and early twentieth century, a small but increasing number of servants risked exercising their rights before the justice of the peace courts in large urban centers such as St. Petersburg and Moscow. Functioning as institutions of mediation, the courts provided the population with a forum in which to air grievances and to resolve disputes. Young servant girls could lay charges against their employers, regardless of the employers' position in society, for being rude and insulting, for not paying wages, and for committing acts of physical violence and sexual harassment.

Frequently such cases were settled in the favor of the domestic. One example involved Maria Alekseevna and her employer, a merchant's wife by the name of Nadezhda Vasil'evna. Upon taking up her position with Vasil'evna, Alekseevna deposited her internal passport with her employer. However, when she decided to quit her job after finding the working conditions unbearable, her employer refused to pay her outstanding wages and return her passport, claiming that the passport had been lost. Without her passport Alekseevna could not attain legal employment. Unprepared to accept the life of an outlaw, Maria Alekseevna put her case to the local justice of the peace, who ruled in her favor. The judge instructed her employer to pay Alekseevna the six rubles owing and to return her passport. In the event the latter could not be found, the judge ordered the police to issue her temporary documents while she secured its replacement.[7]

Unfortunately, statistical records denoting the occupations of both defendants and the litigants do not exist. Consequently, it is impossible to establish conclusively the number of aggrieved domestic servants who appealed to the justice of the peace courts for assistance. Available case descriptions show that many did. Nonetheless, fear of losing their jobs along with the roofs over their heads kept an even greater number of domestics from going to court. Ultimately, the vast majority of urban domestic servants remained isolated and without protection from their employers' exploitation.

Domestic servants were also ignored in the debate over the "woman question" that raged among the intelligentsia in the final decades of Imperial Russia. Both feminists and socialists seemed equally disinterested in engaging in any serious effort to emancipate the female servant from the circumstances that imprisoned her. For feminists there was the unspoken recognition that the continuation of service was a necessary evil in the struggle to liberate other, more educated women from the drudgeries of the home. For socialists there was the assumption that despite their pitiable position, servants were nonworkers who performed unproductive labor in a domestic setting, and as such they were less deserving of the limited available resources than were real workers in factories, in whose hand the future rested.

The poignancy of domestics' plight, their overwhelmingly female composition, and their rapidly growing numbers meant, however, that neither feminists nor socialists could completely ignore them. Feminist solutions to the "servant question" ranged from the traditional provision of philanthropic assistance, to individual servants in need, to the reform of employer attitudes and improvements in working conditions. Socialists, on the other hand, were sometimes more radical in their approach, with individuals like Alexandra Kollontai calling for the institution of communal living in place of the private kitchen. For the most part, however, they emphasized the need for domestic servants to organize in order to establish their rights and safeguard their position. During the period from the late 1880s through 1917 and beyond, all these suggestions for reform were put into play in one form or other.

One of the earliest examples of a recognized organization of domestic servants was the highly structured and exclusive St. Petersburg Cooperative of Male Domestic Servants. It was organized in 1887 by a group of male domestics who sought to protect themselves and others like them from being dependent upon the infamous and predatory employment agencies that out of self-interest favored employers over servants. Membership was open to men under the age of sixty who could boast impeccable behavior, irreproachable character, and no criminal record. Designed to provide "good, experienced and honest male domestic servants" to prospective employers who wished to host events such as dinners, balls, and weddings, the cooperative also ensured that its members worked in safe surroundings and were compensated adequately for their services.[8] Over the seventeen years of its existence, it was active in its efforts to safeguard the interests of its members both inside and outside the workplace.

Broader-based mutual aid societies, concerned either entirely or in part with improving the position of domestic servants, became popular around the turn of the century. These largely philanthropic ventures were spearheaded by upper-class women and others from among the intelligentsia who wished to help women less fortunate than themselves. One example of such an organization was the Russian Society for the Protection of Women. The Society for the Assistance of the Employment and Labor of Domestic Servants in St. Petersburg and the Society for Assisting Young Girls exemplify organizations specifically geared toward helping domestic servants. Mutual aid societies for servants discussed questions of concern to their membership, provided material support to improve the position of servants, offered domestics legal aid, and raised their level of self-awareness and overall knowledge. They sought to provide servants with real relief, and their efforts, though cautious, were not without success.

By the 1905 Revolution, the mutual aid societies for domestics gave way to militant trade unions. For reasons that are not entirely clear, and unlike other service sector groups such as unions involving waiters and tavern staff,[9] domestic service trade unions developed independently from the organizations, cooperatives, and societies that predated them. A notable exception to this pattern, however, was the All-Russian Union for Women's Equality—the first openly feminist organization in Russia. Formed in Moscow after Bloody Sunday (when government troops at the Winter Palace fired upon some tens of thousands of unarmed workers and their families petitioning for better economic conditions and civil rights) by a group of socialist and liberal women frustrated by the failure of male liberals and socialists to support women's rights, the union had grown to twenty-six local chapters by May 1905. Members of this group played a crucial role in the formation of one of the first domestic servant unions—the Moscow-based Professional Union of Female and Male Servants.

When domestic servants found themselves caught up in the flurry of labor protest in 1905, the scale of initial efforts by the more disgruntled among them was much smaller than that of other workers. The realities of the domestic servants' existence militated against greater involvement. Isolated and overworked, domestics had little free time to organize. Moreover, many employers went to great lengths to keep their servants tied to the home and separated from their peers. They threatened them with immediate dismissal if they attempted to assert themselves inside or outside the workplace. The threat of job loss might partly explain why domestics did not initially choose to direct their energies against overbearing employers but rather pitted themselves, as had some of their male predecessors almost two decades earlier, against the much-hated private employment agency.

Outspoken domestics attacked these agencies, accusing them of acting only on behalf of the employers, whose fees kept these private establishments in operation. According to the servants, the agencies were more concerned with ensuring that the employer was provided with a high caliber of domestic than with protecting the servant against exploitation. The domestic was left to chafe under the onerous rules by which the agencies operated, rules that reduced her to little more than a commodity whose medical and criminal history was far more important than her well-being. While an employer had the right to select a servant from a secured pool of candidates, the domestic was required to respond to an unknown prospective employer's summons within twenty-four hours of its receipt or lose her place on the bureau's roster of candidates.

In the face of such inequities, female servants participated in demonstrations in cities such as Ekaterinoslav, Kazan, Kiev, and Moscow throughout February 1905. They called for the immediate closure of private employment agencies and petitioned for their replacement with city-run ones. These protests met with success in only a few cases. The remainder resulted in a number of arrests. In spite of the strong police response, the elimination of private employment agencies remained high on the domestic servant agenda until it was finally achieved in the aftermath of 1917.

By April 1905, as worker militancy among other occupational groups increased, the domestic servant leadership in Baku, Tiflis, and Yerevan called a series of strikes. Each involved thousands of participants, many of whom were rewarded for their efforts with arrests and exile. Isolated incidents of labor unrest continued throughout the next six months as domestics in cities such as Ekaterinoslav, Kazan, and Saratov took to the streets. In Kiev servants "cast aside their stinking kitchens with cockroaches" and marched.[10] They dispersed only when the police moved in and made numerous arrests. By November 1905, the domestics' labor activism had reached a feverish pitch in tandem with the revolutionary events unfolding around them.

A strengthening drive to unionize complemented the unprecedented labor unrest that marked the domestic servant sector in 1905. Domestics heeded the call of female members of the intelligentsia who felt strongly that servants without rights should organize in order to protect themselves. By the summer of 1905 groups of servants in Kiev, Ekaterinoslav, Baku, Tiflis, Yerevan, Kazan, and elsewhere had become increasingly active. This momentum only grew with the release of the October Manifesto and its provision for the existence of unions. The Moscow-based Professional Union of Female and Male Servants, the first and most important union of its kind, quickly spawned locals in a number of Russian cities, most notably in Moscow, St. Petersburg, and Saratov.

The founding meeting of the Professional Union of Female and Male Servants took place in Moscow on 8 November 1905 with over 1,500 mainly female domestics in attendance. It was followed by a succession of meetings throughout the city, the primary purposes of which were to proclaim the union's demands and to develop a plan to secure them. These demands centered on key issues involving terms of employment, compensation, time off, working conditions, living conditions, and the overall treatment of domestic servants inside and outside the home. As an absolute minimum, domestic servants wanted employers to provide formal contracts that specified cash and noncash compensation (i.e., tea, sugar, room and board) and to increase wages. They also reiterated their demand for a dramatically reduced workday. However, whereas a few months earlier they had been willing to settle for a twelve-hour day running from 7:00 a.m. to 11:00 a.m. and 3:00 p.m. to 11:00 p.m., domestics now sought an eight-hour workday with one day off per week and a month's holiday every year. The servants at the inaugural union meeting were also intent on being allowed to use their time off as they saw fit and not as their employer deemed appropriate.

When it came to working and living conditions, union members sought specific changes. They insisted on employers agreeing to fixed times for both lunch and breakfast and above all to refrain from interfering in minutiae of a working kitchen. They wanted employers to provide them with not only a key to the home and a separate room, in which they could live and entertain their guests, but also a mattress, pillow, comforter, and sheets. In terms of board, domestic servants were most concerned that they had a right to fresh food instead of leftovers. Other requests included having the same breakfast as their employer, at least one dish per day that contained meat, and permission to offer their own guests tea and sugar from the household supply.

Additional demands outlined by various locals of the Professional Union of Female and Male Servants included a complete overhaul of the manner in which domestic servants were hired or fired. They called for a minimum of two weeks' severance and reiterated their demand that publicly run employment agencies replace privately owned ones. Union organizers also attempted to address the question of housing for servants who had lost their position and thus their home. The problem of a housing shortage was also chronic for retired domestics, and as such it received increasing attention from those concerned with the domestics' position. Reformers, union organizers, and the rank-and-file union membership felt that servants should be permitted to remain in their former employers' homes while they sought new positions. However, recognizing the infeasibility of that option in some circumstances, they called for the construction of residential buildings that could provide temporary accommodation to servants who had fallen upon hard times. This demand fell largely upon deaf ears in the prerevolutionary period; however, it would appear again in the postrevolutionary period as one of the cornerstones of the domestic servant agenda where it would meet with greater success.

One of the most heartfelt and oft-repeated demands by domestic servants had nothing to do with compensation, or the length of the workday, or even their living conditions. Instead, it centered solely on the question of respect. Domestic servants consistently asked that employers address them in the polite form of *vy* (you) as opposed to the less formal *ty* (you). This demand went hand in hand with the efforts by the All-Russian Union for Women's Equality to invest the domestic servant with recognized protective rights and her position with dignity and respect.

Contemporary newspaper articles provide an insight into the Professional Union of Female and Male Servants' plan of action in detailing the massive strike that followed directly upon the heels of the organizational meetings held in Moscow during the first ten days of November. Over five thousand domestic servants took to the streets. Holding banners, they encircled private apartment buildings and publicly denounced employers known for their exploitative practices. They marched along the city's streets and broke the windows of employment agencies they encountered along their way. They remained resolute in the face of significant police opposition, multiple beatings, and numerous arrests. It was only a matter of days before St. Petersburg domestic servants followed suit. By 18 November 1905 thousands of them had taken to the streets, many of whom risked summary dismissal by their employers. Ultimately, however, this series of strikes in Moscow and St. Petersburg ended more with a whimper than a bang, as domestic servants remained largely unsuccessful in securing their goals.

In the wake of the government's repression of the Moscow uprising of December 1905, the final attempt by workers and revolutionaries to achieve their demands for radical reform, the Professional Union of Female and Male Servants, like other unions in Russia, was compelled to cease all activities. Its membership fell to a small core of committed followers. However, by March 1906, when the revolutionary tide had again turned, the union resumed its efforts to promote its platform and recruit new members. It once more called for the introduction of laws to combat the "evil behavior" of employers, provide assistance for unemployed domestic servants, and create public employment offices for servants.[11] On 22 February 1907 the union lobbied the Second State Duma for the promulgation of special measures to protect domestic servants. It asked the Duma to limit the servants' workday to a maximum of nine to ten hours with a minimum of two hours of breaks and to introduce regulations compelling employers to provide domestics with sanitary lodgings. Reiterating the demand for the creation of free labor agencies that represented the interests of prospective employees and not simply the employers, the union also sought the establishment of an insurance system that would provide assistance in the event of unemployment and injury, along with ten weeks' maternity leave. Finally, in an effort to provide for workplace safety, the union wanted the introduction of a system of inspection of all households employing domestic servants similar to that which monitored working conditions in factories. Unfortunately, the conservative Duma turned a deaf ear to the demands.

Efforts to unionize domestic servants in the aftermath of 1905 were not limited to Moscow, though they met with varying degrees of success in other parts of the country. While a union of domestic servants that included maids, cooks, coachmen, stablers, and janitors was formed in Simbirsk, similar attempts in St. Petersburg and Kiev encountered insurmountable resistance either from municipal officials or from the provincial governor. In the end, unions of domestic servants, like other trade unions, suffered considerable persecution during the years following 1905 and were forced to disband. The only organization to remain was the Mutual Aid Society for Domestic Servants, which for not entirely clear reasons obtained the requisite approval of both the Ministry of Internal Affairs and the Moscow City governor.

The short existence, from 1905 to 1907, of organizations dedicated to the well-being of domestics does not adequately reflect the level of discontent among servants with their lot in life, or the extent of their interest in joining together to improve their situation. A union having an official membership of only three hundred routinely drew over five times that number at public meetings and even more at public demonstrations. Nevertheless, signs of discontent among domestic servants did not readily translate into unionization, if only because prospective recruits were deterred by the cost of joining a union. In addition to the initial enrollment fee, monthly dues amounted to as much as 3 percent of a domestic's salary. Moreover, union organizers during this period had to contend with many of the same obstacles that would hamper their efforts immediately after 1917 and throughout the 1920s.

For example, organizers encountered difficulty contacting servants working in separate households spread throughout a city. The isolation of domestics was compounded by the actions of employers who were determined to thwart all efforts at recruitment. When faced with union organizers going door-to-door to try to enroll new members, employers frequently denied their servants' existence. In cases where employers eventually acknowledged they had a servant, they often barred the organizer from having access to her, fearing that her recruitment would not only disrupt their household routine, but also result in demands for higher wages and better working conditions.

By March 1917 urban domestic servants in Petrograd and Moscow, galvanized by the toppling of the Romanovs, once again banded together to form the Professional Union of Domestic Servants. Along with tailors, barbers, clerks, gold and silver smiths, commercial employees, and metalworkers, they were among the first occupations to organize. Although the euphoria and empowerment that most workers experienced in the wake of the overthrow of the tsar helped to strengthen and extend their actions, the union followed in the footsteps of previous associations and unions. Little was new in the fundamental character of service, or in the perceived need to unite domestics and safeguard their interests. However, while the union's formation was a continuation of earlier efforts to organize domestic servants locally and nationally against the abuses endemic to the occupation, it was also a turning point in that it underlined a more formal introduction of domestic servants into the organizational history of a modern labor force.

An appreciation of the situation of domestic servants in turn-of-twentieth-century Russia allows us to integrate them better into Russian labor history. Crossing traditional gender barriers provides information about the demographic and existential conditions of a substantial part of the Russian labor force that has previously been underrepresented in the historical literature. It also reinstates domestics as actors involved in changing the socioeconomic parameters of the prerevolutionary period. The subsequent participation of domestic servants in the organization history of Russia's postrevolutionary modern labor force reinforces the ongoing need to explore the institutional challenges, gender-related problems, and hermeneutical concerns particular to the occupation of service where the requirements of the servant's self are not easily reconciled with those of the employer's household.

NOTES

Research for this article was carried out in the State Archive of the Russian Federation (GARF) in Moscow and in the Central Historical Archive of St. Petersburg (TsGIA SPb) during the period of 1996–1999. The information presented is primarily drawn from a collection of materials (GARF, f. 6861, op. 1) assembled in the 1920s by members of the Professional Union of Public Catering and Dormitory Workers, otherwise known as Narpit. In an effort to record the history of its domestic-servant members, a commission was established to preserve letters and articles from and about domestic servants during the prerevolutionary period. Not surprisingly, this collection is richest for the period surrounding the Revolution of 1905. Its materials are supplemented by information contained in the Russian State History (RGIA), f. 1261, op. 3.

1. "Otgoloski," *Pridneprovskii krai*, no. 2418 (11 February 1905): 283.

2. In addition to domestic servants, the category of service includes workers in hotels, restaurants, taverns, and inns, as well as gardeners, salesclerks, barbers, cabmen, bath attendants, superintendents, doormen, chimney sweeps, window washers, and floor polishers.

3. Based on 1902 figures compiled by Joseph Bradley in *Muzhik and Muscovite: Urbanization in Late Imperial Russia* (Berkeley: University of California Press, 1985), 27 percent of female domestic servants were literate, as opposed to 19.3 percent of female textile workers and 36.3 percent of female manufacturing workers.

4. While there are numerous examples in Britain of organizations of domestic servants, such as the Servants' Home Society, organized union activities are few and far between. Even in the United States, where the history of domestic servants' unionizing dates back to the washerwomen of New York in 1835, more often than not domestic servant organizing efforts resulted in the formation of clubs rather than unions. Donna L. Van Raaphorst, *Union Maids Not Wanted: Organizing Domestic Workers, 1870–1940* (New York: Praeger, 1988), 192.

5. GARF, f. 6861, op. 1, d. 51, l. 5.

6. Legislation on behalf of factory women, although inadequate, did attempt to address questions of accident and health insurance, maternity leave, medical care, night work, overtime, and even child labor.

7. GARF, f. 6861, op. 1, d. 40, l. 48.

8. *Ustav S-Peterburgskoi arteli domashnei muzhskoi prislugi* (St. Petersburg, 1887), 1.

9. The Moscow Society of Waiters and Other Tavern and Hotel Personnel, formed as a mutual aid society in 1902, grew to have 1,200 members, and by October 1905 it had been effectively transformed into a trade union. Victoria E. Bonnell, *Roots of Rebellion: Workers' Politics and Organizations in St. Petersburg and Moscow, 1900–1914* (Berkeley: University of California Press, 1983), 127.

10. GARF, f. 6861, op. 1, d. 108, l. 98.

11. L. N. Lenskaia, *"O prisluge": Doklad chitannyi vo 2-m Zhenskom klube v Moskve v fevrale 1908 goda* (Moscow, 1908), 19.

SUGGESTED READINGS

Bonnell, Victoria E. *Roots of Rebellion: Workers' Politics and Organizations in St. Petersburg and Moscow, 1900–1914*. Berkeley: University of California Press, 1983.

Bradley, Joseph. *Muzhik and Muscovite: Urbanization in Late Imperial Russia*. Berkeley: University of California Press, 1985.

154   *Rebecca Spagnolo*

Engel, Barbara Alpern. *Between the Fields and the City: Women, Work and Family in Russia, 1861–1914*. Cambridge: Cambridge University Press, 1994.

Glickman, Rose. *Russian Factory Women: Workplace and Society, 1880–1914*. Berkeley: University of California Press, 1984.

Kelly, Catriona. "'Who'll Clean the Boots Now?' Servants and Social Anxieties in Late Imperial St. Petersburg." *Europa Orientalis* 16 (1997): 2.

McBride, Theresa. *The Domestic Revolution: The Modernization of Household Service in England and France, 1820–1920*. London: Croom Helm, 1976.

Rustemeyer, Angela. *Dienstboten in Petersburg und Moskau 1861–1917: Hintergrund, Alltag, soziale Rolle*. Stuttgart, Germany: F. Steiner, 1996.

Van Raaphorst, Donna L. *Union Maids Not Wanted: Organizing Domestic Workers, 1870–1940*. New York: Praeger, 1988.

Chapter Twelve

Plebeian Poets in Fin de Siècle Russia

Stories of the Self

Mark D. Steinberg

*Much has been written about the Russian working class: its heterogeneity in
terms of backgrounds and class consciousness, its daily life, strike activity,
revolutionary aspirations, and radicalization after Bloody Sunday in January
1905 when government troops fired upon unarmed workers and their families
petitioning the tsar for an amelioration of their lives and basic civil rights.
Normally, historians view groups within the working class as sharing a common culture and understanding. Accordingly, they search for the typical or
representative worker. But was there such a being as a typical or representative worker? Was a worker who wrote an autobiography at a time of lower literacy rates exceptional by the very nature of the fact that she or he decided
to leave a written record of her or his experiences? Does it take a personality out of the ordinary to pen a letter or story to a newspaper, even today,
when universal literacy rates have been achieved? To what degree is writing
self-empowering?*

*Normally we do not think about workers writing poetry or prose; yet, as
Mark Steinberg's chapter demonstrates, hundreds and perhaps thousands
certainly did so in the tumultuous years before and during the First World
War. Some were metalworkers, union activists, and party members; others
were artisans, laundresses, and seamstresses; still others had worked in a variety of jobs and had moved around from place to place. These proletarian
writers came from diverse occupations within the working class and expressed themselves in language that was influenced by the stories their families and friends told them, the newspapers and books they read, and the con-
versations they had with others. Most were self-taught, with a modicum of or
no formal education. Many, particularly the men who did not have household
responsibilities, organized themselves into self-education groups, meeting at*

teahouses and taverns or at a patron's home. They wrote about daily life as
well as the philosophical meaning of life.

What do the worker-poets' voices tell the modern reader about the social
dynamics and tensions of the time? Why was their recognition of themselves
as human beings with dignity so subversive in late Imperial Russia? What
mattered to these poets, and why did they feel their alienation so keenly? Can
we talk about the existence of a worker intelligentsia? Were some of them
moral crusaders who shared commonalities with educated, middle-class revolutionaries such as the Bolsheviks, who wished to create a teetotaling and
"civilized" proletarian culture? Might their ideas have clashed at times with
those of other workers?

> An intelligentsia has emerged out of the depths of the life of the common
> people by the strength of its own spirit. . . . Only those who have experi-
> enced all the charms of a life without rights can weep over the people's
> sufferings and rejoice at the people's joys.
>
> —The magazine *Friend of the People*, 1915

> Amidst the prose of everyday life . . . living in dreams, drunk with poetry
> and the thirst for light.
>
> —The worker-poet Mikhail Savin, 1909

Observers of the vitality and instability of Russian life during the final
decades of the old order often noted the remarkable growth of an "intelligentsia" comprised not of educated elites but of urban workers who had little
formal education. By the eve of World War I, most urban workers could read
and write. Part of this growing class of literate working people in Russia, the
worker intelligentsia played increasingly important roles in trade unions, parties, and other social and political movements. But what is most fascinating
and important about these "intellectuals from the people" is less their role or
influence than what they reveal about the human experience of lower-class
life in Russia. A remarkable number of working-class Russians, in fact, were
determined to be heard by others and found their voices in writing. Especially
in the years after 1905, such plebeian writers became a sustained presence in
Russian cultural life. Almost every issue of a trade union or socialist party
newspaper included at least a couple of poems by worker-writers, dozens of
"people's magazines" and newspapers emerged solely to print the work of
"writers from the people," and many popular newspapers and magazines
printed the writings of "self-taught" authors. Most of these plebeian writers
wrote poetry—not only because it was the most familiar, brief, and seemingly
easy genre of writing, but also because poetry was most expressive: it spoke

the language of feeling as well as of fact. The literary merit of most of this work, admittedly, was low. The strength of these writings is their power to reveal much about the inward experiences, ideas, and emotions of lower-class Russians, at least those who aspired to look and reach beyond the day-to-day grind of their lives. As historical sources, these writings offer a rare window onto thinking and feeling in the past, onto a society, and onto individual lives in ferment.

The problems that concerned these plebeian writers included many of the biggest intellectual issues of their day: ethics and morals, the workings of power, the experience of modern urban life, and the meaning of existence. But at the heart of so many of their poetic reflections on the world around them lay the idea of the human self. Like many of their contemporaries, plebeian Russian authors were preoccupied with questions of selfhood. The nature, social place, and moral significance of the individual person was an obsessive topic. Key words such as *lichnost'* (self, person, personality, individual) and *chelovek* (human being, man) saturated their writings, typically as grounding for moral or political appeals. One contemporary observer of prerevolutionary working-class attitudes described these concerns as nothing less than a "cult of the self" and "cult of man" in the discourse of activist and outspoken workers in Russia.[1] This was a subversive and dangerous discourse, even a revolutionary one, but it was also a troubled one, carrying hints of alienated self-absorption, of pessimistic rage, and even of philosophical despair.

Notwithstanding persistent stereotypes about Russian political culture as antagonistic toward the modern liberal notion of the autonomous individual endowed with natural rights and dignity, such a discourse about the self and its social and moral meanings pervaded Russia's flourishing civic life in the final decades of the old order. Since the end of the eighteenth century, though mostly after the middle of the nineteenth, public discussions of ethics and social order in Russia—in journals, newspapers, and literary works; by intellectuals; and at meetings of all sorts—had focused increasingly on the innate worth, freedom, and rights of the individual. The key word in these reflections was the notion of *lichnost'*, a term that denoted not simply the individual, but a person's inward nature and personality, the human self, which made individuals naturally deserving of respect and freedom. This was a subject not without hesitations and disagreement. Many Russians contested the autonomy and moral valence of the individual self, insisting on the moral superiority of the social and the communal. And many feared nurturing the self, noting the darker depths of the human spirit: irrational drives, deviance, and dangerous passions. But the individual and the self were increasingly at the center of cultural attention in late Imperial Russia, and not just among educated elites.

The modern ideal of the self as the inward source of identity, dignity, and rights shared by all human beings occupied a central place in the thinking and arguments of activist workers in Russia in the late nineteenth and early twentieth centuries. Historians of Russian labor have often noted workers' demands for "polite address" and, more generally, for treatment befitting their worth as human beings. These challenges to "humiliation and insult," however, were very often much more than mere items on a list of demands. They were at the heart of an ethical vision with which many workers judged the entirety of social and political life. Variations on these themes pervaded workers' critical writings in the years from 1905 to the revolution. The trade union press on the eve of the First World War reveals a fundamental, even obsessive, preoccupation with questions of honor, conscience, insult, and humiliation, and pervasive demands to be recognized as human beings, not slaves, machines, or animals. Hundreds of articles, essays, and letters by workers repeatedly voiced moral outrage at society's blindness to workers' human personality.

In fiction and especially poetry, worker-writers articulated these same themes. The language of these "voices from the soul"—as a provincial glassworker titled a 1906 poem about the insulted dignity of workers[2]—was filled with the key words and images of this discourse: the pain, insult, and depersonalization of workers resulting from their lack of freedom to act according to their own will; the spiteful disdain of workers' honor; the degradation of workers into "literal automatons"; and the need for the world to see that "we are people, not animals, not cattle," and that "the soul of the worker is no different from that of the educated rulers of the world."[3] A telling elaboration on these themes was offered by the metalworker Aleksei Bibik in his 1912 novel *Toward the Open Road*, the first Russian novel written by a worker. In the midst of a passionate discussion with a comrade from his factory about questions of pride, envy, dignity, art, morality, doubt, and death, Ignat Pasterniak, the young worker who is the semiautobiographical hero of the novel, offers this moral fantasy:

> Imagine a huge hall. Before a crowd of thousands of self-important and conceited people, someone is playing piano. Or violin. It doesn't matter. His playing is so inspired, that everyone is spellbound by his music. They don't even move. Then there is some whispering: who is this, who is he? So he stands up and throws off some sort of cloak he has been wearing and stands there in a simple, dirty blue shirt. He's a worker! . . . Imagine the picture. . . . Everyone would be amazed and he would say to them, "So, you thought that under this dirty blue shirt was emptiness? An animal? What gave you the right to think that? To think that we don't feel or understand beauty? What made you think that only you are the salt of the earth. You are pitiful! I can't bear to stay here anymore with you!"[4]

The seemingly simple identification of the worker as a human being, in Russia as elsewhere in the modern world, was a potentially inspiring and explosive idea. It helped make sense of social structures and relationships, especially subordination and unequal exchange. Most essential in shaping these meanings were the perceived effects these relationships had on workers' inward selves—on their *lichnost'*. It mattered less that these were unequal relationships than that they "trampled in the dirt" workers' "feelings of human dignity"[5]—in other words, that they were relationships of insult and indignity. This was a powerful discourse. It was a force of great interpretive and rhetorical power for workers to be able to see and speak of capitalist social relationships not simply as subordination and unequal exchange, but, as the worker-critic Ivan Kubikov did, as "moral oppression."[6]

Suffering preoccupied Russian worker-writers, for it was strongly intertwined with these ways of experiencing and valuing the self and of deploying these notions critically. Suffering, of course, is interpretation. Physical injury, disease, loss, and death are primarily material facts, while suffering is a category through which people perceive, value, and represent such facts. For the Russian lower classes, suffering had tangible social form and history. The everyday lives of the urban poor in Russia were harsh: crowded and unsanitary living conditions, wide social and political inequalities, low wages and debilitating working conditions, limited social protections, and restricted civil rights. But the organization of these raw facts into a narrative of *suffering* introduced layers of meaning and intent that were not intrinsic.

When literate Russian workers wrote about their lives, they filled their writings with stories and images of suffering, individual suffering in particular. A rich vocabulary of personal affliction saturated the poetry as well as stories and essays of the growing numbers of worker-writers: *grust'*, *pechal'* (sadness); *unynia* (hopeless sadness, depression); *gore* (misery, grief); *skorb'* (sorrow); *muka*, *muchenie* (torment); *stradanie* (suffering); *slëzy* (tears); *bol'* (pain); and, most frequently, *toská* (a mixture of melancholy, sadness, anguish, and depression). Although the 1905 Revolution introduced a more optimistic tone to workers' writings, images of the suffering personality of the worker became more plentiful than ever, filling the pages of the trade union press, popular and populist magazines, and numerous pamphlets and books containing the creative works of lower-class writers. The images and tales of suffering were many, diverse, and imbued with an insistent critical pathos: childhoods ruined and lost (part of a growing view of childhood as a time that should be happy and during which the personality is nurtured); childhoods recalled (or represented) as painful memories of lost joy; sleepless nights yielding only to dreams "tortured by exhaustion" (it would seem that even the most private moments alone with one's self—and away from the "nightmare" of waking life—offered no escape); the frustrated sexuality of male workers from the village who could not afford to keep their wives with them in the city (showing, again, the intimately personal dimension of social suffering); the humiliation of working women by foremen and bosses, the abuse of women as sexual objects, and their "fall" into prostitution; the anguish of a mother watching her children starve; drunkenness as a way to "obliterate this hell on earth"; the beatings, work-related maiming, and death that often occurred in factories; nature itself—especially damp, windy, and melancholy fall—echoing and framing the harsh lives and dark moods of workers, or the beauties of awakened nature becoming inaccessible due to the "anguish, pain and bitterness / in my weary soul." Above all, these writings were filled with constant assertions that "the life of a worker is a chain of suffering / A river of sweat, a sea of tears."[7]

Among the many images of the suffering self in these writings, death is perhaps the most important in illuminating meanings of this discourse on suffering. Images of premature death figured prominently in workers' writings. We see workers dying in factories when crushed by machines; dying of hunger and of diseases associated with poverty, especially tuberculosis (and, adding further insult, being cruelly treated in the public clinics where they sought care); and dying young and innocent. And when they died, one worker-poet suggested, black blood would flow from their mouths, a sign of lifelong suffering.[8] These were complex images. Death was often portrayed also as an answer and an escape, a comfort and a way to freedom. Repeatedly, poems and stories pondered or described suicide, a phenomenon also reported with shocking regularity in the daily press in the prewar years, or voiced prayers that death would come, bringing a long-sought "oblivion" and "rest."[9] But intertwined with these traces of despondency was moral rage. And the suffering self was at the heart of this moral argument. For example, an "epidemic" of suicides around 1910 among tailoring workers was explained not by poverty and unemployment, since conditions were in fact relatively good, but by workers' feelings that life had become a "big, dark, empty and cold barn" in which there is "no one to whom they may tell of their insults."[10] Stories and images of suicide and death, especially of the young and innocent, were strong signs of how much the "spirit ached," of how deeply the self was wounded.[11] Death spoke loudly, as both discursive symbol and material proof, of the denial of the workers' "right," as it was often said, "to live as human beings."

As can be seen, at the intellectual heart of the moral anger in these writings was the self and its ethical value and, more precisely, the modern ideal of the self as the seat of emotions, creative genius, spiritual worth, and individual dignity: hence, the fundamental moral measure. These writers seem to have found in suffering evidence not just of the hard lot of the poor but, even more, of the existence of an inner spirit in the persons of the poor that made their hard lot constitute spiritual injury and moral wrong. To dwell on suffering was at once to remind oneself and one's readers of the evil of conditions that harmed the self. In other words, by casting the everyday brutalities of lower-class life in a language of the injured self, these writers were helping to craft a potent and very usable *moral identity*. Suffering simultaneously defined workers and the poor by an essential common experience, valorized these sufferings as signs of the worthy interior lives of the poor, and condemned poverty and social hardship as harm to the self and hence as violations of a universal ethical truth.

The moral anger fueled by these ideas about the human person was not limited to a critique of social inequities and oppressions. These workers looked beyond "society's" humiliations of the selves of the poor to face workers' own failures to recognize, respect, and nurture their inward personalities and their autonomous wills. Thus, worker-writers focused a steady stream of criticism against the weak, undeveloped, and "fallen" personalities of the majority of lower-class Russians, for which they blamed, at least in part, workers themselves. A huge outpouring of published criticism targeted drunkenness, swearing, cruelty, and lowbrow cultural tastes. Such criticisms echoed the "culturalist" arguments of many elite Russians worried about the dangerous backwardness of the poor. The difference, though not absolute, was telling: when worker-critics of popular culture talked of raising the culture of the poor and nurturing the self and the will, the logic was defiant more than integrative. The goal was to make the poor more dangerous to an unequal social order, not less.

In essays, stories, poems, and other writings, these writers tried persistently to shame their fellow workers away from behaviors and mentalities that were said to degrade the personality and weaken the will. This list was long: drunkenness, thievery, superstition, bigotry, fighting, crass tastes in entertainment, male sexual harassment, female prostitution, dishonesty, and passivity. The Russian vocabulary used was richly moralistic (and difficult to translate directly for so grounded in a particular cultural language of moral judgment): *poshlost'* (self-satisfied crassness), *nravstvennaia padenie* (moral decline), *raznuzdannost'* (licentiousness), *razvrat* (debauchery), *nechesnosti* (dishonesty, dishonor), *durnye instinkty* (low instincts), *skandaly* (scandalous behaviors), *pakosti* (trash, depravities, obscenities), and more.

Drunkenness was a particularly common target and was generally treated as both a sign and an aggravation of a weak self, as a practice that "defaces the image of man" and leads to immorality and depravity. But drunkenness was only the most obvious sin, only one piece of a larger story about the common people's degraded cultural selves. M. A. Loginov, writing in the "people's" journals

he edited, regularly wrote of the "darkness and chaos" he saw in the life of the
common people: the fall in morals, breakdown of families, wasteful and harm-
ful time spent in taverns and *café chantants*, inhuman crimes, cruelty, ignorance, superstition, and fatalism.[12] He described with disgust, for example, "laboring people" resting along the shore of the Volga near Moscow on summer
evenings and engaging in "course swearing, arguments, and fights," "drunkenness, violence, and depravity."[13] A waiter complained that his fellows wasted
their free time on nothing but degrading "buffoonery": "as soon as a few comrades get together, right away they start in with stupid witticisms, obscenities,
card games, drunkenness, and other such trash [*pakosti*]."[14]

These writers blamed society and especially the autocratic state for "dehu-
manizing" workers. But they also saw weakness and disintegration in the very
selves of most workers. The prominent worker-leader of the metalworkers'
union, Fyodor Bulkin, wrote a stinging indictment of workers' "moral non-
chalance," dishonesty, crass literary tastes, and the general "flourishing of
low instincts" among workers.[15] Similarly, the printer Ivan Kubikov complained of finding in many workplaces an "abyss of self-satisfied crassness
and apathy" and "philistine indolence."[16] Workers must take responsibility
for their own failings. As one wrote, "Drunkenness is a disease of the will,
and the will depends on reason. . . . It is all about culture."[17] And, one might
add, for this was implicit, it was about the self.

Paradoxically, as this critique may suggest, part of the inspiration driving
worker-authors to protest social injustice and immorality was a certain estrangement from their own social milieus. In memoirs, these writers often recalled feeling alienated from the crass everyday worlds around them, looking
for truth and meaning in isolated searching, reading, wandering, and thinking.
One worker-writer claimed to have spent his youth feeling so out of place
"amidst the prose of everyday life" that he preferred "living in dreams, drunk
with poetry and the thirst for light."[18] We know from the biographies of these
worker-writers that many in fact took to the road as wanderers and pilgrims:
some went on religious pilgrimages; others "tramped" around the country
seeking happiness or truth, they would later often claim; and a few even
worked their way around Europe. This sojourning and seeking was part of a
familiar cultural tradition in Russian culture: that of roaming religious mys-
tics; lay preachers; holy fools; pilgrims; tramping peasants and workers; wandering artists; and the questing heroes, sympathetic bandits, saints, and
vagabonds of the vast genre of popular literary and folk tales. And they often
had a similar moral resonance. In the lives and writings of workers, wandering had particular meaning and pathos. Proletarian authors elaborated end-
lessly on a sense of alienation from others that bordered on a sort of cultural
and moral nausea. And it was the moral depravity of their fellow workers that

most disturbed such workers. Commenting on a recent story by Maxim Gorky, Ivan Kubikov commented, "How well Gorky portrays the thinking workers' feelings of being alone . . . amidst the gray and backward mass." Seeing "in what filth the soul of man is stewing," the thinking worker feels like "an alien creature among these people."[19]

In the poetry and fiction of lower-class writers—most of which, of course, had a strong autobiographical element—a major theme was the awakened and sensitive individual, estranged from the crass, ordinary people remaining all around them. One fictionalized life story of a sensitive, high-minded, and lonely young worker described the hero's distaste for "the scarcely cultured or literate environment that surrounded him since childhood." As an adult, he had to "always hold himself apart from his coworkers, among whom he noticed many vices." This was not an easy stance. When he refused to join his fellow workers in stealing from the shop, he was ostracized.[20] This sort of conflict had become a cliché in writing by and about worker-intellectuals, but one that was painfully true to life. Sometimes, this estrangement from the workers' milieu extended to an even more painful alienation from one's own social self. The miner and poet Aleksei Chizhikov wrote in 1914 of the "workers' soul," no different in essence from the soul of a tsar or a prince, "imprisoned in a rough worker's hide."[21] However painful this alienation often was, it was also clearly a critical stance: estrangement was an expression of the awakened and moral self.

When these worker-writers felt confident that resistance to the injuries to the self was worth the effort—a confidence most common in periods of social mobilization such as 1905–1907 and 1912–1917—they penned vigorous protests and calls for struggle. Some put their own freedom and lives on the line by taking part in the movements of their day. But this militance was neither universal nor unambiguous. I have suggested that the simple but powerful notion of the human person as endowed by nature (by God, some would say) with natural dignity and rights inspired moral outrage and courage among many lower-class Russians, giving them a mighty and just principle with which to protest and fight, and with which to feel pride and confidence in the justice of their cause. It is no exaggeration to say that this was an idea that helped fuel revolution in Russia. The 1905 Revolution, when the ideal of natural human rights was openly and repeatedly deployed by various groups against social and political inequalities, helped stimulate this positive and militant mood. Almost every worker-writer, especially in the years from 1905 until the war, produced verses, stories, or essays voicing bold moral and political certainty. Hundreds of writings in these years used a similar vocabulary of insistent and self-advertised optimism. They spoke of enthusiasm, boldness, hope, strength of spirit, and faith. Metaphorically, this optimistic spirit was conveyed with repeated images of approaching dawn, the rising sun, and coming spring, and, less often, more original images such as the bold might of the wind and the inexorable power of streams cutting though granite.

But there were other motifs that were not easy to silence, especially within oneself. One needed great faith in human goodness not to lose hope, the worker Mikhail Loginov argued in an editorial in 1910, and he admitted that it was difficult for many to sustain such faith and hope.[22] All too common were the mood and attitudes of "unenlightened melancholy, impenetrable skepticism, and stagnant inertia" that Aleksei Gastev described among his fellow tram workers.[23] Much the same could be said of the mood among the most intellectually active workers. As we have seen, when writing of suffering, these authors tended most often to construct their accounts of misery around socially critical and even defiant narratives of inequality and oppression. But we must not ignore other moments (and there were many) when worker-writers, including those associated with trade unions and socialist parties, felt impelled to speak of more intimate sorrows (a desire for love, the fear of death) and to worry deeply about life's essential meaning. The young socialist metalworker Vladimir Aleksandrovskii explored difficult feelings and thoughts while sitting beside a dying friend. To Aleksandrovskii death appeared not a symbol of an unjust social order or even an escape but the final marker of life's grim and meaningless course: "dark, faceless dread / concealed somewhere, beyond the gloom."[24] The awakening of nature in springtime was sometimes viewed not as a sign of hope but as only a reminder of the "melancholy, pain, and bitterness" in one's "weary soul," or of the truth that life's hardships "have no reason."[25] Many of these writers described lost hopes for a "bright life," growing feelings of anguished melancholy and depression (the term *toská* recurs constantly), and a deepening sense of the pointlessness of life.[26] Like so many of these proletarians, Sergei Obradovich, a socialist worker whose poems appeared in many labor journals, shared with readers dark thoughts about self and existence:

> I thought to myself: in this world of vanities
> I am a hollow and superfluous thing,
> Nothing and unnoticed
> Beneath the weight of suffering and misfortune . . .
> Loving all that the soulless world despised,
> I called upon death as if it were joy,
> And, in that indifferent darkness, in anguished doubt,
> I sought an answer to my question:
> Is there a place where life shimmers,
> Or are we fated to suffer forever.
> There was no answer.[27]

Like Obradovich, many "called upon death." But there remained still another, more positive answer, however ambiguously mixed with moments of doubt and despair. For even within these troubled thoughts, the importance and value of speaking aloud about the inner life of the self remained clear. As a great deal of modern social and political history makes evident, this discourse about the self had powerful critical and subversive potential. At the very least, even when despair lurked around the corner, there was a certain pleasure and pride in the ability to feel and express one's inner torments. It demonstrated the sensitivity and hence worth of one's inner self and creative powers. In profoundly unequal societies like prerevolutionary Russia, even this was a dangerous discourse.

NOTES

1. L. M. Kleinbort, "Ocherki rabochei demokratii," part 1, *Sovremennyi mir* (March 1913): 32–44, and part 5 (November 1913): 178–85.

2. E. Nechaev, "Golos dushi," *Zhurnal dlia vsekh* (1906), reprinted in *U istokov russkoi proletar'skoi poezii* (Moscow: Sovetskii pisatel', 1965), 88.

3. These quotations are from workers' poems and other writings in a variety of contemporary magazines and newspapers, including *Rodnye vesti*, 1912, no. 4:7; and *Nash put'*, 1911, no. 17 (23 May): 8–9.

4. A. Bibik, *K shirokoi doroge (Ignat iz Novoselovki)* (St. Petersburg: Tip. M. Pivovarskii i A. Tipograf, 1914), 80. The novel was first published in 1912 in the leftist journal *Sovremennyi mir*.

5. *Golos portnogo*, nos. 1–2 (10 May 1910): 10.

6. *Pechatnoe delo*, no. 24 (11 September 1910): 2.

7. From a variety of contemporary publications, including *Bulochnik*, no. 2 (26 February 1906): 20–22; *Balalaika*, 1910, no. 18:2; *Dumy narodnye*, no. 7 ([13 March] 1910): 5; *Golos portnogo*, nos. 1–2 (10 May 1910): 10; *Pechatnoe delo*, no. 24 (11 September 1910): 3–4; *Chelovek*, no. 4 (24 April 1911): 32; *Rodnye vesti*, 1911, nos. 3–4:5–6, and 1912, no. 3:4–5; *Metallist*, 1911, no. 4 (10 November): 7–8; *Narodnaia sem'ia*, no. 5 (4 March 1912): 13–14; *Zhivoe slovo*, no. 10 (March 1913): 6; *Zhizn' pekarei*, 1914, no. 1/4 (10 March): 2; and *Pervyi sbornik proletarskikh pisatelei* (St. Petersburg: Príboi 1914), 56–61, 91–92.

8. *Nash put'*, 1911, no. 17 (23 May): 8–9; *Zvezda utreniaia*, no. 21 (20 June 1912): 7; *Rodnye vesti*, 1912, no. 3:2–3.

9. For example, *Dumy narodnye*, no. 7 ([13 March] 1910): 5; *Narodnaia mysl'*, no. 2 (February 1911): 107; *Rodnye vesti*, 1912, no. 3:2–3.

10. *Golos portnogo*, no. 3 (10 July 1910): 3–4, 8.

11. *Kolotushka*, 1911, no. 1:3, and no. 2:4; *Chelovek*, no. 3 (27 March 1911): 11.

12. *Dumy narodnye*, no. 2 ([February] 1910): 1; *Zvezda iasnaia*, no. 6 (29 February 1912): 2–4; *Zvezda utreniaia*, no. 17 (23 May 1912): 2.

13. *Dumy narodnye*, no. 1 ([February] 1910): 2.
14. *Chelovek*, no. 3 (27 March 1911): 12.
15. *Nash put'*, no. 11 (20 December 1910): 7–8.
16. *Pechatnoe delo*, no. 24 (11 September 1910): 6.
17. *Pechatnoe delo*, no. 13 (24 November 1909): 10–11.
18. *Gallereia sovremennykh poetov* (Moscow, 1909), 11.
19. *Novaia rabochaia gazeta*, no. 5 (13 August 1913): 2.
20. *Samopomoshch'* 2, no. 1 (December 1911): 6.
21. A letter to *Pravda* in RGASPI (the Russian State Archive of Social and Political History), f. 364, op. 1, d. 315, l. 1–3 (quote p. 4).
22. *Dumy narodnye*, no. 2 ([February] 1910): 1.
23. *Edinstvo*, no. 12 (21 December 1909): 11.
24. *Novaia rabochaia gazeta*, no. 9 (18 August 1913): 2.
25. *Chelovek*, no. 4 (24 April 1911): 32.
26. For example, poems by V. Vegenov in *Novoe pechatnoe delo* in 1911 and 1912.
27. *Severnoe utro*, no. 52 (6 March 1913): 2.

SUGGESTED READINGS

Brooks, Jeffrey. *When Russia Learned to Read: Literacy and Popular Culture, 1861–1917*. Princeton, NJ: Princeton University Press, 1985.

Engelstein, Laura, and Stephanie Sandler, eds. *Self and Story in Russian History*. Ithaca, NY: Cornell University Press, 2000.

Frank, Stephen, and Mark Steinberg, eds. *Cultures in Flux: Lower-Class Values, Practices, and Resistance in Late Imperial Russia*. Princeton, NJ: Princeton University Press, 1994.

Kleinbort, L. M. *Ocherki rabochei intelligentsii*. 2 volumes. Petrograd: T-vo Nachatki znanii, 1923.

Offord, Derek. *"Lichnost'*: Notions of Individual Identity." Pp. 13–25 in *Constructing Russian Culture in the Age of Revolution: 1881–1940*, edited by Catriona Kelly and David Shepherd. Oxford: Oxford University Press, 1998.

Pervyi sbornik proletarskikh pisatelei. St. Petersburg: Priboi, 1914.

Rubakin, N. A. *Chistaia publika i intelligentsia iz naroda*. 2nd ed. St. Petersburg: Palada, 1906.

Sbornik proletarskikh pisatelei. Petrograd: Parus', 1917.

Steinberg, Mark D. *Proletarian Imagination: Self, Modernity, and the Sacred in Russia, 1910–1925*. Ithaca, NY: Cornell University Press, 2002.

Zelnik, Reginald. *A Radical Worker in Tsarist Russia: The Autobiography of Semen Ivanovich Kanatchikov*. Stanford, CA: Stanford University Press, 1986.

Index

abolitionist movements, xv
abolition, of serfdom, xi, 51, 85, 101.
    See also emancipation, of serfs
abortion, 69
absolute monarchy. *See* autocracy
accessories, 6
accidents, reports on, 104–5
adultery, 118
advertising, 7, 10
Afanasev, Nil, 59, 65
Akinfiev, Gurian, 59, 62, 63–64
alcohol consumption, 87
Alcott, Louisa May, 78
Aleksandrovskii, Vladimir, 164
Alekseev Brothers, 10
Alekseevna, Maria, 145–46
Aleksei Michailovich (Tsar), xiv, 1
Alexander I (Emperor), 56, 72
Alexander II (Emperor), 72, 77, 78, 85,
    91; assassination of, 79, 82n22, 94
Alexander III (Emperor), 87, 89; Siberia
    reform reply by, 95–96
Alexander Nevsky monastery, 29
alienation, 162–63
All-Russian Union for Women's
    Equality, 147, 150
Andronik (Archimandrite), 17
anonymity, 106
Antonova, Mariia Semenovna, 21

Antonov, Vasilii, 59, 64
architecture, xiv
arrests, reports on, 106
artel, 78–79
artisans, foreign, 6–7
assault, 103, 107–8
Astrakhan, xvi
autocracy, new areas and, xvi
autonomy movements, x

Baker, Keith, 51n4
Bakst, Lev, 9
Ballets Russes, 9
balls, 5, 47, 72, 77–78, 81
Bashmakova, Aleksandra, 104
Bauer, Evgenii, 104
Belozerskaia, N. A., 76
Bernovo, xii–xiii, 56; marshal
    investigation of, 61; marshal
    petitioned by, 59–60; mistreatment
    claimed by, 60–61; peasant uprising
    at, 57; population of, 57; rents
    charged to, 60; sheriff demonstration
    by, 62; sheriff investigating peasants
    at, 61–63; tsar petitioned by, 60, 62,
    63; Vul'f, I. I., ruling, 57
Beshentsov, Ivan, 20–21
Bibik, Aleksei, 158
Black Repartition, 79, 82n22

About the Contributors

Rodney D. Bohac is associate professor of history at Brigham Young University. He has authored numerous articles and book chapters on various aspects of Russian serfdom, including peasant resistance, the military draft, serfs' inheritance strategies and agricultural practices, and serf owners' attempts to force widows to remarry.

Barbara Alpern Engel is professor of history at the University of Boulder, Colorado, and the author of *Mothers and Daughters: Women of the Intelligentsia in Nineteenth-Century Russia* (1983); *Between the Fields and the City: Women, Work, and Family in Russia, 1861–1914* (1994); and *Women in Russia, 1700–2000* (2004).

ChaeRan Y. Freeze is associate professor of history at Brandeis University. She is the author of *Jewish Marriage and Divorce in Imperial Russia* (2002) and coeditor with Paula Hyman and Antony Polonsky of *Jewish Women in Eastern Europe* (2005).

William B. Husband is professor of history at Oregon State University and the author of *Revolution in the Factory: The Birth of the Soviet Textile Industry, 1917–1920* (1990) and *"Godless Communists": Atheism and Society in Soviet Russia, 1917–1932* (2000).

Laura L. Phillips is professor of history at Eastern Washington University and the author of *Bolsheviks and the Bottle: Drink and Worker Culture in St. Petersburg, 1900–1929* (2000).

David L. Ransel is professor of history at Indiana University. He is the author of *Politics of Catherinian Russia: The Panin Party* (1975); *Mothers of Misery: Child Abandonment in Russia* (1988); *Village Mothers: Three Generations of Change in Russia and Tataria* (2000); and *A Russian Merchant's Tale: The Life and Adventures of Ivan Tolchënov, Based on His Diary* (2008).

Christine Ruane is professor of history at the University of Tulsa. She is the author of *Gender, Class, and the Professionalization of Russian City Teachers, 1860–1914* (1994) and *The Empire's New Clothes: A History of the Russian Fashion Industry, 1700–1917* (2009).

Rochelle G. Ruthchild is professor of graduate studies at the Union Institute and University and a research associate at the Davis Center for Russian and Eurasian Studies at Harvard University. She has written numerous articles and book chapters on Russian feminism, including most recently "Women's Suffrage and Revolution in the Russian Empire, 1905–1917," *Aspasia* 1 (2007): 1–35. She is also the compiler of *Women in Russia and the Soviet Union: An Annotated Bibliography* (1994).

Rebecca Spagnolo is assistant dean in the School of Graduate Studies at the University of Toronto. She is completing a dissertation on domestic servants in Russia in the revolutionary period and is the author of "When Private Home Meets Public Workspace: Service, Space, and the Urban Domestic in 1920s Russia," pages 230–55 in *Everyday Life in Early Soviet Russia: Taking the Revolution Inside* (2006), edited by Christina Kiaer and Eric Naiman.

Mark D. Steinberg is professor of history at the University of Illinois, Urbana–Champaign. He is the author of several books, including *Moral Communities: The Culture of Class Relations in the Russian Printing Industry, 1867–1907* (1992); *Voices of Revolution, 1917* (2002); and *Proletarian Imagination: Self, Modernity, and the Sacred in Russia, 1910–1925* (2002).

Elise Kimerling Wirtschafter is professor of history at California State Polytechnic University and the author of *From Serf to Russian Soldier* (1990); *Structures of Society: Imperial Russia's "People of Various Ranks"* (1994); *Social Identity in Imperial Russia* (1997); and *The Play of Ideas in Russian Enlightenment Theater* (2003).

Christine D. Worobec is Board of Trustees Professor and Distinguished Research Professor at Northern Illinois University. She is the author of *Peasant*

Russia: Family and Community in the Post-Emancipation Period (1991) and *Possessed: Women, Witches, and Demons in Imperial Russia* (2001). She is also coeditor with Barbara Evans Clements and Barbara Alpern Engel of *Russia's Women: Accommodation, Resistance, Transformation* (1991) and coeditor with Mary Zirin, Irina Livezeanu, and June Pachuta Farris of *Women and Gender in Central and Eastern Europe, Russia, and Eurasia: A Comprehensive Bibliography*, 2 volumes (2007).